Management Planning for Archaeological Sites

An International Workshop Organized
by the Getty Conservation Institute and
Loyola Marymount University
19–22 May 2000
Corinth, Greece

*Edited by Jeanne Marie Teutonico
and Gaetano Palumbo*

THE GETTY CONSERVATION INSTITUTE
LOS ANGELES

Cover: Temple of Apollo, Corinth, Greece.
Photograph by Gaetano Palumbo, 2000.
© 2000 J. Paul Getty Trust.

Jeanne Marie Teutonico and Gaetano Palumbo, *Editors*
Michelle Ghaffari, *Copy Editor*
Anita Keys, *Production Coordinator*
Jeffrey Cohen, *Series Designer*
Hespenheide Design, *Book Designer*

The Getty Conservation Institute (GCI) works internationally to advance conservation and to enhance and encourage the preservation and understanding of the visual arts in all of their dimensions—objects, collections, architecture, and sites. The Institute serves the conservation community through scientific research; education and training; field projects; and the dissemination of the results of both its work and the work of others in the field. In all its endeavors, the Institute is committed to addressing unanswered questions and promoting the highest possible standards of conservation practice.

The GCI is a program of the J. Paul Getty Trust, an international cultural and philanthropic organization devoted to the visual arts and the humanities that includes an art museum as well as programs for education, scholarship, and conservation.

Published by The Getty Conservation Institute, Los Angeles, CA 90049-1684
© 2002 J. Paul Getty Trust.
Printed in the United States of America
10 9 8 7 6 5 4 3

Library of Congress Cataloging-in-Publication Data

Management planning for archaeological sites : an international workshop organized by the Getty Conservation Institute and Loyola Marymount University, 19–22 May 2000, Corinth, Greece / edited by Jeanne Marie Teutonico and Gaetano Palumbo.
 p. cm.
Includes bibliographical references.
  ISBN-13: 978-0-89236-691-0
  ISBN-10: 0-89236-691-5
1. Excavations (Archaeology)—Congresses. 2. Historic sites—Management—Congresses. 3. Historic sites—Conservation and restoration—Congresses. 4. Archaeology—Methodology—Congresses. 5. Archaeology—Field work—Congresses. 6. Excavations (Archaeology)—Greece—Corinth—Congresses. 7. Corinth (Greece)—Antiquities—Congresses. I. Teutonico, Jeanne Marie. II. Palumbo, Gaetano. III. Getty Conservation Institute. IV. Loyola Marymount University.
CC76 .A76 2002
930.1'028'3—dc21
                                                              2002013572

Contents

Timothy P. Whalen — v — Foreword

Jeanne Marie Teutonico and William Fulco — vii — Preface

PART ONE
Background Papers

Gaetano Palumbo — 3 — Threats and Challenges to the Archaeological Heritage in the Mediterranean

Randall Mason and Erica Avrami — 13 — Heritage Values and Challenges of Conservation Planning

Martha Demas — 27 — Planning for Conservation and Management of Archaeological Sites: A Values-Based Approach

PART TWO
Case Studies

Jeanne Marie Teutonico — 57 — Introduction

Experiences from Europe and Latin America

Christopher Young — 60 — Hadrian's Wall, United Kingdom

Carolina Castellanos — 68 — Chan Chan, Peru

Three Sites in the Region

Esti Ben Haim — 83 — Masada, Israel

Aysar Akrawi — 98 — Petra, Jordan

Guy Sanders — 113 — Corinth, Greece

Jeanne Marie Teutonico and Gaetano Palumbo	126	Summary of Discussions
Martha Demas	129	Annotated Bibliography
	155	List of Participants
	157	Author Biographies

Foreword

IT IS MY PLEASURE to present this newest addition to the Proceedings series of the Getty Conservation Institute (GCI). The series has a long history and has dealt with a great variety of topics from wallpaintings conservation to the study of ancient and historic metals to the conservation of grotto sites on the Silk Road. It is one of the many publication venues through which the GCI seeks to advance the conservation and protection of the world's cultural heritage by disseminating information to a broad professional audience.

Under the dedicated editorship of Jeanne Marie Teutonico and Gaetano Palumbo, this most recent volume contains the proceedings of a workshop entitled "Management Planning for Archaeological Sites," jointly organized by the GCI and Loyola Marymount University (LMU) near the site of Corinth, Greece, in May 2000. The workshop was attended by more than thirty participants from fourteen countries who gathered together for four days of presentations, site visits, and small group discussions focused on issues of archaeological site conservation and management in the eastern Mediterranean.

The GCI has a long-standing commitment to the conservation and management of archaeological sites that is reflected in years of research, teaching, and field projects. In many ways, the Corinth workshop can be seen as a logical outcome of the 1995 conference "The Conservation of Archaeological Sites in the Mediterranean Region," which first brought together a group of professionals from the region to debate the merits of a values-based planning approach. Building on the results of that experience, the Corinth workshop provided an opportunity to focus in a more detailed way on the realities of the region in relation to the theoretical planning model. It is our hope that this publication will promote critical discussion, inspire further research, and advance the conservation and management of archaeological sites worldwide.

As always, events such as the Corinth workshop require the intelligence, talent, and enthusiasm of many people. First and foremost, thanks are due to the workshop participants, many of whom are represented as authors in this volume. From the outset, they embraced the workshop's aims and brought energy, ideas, and a spirit of openness to the proceedings. The event and this publication would not have been possible without them.

Our partner in the event, Loyola Marymount University, brought an invaluable knowledge of the region and its archaeological heritage and promoted the idea of a collaboration with the GCI. Special thanks are extended to Dr. William Fulco, NEH chair in Ancient Mediterranean Studies, who worked closely with GCI staff to develop, organize, and deliver the event, and to Dr. Joseph Jabbra, academic vice president, who supported the institutional collaboration and enthusiastically participated in the workshop. Thanks, too, to Sandra Scham in Jerusalem for facilitating early contacts.

Grateful acknowledgment is also due to Yad Hanadiv (The Rothschild Foundation) and to its representative Ariel Weiss for providing initial funding support for the event and for consistently emphasizing the importance of dialogue.

The workshop would not have been possible without the assistance, collaboration, and hospitality of the local and national authorities in Corinth. We are especially grateful to Angelos Manolakis, prefect of Corinth, who welcomed us to the city and provided the workshop participants with a generous reception in their honor. We thank Elisabeth Spathari, director of the IV Ephoreia of Prehistoric and Classical Antiquities, and her colleague Zoe Aslamatzidou for their help in organizing the event and for sharing their knowledge of Corinth and of the administrative framework in which conservation takes place in Greece.

We were also very fortunate to count on the collaboration of Guy Sanders, director of the Corinth excavation for the American School of Classical Studies at Athens, who provided invaluable assistance in organizing the site visit to Corinth and the event in general. We also acknowledge the assistance of Nancy Bookidis, who, together with Guy Sanders, provided the workshop participants with an extraordinary in-depth visit to the site.

Recognition must also be given to the GCI staff who worked hard over a long period to realize this project. Giora Solar, formerly head of field projects at the GCI, fostered the early partnership with LMU and eventually participated in the workshop as a representative from Israel. On Giora's departure from the GCI, leadership for the event was taken up by Jeanne Marie Teutonico, associate director of the GCI, who worked with an extraordinarily dedicated team of professionals including Gaetano Palumbo, Martha Demas, Randall Mason, Erica Avrami, and Françoise Descamps to prepare and deliver the workshop. Their knowledge, experience, and commitment were critical in giving structure and substance to the initial concept. On the logistical side, the team was ably assisted by Chris Seki of the GCI and Tammy Jones of LMU, who managed to meet numerous administrative and organizational challenges with exceptional grace and efficiency.

Finally, in addition to the volume editors, we are indebted to Michelle Ghaffari, who copyedited the manuscript; to Kristin Kelly, head of Public Programs and Communications at the GCI; and to our colleagues at Trust Publications for getting these proceedings into print.

Timothy P. Whalen
DIRECTOR
The Getty Conservation Institute

Preface

IN MAY 2000, an international group of architects, archaeologists, tourism professionals, and government officials met in Loutraki, Greece, near the ancient site of Corinth, for a workshop on archaeological site management planning that was jointly organized by the Getty Conservation Institute (GCI) and Loyola Marymount University (LMU). The purpose of the workshop was to explore management planning concepts that might be useful in addressing the many threats facing archaeological sites in the eastern Mediterranean.

For several years, the GCI has taken a leading role in developing, utilizing, and advocating a values-driven planning process for the management of archaeological sites based largely on the Australia ICOMOS Burra Charter. A particularly important event in the development of this approach was "The Conservation of Archaeological Sites in the Mediterranean Region," a conference organized in 1995 in collaboration with the J. Paul Getty Museum. The conference brought together conservation specialists, policy makers, and tourism authorities to explore site management needs and issues in the region. The proceedings of that conference (de la Torre 1997) are an important reference, which reflect the most current thinking of the time. Since then, the GCI, in collaboration with various national and international organizations, has continued to explore and to refine this approach to site management planning based on research, teaching, and field experience.

LMU is committed to scholarly research in Near Eastern archaeology and is currently developing an interdepartmental graduate program in scientific archaeology and conservation studies. In 1998, in the context of a conference entitled "Near Eastern Archaeology into the Twenty-First Century," LMU invited the GCI to present a session on site management planning in order to broaden the dimension of the event to include a consideration of heritage conservation and management issues. The seeds of the collaboration that subsequently materialized in the Corinth workshop were sown at that time.

Building on each institution's past experiences and with additional funding support from Yad Hanadiv (The Rothschild Foundation), the Corinth workshop was designed to disseminate the most current management planning concepts, to explore their applicability in the countries of the eastern Mediterranean, and, in so doing, to foster cross-cultural dialogue. The workshop participants included professionals from Albania, Egypt, Greece, Israel, Jordan, Lebanon, Macedonia, Palestine, and Saudi

Arabia, as well as GCI and LMU staff and professionals from other parts of the world with experience in the development of management plans. In order to promote an interdisciplinary and dynamic exchange and, perhaps, to influence future work in the region, an effort was made to include participants from a variety of disciplines (archaeology, conservation, and tourism) with knowledge of significant sites in the region, responsibility for their care, and, most importantly, decision-making authority. Corinth was chosen as the conference venue both for its relatively central location and because the site offered an ideal focus for discussion of the multiplicity of values and issues that must be considered in the formulation of any management plan.

Structure of the Workshop

The workshop extended over a four-day period and was structured to include general presentations, small group discussions, and a comprehensive site visit. The first day included background presentations on values and a theoretical model for site management planning that advocates active participation of stakeholders and the assessment of values and significance as central elements of the process. This was followed by two case studies from very different parts of the world—Chan Chan in Peru and Hadrian's Wall in the United Kingdom—which illustrate the practical development and implementation of site management plans in complex social and political environments.

Succeeding days were devoted to presentations on major archaeological sites in the eastern Mediterranean—Masada in Israel, Corinth in Greece, and Petra in Jordan—and structured small group discussions where participants could debate and expand on issues emerging from the case studies. Participants also visited the archaeological site of Corinth, which subsequently served as the focus of an exercise regarding the identification of stakeholders and the role of values in management decisions. The workshop concluded with a discussion of barriers to the application of integrated planning in the region and recommendations for the way forward.

About This Publication

As in the case of the Mediterranean conference of 1995, much of the value of the Corinth workshop was derived from the discussions and the interaction of participants. It is difficult, if not impossible, to capture this in a publication. Nonetheless, it seemed important to all of the workshop participants that some attempt be made to record the event, both as a contribution to the literature on site management planning and as a possible catalyst to further activity in the region. Thus, while not proceedings in the traditional sense of the term, this publication gathers together all of the official presentations made at the workshop and attempts to present some of the more important ideas that emerged from the discussions.

Part 1 includes a number of background papers that address the overall themes of the workshop: threats to the archaeological heritage, the concept of heritage values, and a methodology for the conservation and management of archaeological sites. Part 2 is devoted to case studies where site management plans have been developed and implemented or where their use is under discussion. Cases include both sites in Europe and

Latin America as well as several examples from the region. The volume concludes with a summary of the main points emerging from the discussions and an annotated bibliography on site management planning.

In many ways, the Corinth workshop provided an opportunity to coalesce some of the thinking regarding values and values-driven planning that has been developing during the last decade. In addition, through a series of case studies, it promoted critical reflection on why and how the management planning process has been successful (or not) in various situations. In terms of the Eastern Mediterranean in particular, the workshop also provided an opportunity to confront a theoretical model with the practical needs of a diverse group of professionals from different countries and disciplines, and for those professionals to compare experiences and to advance their thinking regarding the management planning process. It is our hope that this publication will record, in some way, the intellectual content and energy of the Corinth workshop, contribute to the existing body of knowledge regarding site management planning, and promote a better and more informed stewardship of the world's archaeological heritage.

Jeanne Marie Teutonico
ASSOCIATE DIRECTOR
The Getty Conservation Institute

William J. Fulco, S. J.
NEH CHAIR IN ANCIENT
MEDITERRANEAN STUDIES
Loyola Marymount University

PART ONE

Background Papers

Threats and Challenges to the Archaeological Heritage in the Mediterranean

Gaetano Palumbo

THIS ARTICLE IS LARGELY BASED on a presentation given at the Corinth workshop held on 19–22 May 2000, in Corinth, Greece, which listed threats and patterns of destruction affecting archaeological sites. With that analysis as a starting point, this article examines the causes and effects of these threats and proposes a series of responses aimed at reducing their impact.

It is clear that threats to the survival of this heritage come from a vast array of sources, but most of them are linked to the way modern societies are developing. Conservation efforts are still, in many cases, trying to address only one of these threats, the one that is most visible: material decay. This article will show that assessing the causes of the deterioration of our archaeological heritage and responding to these threats by including the archaeological heritage in development and management planning processes is the only way to minimize the effects of the many factors of decay. In other words, while threats cannot always be eliminated, they can certainly be managed.

Which Threats?

The International Council on Monuments and Sites (ICOMOS) recently published a document entitled *Heritage at Risk: ICOMOS World Report 2000 on Monuments and Sites in Danger* (ICOMOS 2000). This document will be updated each year on the ICOMOS Web site. The threats identified by the report range from natural causes to those related to development, including pollution and mass tourism. In addition, the report specifies threats related to the loss of handicraft traditions and overzealous restorations, a point also made in this article. Although many would argue that "universal" concepts of heritage, conservation, and preservation of ancient monuments are not only a myth but a myth based on Western concepts, it is fair to say that with some variation in philosophy, the idea that archaeological sites should be conserved is common among all the Mediterranean countries. In some cases, this stance probably has a justification in the development of cultural tourism and its economic importance, while in others, it responds to a political agenda and more entrenched intellectual positions. In other words, there is no single justification for conserving a site, and people believe in conserving the past for very different reasons.

Threats can easily be identified just by observing the patterns of destruction affecting our archaeological and historic sites. The distinction made at Corinth between man-made and natural threats is only practical, as most natural phenomena, such as floods, are often made worse by the violent and irreversible changes caused by years of overexploitation of natural resources and the systematic destruction of our cultural landscapes. Only the natural decay of materials and some disastrous, although rare, natural phenomena such as earthquakes and tornadoes are independent of human intervention. This concept was discussed by Alessandra Melucco Vaccaro in 1989 when she referred to extreme natural phenomena as catastrophic for the survival of heritage sites when combined with a lack of risk mitigation in such events. There is widespread agreement among heritage managers about the general causes of decay of cultural resources. Less clear, however, is how to measure the level of threat. The concept of risk can provide this measuring stick and has been used in some recent assessments of cultural heritage conditions, such as *The Risk Map of Cultural Heritage* (ICR 1997) of the Italian Istituto Centrale per il Restauro; *MARS: The Monuments at Risk Survey of England, 1995: Main Report* of English Heritage (Darvill and Fulton 1998); and *Heritage at Risk: ICOMOS World Report 2000 on Monuments and Sites in Danger* (ICOMOS 2000). The first two are surveys conducted by national heritage organizations regarding the conditions affecting the survival of heritage sites and are supported by periodic reports (ICR 1996a, b, c, d; 1997; 2000; Darvill and Fulton 1998; 2000), while the third is a report on current threats to cultural heritage (ICOMOS 2000).

The Impact of Development

Development is undoubtedly one of the main causes of destruction of our archaeological heritage. Demographic growth and the need for land for the expansion of settlements, for agricultural purposes, and for the growth of infrastructure are some of the most important causes of depletion of

Figure 1
New construction beside Roman ruins, Amman, Jordan. Much legislation does not include adequate provision for buffer zones between archaeological areas and other uses.

our cultural landscapes and of the indiscriminate bulldozing of thousands of unrecorded sites. The encroachment of archaeological sites and the unsympathetic growth of our cities and rural areas are the most visible effects of these phenomena. Subtler, but no less destructive, is the damage caused by the abandonment of the countryside following urbanization processes in many developing countries. The mechanization of agriculture and the loss of the human component in our rural areas contribute to the decay of sites and landscapes. Many antiquities authorities resort to salvage excavations to limit damage, but this practice is incredibly costly and unsustainable in the long run. This is because of the huge gap that exists between the vast areas to be salvaged and the limited number of available personnel. It is also due to time and financial constraints that demand shortcuts in the excavation and recording phases that are unacceptable from a professional and ethical point of view. In many cases, the loss of the archaeological heritage might have been avoided by adding this component to already existing territorial or urban zoning or planning strategies. Unfortunately, many times this does not happen because of the poor integration of cultural heritage within the economic and development spheres of society. In the case of existing sites, the lack of adequate planning measures also means that such sites quickly become "islands" of a past without any connection to the present, obstacles to "beautification" or gentrification initiatives, or, in the worst case, garbage dumps and places to avoid. It is the ultimate irony that these places are sometimes fenced in to protect people from the danger of open pits and crumbling buildings, perhaps more than to save these remains for a disinterested public.

Pollution and the By-Products of Development

It is impossible to separate development from pollution. In our society, pollution has become a measure of development: while developed countries pollute in huge measures, it is in developing countries where the effects of pollution are much more evident due to poor planning and the lack of means to reduce the visual effects of pollution.

Figure 2
The Antonine Column, Rome, after conservation. In places one can see vestiges of its blackened condition that remain after cleaning.

Both high and low water tables are the direct effect of human intervention and both cause great damage to the archaeological heritage. In Beirut, the high water table affects all the structures excavated within the urban center mitigation project, which are often submerged in sewage or highly polluted water. The salinization of soils, caused by excessive use and indiscriminate application of fertilizers, has destructive consequences on archaeological structures. Acid rains have caused immense damage to marble and stone monuments, such as Trajan's Column in Rome, where the finest details, still visible only fifty years ago, are now lost. Black crusts have formed on the surface of many stone monuments within recent years, often causing within a short time span damage that is much worse than the decay observed over hundreds of years. These crusts are a concentration of pollutants and their removal can sometimes place the monument at even greater risk of decay.

Tourism and Site Conservation

The development of mass tourism is strictly linked to physical development and its economic dimension. Such threats range from the sheer number of tourists accessing fragile sites (with concomitant damage to decorated surfaces and other features) to unsympathetic behavior by visitors. This is the case of Volubilis, Morocco, where tourists often climb walls to take better pictures of the mosaic floors, or of many other sites, where they collect pottery fragments or mosaic tesserae to take home as souvenirs. Sometimes this behavior has to do with the lack of facilities at the archaeological site: the lack of signage, clear paths, and maintenance undoubtedly have a psychological effect on visitors. An "abandoned" site, or one perceived as such, gives the visitor an "everything is allowed" attitude, which often translates into behavior close to vandalism. Tourism pressure also translates into the encroachment of sites with visitor facilities and hotels, as well as excessive reconstructions. Vandalism is often associated with touristic activities, in the form of graffiti, gratuitous breaking of objects, and so on. In these forms, it is a consequence of ignorance and stupidity; however, vandalism is sometimes committed on purpose for reasons that are more appropriately described under the category of social unrest.

Figure 3
Tourists in the Roman baths of Pompeii, Italy. Lack of sensitivity to conservation issues, such as the damage caused by visitors sitting on delicate masonry and marble pictured here, is a threat to conservation.

Figure 4
Reconstruction of a columned portico, Machaerus, Jordan. Projects like these are aimed at attracting tourists rather than achieving authenticity and philological anastylosis.

The Impact of Social Unrest on Cultural Heritage

Vandalism committed for political or social reasons is not a casual act and is often highly destructive: sites may be targeted for the value they hold in the eyes of certain groups of people against which the act is directed. Vandalism can take the form of looting, such as in Lebanon during the Civil War (1975–92), when sites in the Biqaa Valley were bulldozed to obtain artifacts to sell on the antiquities market in order to finance the purchase of weapons. Another such case occurs in Pakistan, where a large number of antique objects come in from Afghanistan. Vandalism can also take the form of the systematic destruction of the symbols of another community during an armed conflict, in order to deny that community's right to the land. This was the case of the destruction of mosques in Bosnia and of the famous Bosnian bridge in Mostar, and the attacks on mosques and synagogues (including those in archaeological sites) in Israel and Palestine, and on churches and mosques in Cyprus.

In addition to the effect of these acts of war on archaeological sites, there is the selection of archaeological sites for military purposes. For example, Anjar, a World Heritage site located in Lebanon, is currently occupied by a Syrian military camp that is damaging many of its monuments. Furthermore, the staff of many antiquities departments are not well trained in emergency activities, which consequently results in great damage to heritage in crisis situations (such as taking objects off display without proper recording and storing them in inappropriate conditions).

Situations involving a conflict of values can also have sad consequences for archaeological sites. For example, the tension accumulated in Piazza Armerina in Italy over a contract for building extra parking lots around the site finally became explosive when a group of contractors who either were excluded from the bidding or felt that the competition was unfair vandalized some of the site's mosaics (Ciliberto et al. 1995). Similarly, tensions were extremely high when the Neolithic temples of Mnajdra, Malta, were seriously vandalized by hunters in response to drastic limits imposed on hunting activities in and around the site (Debono 2001).

The Problem of Looting

Looting merits a category on its own because, in some countries, this is the single most important cause of the depletion of cultural resources. Looting is caused by the huge demand for archaeological objects in the international antique markets. Often associated with organized crime, the traffic in antiquities takes advantage of poverty in rural areas and of the connection of middlemen with the higher social classes of the ruling elite. Another reason for the difficult control of clandestine archaeological activities is that while the Western public's interest in archaeology is deeply rooted, people from other parts of the world perceive archaeology as a foreign import or an activity practiced by the elite, and for this reason, as something to mistrust. Archaeologists are often seen as treasure hunters with whom to enter in competition. While this is not the place to expand on this topic, oftentimes looters do not see themselves as guilty of wrongdoing, especially when the foreigners are perceived to be engaged in exactly the same activity. This might be called the "treasure hunt" syndrome. The idea that foreigners are there to find gold is very common across the Mediterranean; unfortunately, the usual response is to dig after the archaeologists, or better before them, in the hope of finding the treasure that "the foreigners" must be after. The looting of Daunian cemeteries in Apulia, Italy, using bulldozers, or the destruction of Bronze Age cemeteries in the Jordan Ghor by treasure hunters are some examples of this phenomenon.

Archaeological Excavations: A Damaging Factor

Archaeological activities are one of the main causes of decay of archaeological sites. In too many cases, excavation projects do not take into consideration the conservation of the structures found. Even worse, they do not provide for the consolidation and protection of the structures from one project season to the next. The result is not only that "completed" archaeological projects soon look like a collection of abandoned and collapsing structures and pits but also that archaeological evidence is lost because of the uncontrolled erosion and decay taking place.

Simple and inexpensive procedures exist to secure the safety of a site during excavation and in the period immediately following the end of a project (Pedelì and Puglia 2002; Stanley Price 1995), but, unfortunately, archaeologists do not always believe that it is their ethical responsibility to ensure the survival of the site they investigate. This is often compounded by the scarce coordination between scientific missions and local antiquities services, with the latter in many cases exerting little control and imposing loose regulations on excavation projects. It is important to emphasize this point, as archaeology carried out purely for research objectives, and not justified under salvage schemes, is a common phenomenon in the Mediterranean, one that attracts many foreign teams to various countries in the area. For this reason, it is even more important that excavation teams provide for conservation, site stabilization, and backfilling (where necessary) to take place at their sites with the involvement of conservation professionals.

Figure 5
Eroding structure at Dura Europos, Syria. The abandonment of archaeological excavations without preventive conservation measures causes rapid decay.

Damage Caused by Inappropriate Interventions

It is ironic that conservation activities, although often carried out with good intention, may have disastrous effects on the structures meant to be preserved. Untrained personnel, the application of outdated methodologies or incompatible materials, and undocumented reconstructions disguised as restorations have made conservation, in many cases, a threat to sites and monuments. For example, despite claims to the contrary, cement continues to be widely used in many countries for stabilization and conservation projects even though it is a material that contains high quantities of salts and is incompatible (being too strong and rigid) with traditional lime-based mortars. The application of such incompatible materials is sometimes dictated by the absence of valid alternatives, but is more often the consequence of poorly trained personnel being given responsibility for major conservation projects.

Also problematic, driven by the desire to show monumental architecture to the visitor, is the issue of reconstruction on archaeological sites.

Figure 6
The Islamic castle of Dablah, Syria. Lack of resources and the scale of intervention required for some major monuments led to the disappearance of many "lesser" monuments.

Figure 7
Capping of mud brick structures at Tumacacori, Arizona.

Figure 8
Vegetation overgrowth in Ostia Antica, Italy.

Figure 9
Decay of mural painting, Pompeii, Italy. Lack of maintenance is often the cause of damage to cultural heritage.

Figure 10
Vegetation damage on mosaic floor in Tel Itztaba, Israel. Lack of maintenance causes damage to many in situ mosaic pavements.

Some reconstructions are made with the intent of protecting the site, returning it to an ideal "original" condition, or making it more understandable to the visitor. Reconstructions are, however, often irreversible, do not improve the understanding of the site, and may be historically and archaeologically incorrect. Reconstructions, but also "improvements" such as heavy wall cappings, partial reconstructions of walls, and the erection of columns using "spare parts" or new material, show, historically, how fast our taste changes in conservation and also how easy it is to do damage that is difficult to repair.

The opposite of excessive conservation intervention, that is, the lack of maintenance, is certainly a cause of the destruction of many heritage sites. Vegetation growth, accumulating dirt, and stagnating water are factors that contribute to material decay. It is not uncommon to see grass and bushes growing out of mosaic floors or on walls. In the same way that a house needs continuous maintenance to avoid large-scale problems, so do archaeological sites.

Lack of Administration and Legislation as Factors in Heritage Loss

The lack of administrative and legislative frameworks within which to carry out the conservation process causes tangible threats to heritage sites. Examples include the unclear definition of the status of archaeological remains on private property, the lack of consideration for site context, and vague criteria for designating protection zones, as well as the poor integration of physical heritage into urban and development plans. In addition, there is the thorny issue of adequate training of personnel in the organizations responsible for site protection, adequate retribution, and other incentives to promote improved job performance.

Discussion

After such an extensive list of man-made threats, those caused by nature seem not only obvious but also more manageable; however, this is not the case. Destructive phenomena such as earthquakes, fires, floods, landslides, and volcanic eruptions often cause extensive damage to human life and property that needs to be dealt with first, before attention can be directed to archaeological and historic sites. The slower, cumulative effect of other natural phenomena such as erosion, material decay, and pests can be as destructive as catastrophic events. *Save Our Sites: The Fragility of Archaeological Sites and Monuments*, an exhibition organized by the Centro di Conservazione Archeologica in Jordan and Syria, defined two categories of threat: those having an immediate and catastrophic effect and those having slow and cumulative effects (Nardi et al. 2000). It also identified the importance of preventive conservation and pointed to training, administration, consciousness-raising, maintenance, and emergency plans as specific areas of intervention to reduce the effects of damaging phenomena.

The ICOMOS *Heritage at Risk* survey is more articulate in suggesting responses to different types of threats. These range from maintenance, monitoring, and promotion of traditional and modern preventive technologies to limit the impact of natural decay processes, to the development of legislation for planning, pollution control, and for ensuring the existence of buffer zones around sites. The stated aim of such measures is also to "promote and improve the implementation of international conventions," "promote cultural diversity," and "promote the recognition of cultural diversity." There is some contradiction in promoting the use of international conventions as a measure of good practice while decrying the threats of globalization. This contradiction is a fundamental one, since a stance that recognizes the existence of diverse heritage and perceptions of heritage also insists on a single standard for conservation (ICOMOS 2000).

The approach advocated in these proceedings, which characterized the entire Corinth workshop, does not stop at simply responding to perceived threats. It recognizes the need for planning, prevention, maintenance, and monitoring in cultural heritage management; at the same time, it also maintains that the process must be based on the recognition of values that often go beyond the traditional areas of scientific research and aesthetic importance. These values have an impact on the way a site is perceived, understood, and, ultimately, managed. If this is a first step toward a less mechanistic view of heritage conservation and management, the second and more radical step is the recognition of the people behind the expressions of values attached to the heritage resources, and the way in which these values influence the significance of the resource. By describing the variety of threats affecting cultural heritage, this paper has demonstrated the importance of assessing and understanding the present conditions of cultural resources prior to the formulation of long-term management plans.

The papers by Erica Avrami and Randall Mason, and Martha Demas further elaborate this approach to heritage management. It is sufficient to anticipate here that taking measures to reduce threat is relatively simple: the idea of preventive conservation and maintenance is gaining consensus on a large scale, although its practical development is still uneven. What is more difficult to achieve, however, is the development of a conceptual framework for heritage management planning that looks at value and stakeholder recognition (and participation) as the core elements for developing plans that are sensitive to local conditions and sustainable in the long term.

References

Ciliberto, E., R. Chillemi, S. Sciuto, G. Spoto, C. Puglisi, G. Villari, and A. Bombaci
1995 "Acts of Vandalism on Archaeological Monuments: The Case of the 'Villa del Casale,' Piazza Armerina." In *Science and Technology for the Safeguard of Cultural Heritage in the Mediterranean Basin*, 1:785–88. Rome: CNR.

Darvill, T., and A. Fulton
1998 *MARS: The Monuments at Risk Survey of England, 1995: Main Report*. Bournemouth: Bournemouth University and English Heritage.

2000 *MARS: The Monuments at Risk Survey of England*. See http://csweb.bournemouth.ac.uk/consci/text_mars/marsint.htm.

Debono, F. G.
2001 "Vandals Cause 'Irreparable' Damage to Mnajdra Temple." *The Sunday Times of Malta*, 15 April, 1.

ICOMOS
2000 *Heritage at Risk: ICOMOS World Report 2000 on Monuments and Sites in Danger*. See http://www.international.icomos.org/riskindex_eng.htm.

ICR
1996a *Carta del Rischio del Patrimonio Culturale: La Cartografia Tematica*. Rome: Bonifica S.p.a.

1996b *Carta del Rischio del Patrimonio Culturale: La Metodologia per il Calcolo del Rischio*. Rome: Bonifica S.p.a.

1996c *Carta del Rischio del Patrimonio Culturale: Il Rischio Locale*. Rome: Bonifica S.p.a.

1996d *Carta del Rischio del Patrimonio Culturale: Il Sistema Informativo della Carta del Rischio*. Rome: Bonifica S.p.a.

1997 *The Risk Map of Cultural Heritage*. Rome: Bonifica S.p.a.

Carta del Rischio del Patrimonio Culturale. See http://www.icr.arti.beniculturali.it/rischio/rischio00e.htm.

Melucco, Vaccaro, A.
1989 *Archeologia e Restauro*. Milan: Il Saggiatore.

Nardi, R. et al.
2000 *Save Our Sites: The Fragility of Archaeological Sites and Monuments*, exh. cat. Amman/Damascus: Centro di Conservazione Archeologica.

Pedelì, C. and S. Puglia
2002 *Pratiche Conservative sullo Scavo Archeologico: Principi e Metodi*. Florence: All'Insegna del Giglio.

Stanley Price, N., ed.
1995 *Conservation on Archaeological Excavations*. 2nd ed. Rome: ICCROM.

Heritage Values and Challenges of Conservation Planning

Randall Mason and Erica Avrami

Why Is the Conservation Field Concerned with Values?

THOSE OF US WORKING in the cultural heritage field believe that conservation provides a benefit to society. The physical products and remains of our past serve as an important reminder of where we come from, who we are, and who we want to be. Conservation of cultural heritage is essential because it provides us with a greater understanding of our identity, of continuity, of the human condition, and of our place in the world and in time. In addition, cultural heritage has the potential to bring us together as communities, to foster tolerance among communities, and, ultimately, to make us better citizens. Heritage, however, also has the potential to divide us. This Janus-like nature of heritage as a social phenomenon highlights the need to understand the *process* of heritage conservation—who participates, why, and how? It is our belief and assumption, as conservation professionals, that heritage conservation yields important and unique social benefits. Our continuing practical work, advocacy, and research efforts are motivated by this belief.

Archaeological sites constitute an important form of cultural heritage and they form the focus of this publication. Archaeology offers, among other things, a window to the distant past that enhances our understanding of human, social, and technological development. For professionals, academics, and the public at large, archaeological sites provide valued information and experiences, which most of us hope to keep available to future generations as well. Thus, there is increasing and well warranted concern about the long-term preservation of archaeological sites and about the intergenerational responsibility conservation professionals and decision makers have to ensure that preservation is meaningful in the present and sustainable in the long term.

There are many challenges to making the conservation of archaeological heritage possible, meaningful, and sustainable (see "Threats and Challenges to the Archaeological Heritage in the Mediterranean" by Gaetano Palumbo in this volume, which outlines a number of specific, observable threats). From a technical perspective, the range and complexity of archaeological materials and constructions, their condition, their use, and their exposure to the elements make conservation a formidable task. From a philosophical perspective, conservation poses a number of thorny dilemmas—how to conserve, to what degree of intervention, and with what objectives in mind. Technical problems are further compounded by social factors such as looting, unchecked urban development and encroachment, increased tourism, the violence of war and civil unrest, rampant excavation, lack of financial and human resources, political controversy, and the like.

In the face of these challenges, conservation can often seem like a low priority, if not a virtual impossibility. As a professional field that is still developing, conservation is in a period of evolution and experimentation with new ideas and methods. We assert that the issues of heritage values—the many, sometimes conflicting kinds of values, how values are articulated, who decides which values take precedence—are paramount to positively engaging this moment in the field of heritage conservation.

To what is the values-based approach responding? What are the salient social contexts in which conservation is enacted today? These questions can be summarized by noting the three closely related contextual challenges that follow:

1. At the largest scale there is the context of globalization, which is characterized in briefest terms by marked increases and effects of transnational migration; mobility of ideas, capital, and people; and the digital technology enabling it. Generally, these processes are understood as driven by political-economic factors: the innovations and depredations of the global economy and the power of multinational corporations. The role of culture and identity in globalizing society is difficult to discern and often contradictory. Exchange among cultures at all scales is rampant; however, the mode of exchange often requires the commodification, decontextualization, and debasement of culture. Culture and identity—and, therefore, heritage—are often controversial, contentious subjects. With culture seeming more changeable, debated, and marketed, many of us feel a greater desire for heritage as an anchor against change. Clashes between economic and cultural forces—between stasis and change—present daily challenges in the heritage field and elsewhere, seeming to invade the once-insulated field of conservation.
2. At the scale of human communities, the social contexts of heritage "on the ground" present myriad obstacles and complexities to heritage conservation activities. All heritage or conservation decisions are bound by empirical contexts, such as land ownership, financial needs, development pressures, environmental features, and claims by culture groups or politicians to use heritage for specific, and sometimes divisive, symbolic purposes.
3. The conservation field itself constitutes a third important context. The information infrastructure of the field needs to keep pace with changes in the social contexts of conservation, in addition to technical advances. The question must continually be asked: As a field, what do we need to learn that we don't already know? The knowledge and skills required to conserve

material heritage fall into three broad categories, and the field needs to pursue research in all three. These include the physical condition of heritage artifacts, buildings, and so on; the management context in which conservation projects are developed and carried out; and the cultural significance, or more generally, how the meaning and value of heritage is expressed and weighed. Currently, those of us in the conservation field know the least about this third front of knowledge; a values-based approach to conservation theory advances our understanding here.

Stated differently, those of us working in the conservation field are quite comfortable figuring out *how* to conserve something (technical questions, mostly concerning physical conditions), but we are just beginning to look more seriously for answers to the questions of *what* and *why*. What things become objects of conservation interest and precisely why? A discussion of values opens our eyes to these other questions, enabling cross-disciplinary, cross-cultural dialogue about the decisions on what, why, and how to conserve. Discussion of values is necessary because these questions do not have one optimal answer. Rather, the solution to the question of *what* will be subjective, context-dependent, and political. Values gives us an analytical tool, a lingua franca, to organize research and practice in this subjective, political terrain.

Values in Conservation

Clarifying what is meant when we speak of values is a necessary first step in the explanation of values in conservation. *Value* is a multifaceted and even tricky term. There are two main senses of the noun *value* (the meaning of *value* as a verb is considered below). First, and perhaps most often, *value* refers to morals, principles, or ethics—ideas that serve as guides to action. All people and organizations, it can be said, have and act on a set of these values even if they are often tacit. These values are sometimes codified in a "code of ethics," mission statement, profession of religious belief, philosophical statement, and so on.

Second, *value* refers to the characteristics of things or objects. In this sense, one can speak of values as the qualities of the places (sites, buildings, artifacts, and landscapes) we refer to as heritage. As detailed below, these characteristics range widely from the economic to the aesthetic or the symbolic. It is this definition of *values* on which the present discussion is built.

The following observations should be made to reveal the assumptions and principles that guide our discussion of values as characteristics of heritage:

- A heritage building or site has several different kinds of value all at once. Simply, they are the different qualities that motivate the labeling of some object or place as "heritage" and, further, they motivate conservation of that object or place.

- For the most part, heritage values are not intrinsic but rather subjective, context-bound, changeable, and malleable. This is not to say that heritage objects have no objective qualities; age, size, and other factors are some of these. The values we speak of here, however, are the opinions about characteristics—not separable from someone ascribing and describing the value. There are many different kinds of value attached to one heritage site and they are very tightly connected. The different kinds of value are not necessarily exclusive; and sometimes they are in conflict.
- Assessments of value can differ greatly depending on who is doing the assessing. The way one talks about and expresses heritage values depends a great deal on one's perspective: a citizen with strong emotional attachment to the site, an economist working for a bank, an academic from another country, a teacher from a local school, and so on.

The discussion of values is not new in the heritage field—the Venice Charter, for instance, was greatly concerned with values. In general, however, values usually are invoked as something fixed, whereas the more important insight, we believe, is that values are most often in flux and contested, and do not submit easily to measurement and assessment.

To support a discussion of heritage values, it is useful to suggest a typology as a common reference point. Most heritage sites have some measure of most kinds of the following values. This list is not all-encompassing or essential. Several of the value-types overlap and cannot be totally separated from one another. Furthermore, no typology can accurately describe the values of every site—on the contrary, a value typology needs to be specific to a particular project or site.

Historical and artistic values

Heritage embodies historical values by simply providing a physical connection to the past. By representing the passage of time in material form, heritage has historical value (for example, the Pantheon in Rome). In terms of artistic values, heritage embodies value stemming from its sensate qualities—its capacity to stimulate the senses (for example, the value of the beauty and artwork of a site such as Central Park in New York or the Duomo in Florence).

Social or civic values

Heritage often supports and symbolizes our sociability: the way in which different parts of a society group, live, and work together and relate. It serves as an organization point for political action or otherwise creates the conditions for civil society (for example, the central plaza in Guanajuato, Mexico—or the plaza of just about any other city).

Spiritual or religious values

Heritage has spiritual value when it is integral to the beliefs or practices of a religious group (for example, ancient Corinth's religious value to Christians as the place where the Apostle Paul ministered and wrote his letters to the Corinthians).

Symbolic or identity values

The term *symbolic values* refers to the capacity of a heritage site to stimulate or maintain group identity and other social relations built through association with a heritage site (for example, the value of ancient burial sites to Native American groups in the United States).

Research values

Heritage sites—archaeological sites in particular—are valued as records of the past. The information uniquely contained in them has real and potential value for research, education, and the generation of knowledge (for example, any archaeological resource, such as Chaco Canyon in New Mexico).

Natural values

The natural value of heritage stems from the role it may play in the ecology of a particular natural community. In addition to its social (human-constructed) values, a heritage site may also function as a natural resource —as open, green space or as part of a watershed (again, consider Chaco Canyon in New Mexico as an example).

Economic values

Economic values constitute a distinct, powerful perspective on heritage values. Any heritage site is an asset in the economic sense: it requires investment to acquire and maintain; it yields a flow of benefits (for example, the fee paid to visit an historic site, such as the Roman Forum; or the increased value of real estate in a district of well-preserved houses). Some of these benefits can be traded on markets and, therefore, can be expressed in prices, while others cannot. Economic values are often used to describe all other kinds of value in terms of a single variable—price. This is a problematic assumption (see Mason 1998).

Why It Is Necessary to Integrate Values into Conservation Planning

Values Shape Conservation and Conservation Decisions

Conservation is a complex and often controversial process that involves determinations about what constitutes heritage; how it is used, cared for, interpreted, and invested in; by whom and for whom. Decisions about *what* and *how* to conserve are largely defined by cultural contexts, societal trends, and political and economic forces, which themselves are continually changing. Cultural heritage is thus a medium for the ever-evolving needs, beliefs, and attitudes of social groups, be they disciplines or professional groups, communities residing in a certain territory, ethnic groups, or entire nations. Social groups are embedded in certain places and times, and, as a matter of routine, use *things* (material heritage) to interpret their past and their future. In this sense, conservation is not merely about saving the physical remains of the past; it is about telling something about ourselves to present and future generations—what is important to us, what we value about our history, and why we are connected to our various groups. Because social attitudes and beliefs can change with time, one would expect the meaning and values ascribed to cultural heritage to change as well.

As argued above, material heritage is valued for the connections it provides to the past. This is not the only reason it is valued, however. The investigation and conservation of archaeological sites strongly shape and reshape these values of heritage. Selecting where to excavate and what occupation period to investigate, determining methods and levels of intervention of conservation treatment, deciding where and how to give access to the public—these very typical examples demonstrate the ways in which different values come into play at archaeological sites.

Changes in the Conservation Field

The conservation field has made significant advances in grappling with these challenges in a holistic way in the last twenty years. This is particularly true vis-à-vis the conservation of architecture and historic and archaeological sites. Through comprehensive planning for "cultural resource management" (otherwise known as conservation management or site management), integrated, interdisciplinary approaches to the preservation of the built environment have been developed to address the changed conditions of contemporary society.

Critical to this trend in conservation has been the evolving notion of "cultural significance." The Venice Charter, adopted in 1964, made initial reference to "cultural significance" and "aesthetic and historic values" within the context of a set of guidelines for professional practice. It was not until the early 1980s, however, that the assessment of values or cultural significance was distinguished as a discrete part of the conservation process in policy documents, namely the United States Secretary of the Interior's Standards for Rehabilitation and the Australia ICOMOS Burra Charter. The Burra Charter, in particular, elucidated the notion that conservation is a value-driven process centered on the notion of cultural significance and provided a systematic approach to conservation planning that reflected this.

Both the Burra Charter and the Secretary of the Interior's Standards represent the policies of specific countries, but subsequent documents, especially the Nara Document (1994) and the Declaration of San Antonio (1996), resulted from international and regional discourse on values and the not-so-fixed concept of authenticity. As a matter of practice, integrated planning methodologies that attempt to incorporate values more effectively in conservation decision making have been developed by

Australia ICOMOS, the United States National Park Service, Parks Canada, English Heritage, and many other governments and nongovernmental agencies (NGOs). These planning approaches foreground issues of values and aim to integrate values with other contextual considerations, such as available resources, legislative environment, and so forth, as well as the more technical issues of physical condition. The underlying tenet is that a thorough, holistic, and integrated analysis of all these considerations paves the way for clear conservation policy that is sustainable in the long term.

The application of these holistic approaches results in management plans that serve as vital instruments for the ongoing conservation process. Management plans themselves vary in scope and content; some are site-specific while others deal with several sites or entire regions. Some are developed as short-term operational plans that are redeveloped every few years, while others entail a longer horizon with periodic adaptation. The level of detail also varies from plan to plan; while some may provide specific designs for how the different aspects of site management are undertaken, others outline general objectives and terms of reference for different program areas.

Ultimately, the importance of a plan is its use as a decision-making tool over a period of time. A plan should represent a collective vision for the site and engender support for continued investment by engaging the range of stakeholders early on in and throughout the planning process. What is most critical about management plans is that they should be value-driven and developed through a participatory and interdisciplinary process. This participatory process of *planning*—of making, implementing, monitoring, and reevaluating the plan—can be as important to long-term conservation as the plan itself.

As professionals in this field, we face numerous challenges in promoting this type of integrated approach to conservation. On the broadest level, the conservation field has not been successful in translating its own issues and beliefs so that they are understood in relation to the beliefs of the broader public. If we are to advocate a participatory conservation process, we must become better at articulating our own beliefs, assumptions, and working principles. Conservation often fails on a second front as well: although we recognize that assessment of values and other contextual issues is imperative, we have not as yet developed professional tools and methods for this type of analysis, as we have, for example, for technical matters, such as the analysis and recording of condition. To a great extent, these new tools for integrated planning will only be developed through an ongoing dialogue between the empirical implementation of planning processes and the continued research and refinement of methodological approaches. Our great hurdle is this paradox: we have not yet developed a body of knowledge to inform the implementation of values-centered, integrated planning processes, and we have yet to accumulate enough experiences of planning processes to build the knowledge base. Our field is, therefore, in a period of experimentation, as mentioned at the outset. As value-driven methodologies are applied and adapted to local contexts, we will learn more about the advantages and challenges of implementation, and ways to improve our approaches.

In the face of this dilemma, the Getty Conservation Institute (GCI) has attempted to address issues on both sides of the paradox: by advocating, teaching, and monitoring value-driven planning approaches used in different parts of the world; by promoting national and regional conservation policies that incorporate values; and by undertaking and publishing research regarding values in conservation. This workshop is part of a series of efforts that ranges from courses to conferences to research publications. In particular, "The Conservation of Archaeological Sites in the Mediterranean Region," a conference organized by the GCI in 1995, brought together policy makers from the Mediterranean (including archaeologists, conservation specialists, and tourism professionals) to explore site management needs and issues of the region. Through the Corinth Workshop, the GCI hoped to develop some of the concepts put forth in the Mediterranean Conference, in particular the issues of values and value-driven planning processes for conservation. This publication is intended to sustain the momentum for integrated conservation planning in and around the region.

Incorporating Values into Conservation Planning Practices

The balance of this paper discusses issues raised in applying these abstract notions about values and valuing to the practices of making conservation plans. Today's climate of globalization, technological advancement, political conflict, and population mobility, along with the spread of participatory democracies and market economies, makes for rapidly changing cultures and communities. Although none of these processes is totally novel, in combination they constitute a climate substantially different from the social relations that previously governed the conservation field—the dominance of the West, state institutions, and so on. We often find that cultural heritage is "at risk." These changing social conditions compel us to act strategically—instead of simply reacting—to ensure that heritage conservation is responsive to cultural values and conditions, and that it remains a sustainable process.

What specific concepts and issues must be worked out in adopting a "values-based model of conservation planning and management"? Why do the GCI and others in the conservation field see values as an important issue for advancing conservation practice? The questions discussed in the balance of this paper connect more detailed discussion of the management planning process itself by Martha Demas with Gaetano Palumbo's exegesis of the threats facing archaeological heritage.

The Valuing Process: "Value" Is Also a Verb

Conservation of material heritage, in some form, is a practice observable in all cultures, reinforcing the notion that preserving things and places of the past is a vital function of society, a contributor to human and social development. An important corollary to this, which is not expanded on here, is that every culture will pursue the conservation of heritage differently—sometimes drastically so as seen in the contrasts, for instance, between Western and Eastern notions of what constitutes heritage. Cultural materials and artifacts of the past, one can say, have an inherent "story telling" capacity. In the case of archaeological sites, this is poignantly evident. As the legacy of a past civilization, as a collection of artifacts and settings with inherent narrative power, archaeological sites have an intrinsic potential for providing, among other things, historical information. This enduring potential to inform our understanding of human and social evolution speaks to a universal quality of cultural heritage that cannot always be related to a specific context.

Acknowledging the context-bound valuing of cultural heritage, without subverting the potential for collective and even universal meaning, is critical to conservation decision making. To achieve balanced decisions, there is a need for increased cooperation among the many professionals, decision makers, and community members that influence the outcomes and sustainability of conservation efforts. These different persons are often referred to as "stakeholders" in conservation processes; they each have a "stake," or vested interest, in the site and how it is used, preserved, and developed. Giving voice to their varied perspectives through a participatory process helps to ensure that conservation is responsive to professional and academic ideals as well as to social needs and concerns. As conservation professionals, we can play a very important role in facilitating participation and guiding the conservation process.

The notion that the values of cultural heritage are subjective and mutable is taken for granted in many academic circles today, although this notion is still debated in the conservation field. More than a generation of scholarship affirms that culture is better understood as a set of processes rather than a collection of things, thus reinforcing the notion that artifacts and sites are not static embodiments of culture but rather conduits for evolving notions of identity and history. Taken to its extreme, this insight suggests that cultural heritage is simply a social construction, which is clearly problematic. The sheer physicality of heritage—as a tangible, handed-down vestige of material culture—seems to contradict this and gives rise to the sentiment that it is in fact imbued with some objective, universal, intrinsic qualities.

The concept of values has been developed here in a fairly static way—as a characteristic of a site that can be fairly described and even measured. This concept becomes most useful, however, when it is connected to the process of valuing. Who ascribes value? What are the conflicts and correspondences between different kinds of value and ways of describing and measuring them? The real usefulness of the values concept for planning resides precisely in this connection between the characteristics of sites and the processes through which different stakeholders express and act on those values.

Who Does the Valuing?

Discussion of "values" inexorably leads to questions of "valuing." Who is ascribing the different values to heritage? Who is balancing and prioritizing and advocating them? In the most general sense, the answer is "stakeholders"—the many individuals, groups, and institutions with an interest in the outcome of heritage and conservation issues.

Values are not objects themselves; rather, they are assessments and interpretations of objects. The processes shaping heritage values—

those processes that shape these ideas—are thus exceedingly important, not just as an intellectual exercise but because this focuses attention on how decisions and actions are motivated, how different stakeholders stake their claim, and more specifically, what role we as professionals play in the value-formation and decision processes.

Different kinds of value—not to mention differing interpretations of any particular kind of value—often correspond to different stakeholders. The correspondence is seldom one for one (that is, only investors are interested in articulating economic values, only artists see artistic value). There is, however, an essential connection between the interpretation and articulation of values and the interests of different stakeholders, a connection that makes values so central to planning and decision making. Accounting for the full range of heritage values for a given project or plan will, therefore, require an understanding of who is doing the valuing of the heritage in question.

It is, therefore, important to know who the stakeholders are. Traditionally, political officials and investors have been the most influential stakeholders, while conservation experts have perhaps been the most vocal. The net must be cast more broadly, however. Thinking in terms of social equity, the stakeholders should include those whose voices on political and planning matters are usually soft or silent (the poor, minorities, and other disenfranchised groups). Further, stakeholder groups may extend beyond the people located around a site. Indigenous peoples worldwide, one could argue, have a stake in the conservation of indigenous-culture heritage sites on any continent. Stakeholders may include specialists with an interest in the site (that is, research and spiritual value); they may also include people who used to live near the site but who have since moved away.

Focusing on stakeholders opens the issue of broadening *participation* in conservation. Demand for wider participation is perhaps the most pressing political issue facing conservation planners, site managers, and policy makers; however, the nature of participation is its own considerable question. The quality of participation can vary widely—from less-meaningful large public meetings to more meaningful involvement on steering committees and work teams—so it is important to follow vague guarantees of greater participation with specific measures. The end goal is bringing a meaningful representation and balance among heritage values as held by outsiders as well as insiders to the process of decision making and planning.

Assessing and Balancing Values

The connections among site attributes, values, and stakeholders present the conservation professional with two specific challenges vis-à-vis planning and management: *assessing* and *balancing* values.

What tools do we have for speaking of, communicating about, and dealing with values? "Cultural significance," the conservation field's traditional way of articulating the values of heritage, is inadequate as it is generally used. For the most part, cultural significance refers to a narrow range of the heritage value spectrum. For instance, significance tends to neglect economic values, but where decision making is concerned these values of course cannot be ignored. Significance is conceived as a static and timeless assessment of value, which speaks to conservation professionals not to cultures. It fixes the meaning of a site, mostly according to expert assessments, whereas most would agree that the meaning of a site is usually a bit contentious and always shifting and changing. Finally, cultural significance assessments tend to include only the expert voices in the conversation so that assessment of any particular kind of value—say, historical—is not seen from a variety of perspectives. Or rather, the final assessment is "resolved" and does not reflect real differences in different stakeholders' assessments of the value of a site.

While we do not need to discard "cultural significance," we do need to be more rigorous and inclusive about determining what is significant, to whom, and in what ways. How can this be accomplished? First, the net of values considered in assessments of significance must be widened. Second, the range of stakeholders consulted and included in the process must be widened. Conservation planning can be better informed about methods for achieving this by examining parallel fields and how they have sought wider participation. For instance, the fields of town planning, environmental conservation, rural development, and public health have all developed tools for addressing similar challenges to their own canonical ways of practice.

Heritage conservation is an essentially multidisciplinary field; therefore, research must also be devoted to integrating the tools, methods, and ideas of allied disciplines. In particular, those of us in the conservation field face a steep and productive learning curve in adapting and using the work of allied disciplines of anthropology, economics, and philosophy. Each of these fields has specific methods for assessing and articulating values from which we can learn. Our sense, in working with professionals from these fields, is that overlaying different perspectives on value and heritage—folding together the methods of economists, anthropologists, and heritage professionals—is a very promising direction of research. The GCI has been working to develop specific, hybrid assessment tools to be integrated into the kind of planning models that Martha Demas addresses in her paper. The goal of such tools is not only to give the best possible accounting of the full range of heritage values but also to make the values of heritage understandable to as many people as possible. In both these senses, we believe that a dialogue about heritage values can function as a lingua franca for the many stakeholders in heritage conservation.

Another significant challenge for conservation planning is finding ways to incorporate the participation of "insiders" and "outsiders," respectively those stakeholders traditionally included in the conservation decision-making processes and those who are not. The outsiders include local residents, experts from disciplines other than heritage conservation (environmental conservation, economic development, and public health, for instance), and even conservation professionals in instances where they are not consulted or given a say in decisions.

Once heritage values are assessed, the question becomes one of balance: how do the different values get prioritized, traded, and balanced in the course of making and carrying out plans? Balancing values is indeed a primary goal of conservation plans—alongside ensuring the stewardship of the heritage itself. If we are to weigh, balance, and manage the conservation of values, and employ an integrated approach, what is our guide? This is a difficult question on two levels: first, the value assessments will not likely be easily commensurable. They will likely be in different terms (dollars, historical significance, beauty, symbolic power, and so on). It is also likely that they will conflict in that maximizing one type of value will mean minimizing other types of value. Finally, any particular balance will be decided on (or trumped) politically, not as a matter of an optimal, objective solution.

To guide the work of conservation professionals and decision-makers in striking a balance of the many stakeholders and values, one suggestion is the notion of *sustainability*. Although rooted in environmental conservation—balancing economic, ecological, spiritual, and aesthetic values of the natural environment—sustainability is beginning to be developed in terms meaningful to the practice of heritage conservation. A few sustainability principles can serve as a useful guide—or set of tests—to strengthen the long-term and social benefits of heritage conservation as they flow out of conservation planning and management processes.

Based on the work of David Throsby (2002), sustainable heritage conservation should do the following:

- Promote *intergenerational equity*: take into account the needs of *future* generations;
- Promote *intragenerational equity*: a notion that aspires to fairness, equality in distribution of benefits and costs, and wide participation in conservation planning processes;
- Maintain *diversity*: parallel to the notion of biodiversity in the environmental realm, a measure of cultural diversity is essential for cultural health, and individual decisions can be evaluated in terms of whether they increase or decrease the overall diversity of the culture;
- Generate *tangible and intangible benefits*: recognize the economic and cultural, use and nonuse benefits of heritage conservation;
- Use scarce *resources* wisely and strategically: this applies to financial, human, and environmental aspects;
- Abide by a *precautionary principle*: recognizing that some actions are irreversible, this principle dictates that they be approached with extreme caution;
- Recognize *interdependence*: heritage is part of a system connected to society and environment; it is not a realm apart. Conservation must, therefore, be approached holistically, considering the many values of heritage and seeking to integrate heritage into other social activities (development, education, and so on); and
- The *currency* of conservation: assure some relevance and responsiveness of conservation measures to current/near-term cultural conditions. Without such relevance, support for conservation will remain scarce and fleeting; educational measures, in the broadest sense, can demonstrate the relevance of conservation to contemporary society.

Conclusion

In this paper, we have advanced the idea that a discussion of values is important—even essential—to the field of conservation. More specifically, grappling methodologically with the issue of values is central to planning for archaeological and other heritage sites.

The rationale for a discussion of values in conservation stems from challenges arising from understanding conservation planning as a social and political process, as opposed to a technical problem to solve. Conservation shapes the society in which it is situated; in turn, it is shaped by the needs and dynamics of that society. Ultimately, we conserve heritage because of the values imputed to it, not for the sake of the material itself. What we are conserving, ultimately, are the values of heritage. If we focus on, or try to conserve, the material itself without its contexts, we lose sight of the material's values. At such a point, conservation becomes merely a self-serving interest of conservation professionals instead of the robust, meaningful struggle with representing memory and identity that is conservation's central social function.

Values constitute a lingua franca for understanding and talking about the different (although often incommensurable and often contested) interests and stakeholders attached to a particular site. A values framework such as that discussed here builds a realistic picture of stakeholder interests and begins to provide a basis for comparing and balancing them. A values framework also lends itself to understanding comparatively the meanings that different cultures attach to conservation.

The best decisions and plans are those that preserve values for the long term and for as many stakeholders as possible. A values framework achieves the pragmatic goal of setting the context for conservation decision making and planning by (1) acknowledging and framing different positions in a comprehensive, mutually intelligible framework; and (2) helping to clarify trade-offs in the sense that conservation measures will cultivate some values and not others. Using a values framework in conservation planning enables professionals and decision makers to better understand how to balance technical, administrative, financial, aesthetic, and social concerns of heritage conservation, by putting these needs and decisions in the context of who cares, who values, and why.

The principles behind a values framework also provide a useful reminder that there is no simple, technical, objective way to make decisions about what heritage gets preserved and how. A values framework does not pretend to be a scientific method for resolving stakeholder clashes or anointing one best solution; rather, it presents a way of enabling discussion and negotiation of positions, interests, and values. It makes room for laypersons to collaborate with experts, for experts in different fields to be mutually intelligible, and for a discussion about "apples and oranges" to become one about "fruit."

Finally, most would agree that a more sustainable model of conservation planning is our shared goal. A planning process based on values in the full sense argued here is a model for sustainable conservation, which is to say it promises to be meaningful and resonant to many stakeholders, open to wide participation, future-focused, realistic, and flexible but not totally subjective.

A Look to the Future

Through the application and evaluation of planning processes that utilize this sort of value-based approach, we can build a body of knowledge to refine methodologies of conservation planning. In addition to such advancement of the field and profession, value-based, participatory planning approaches will also serve to create stronger public support for the work of conservation and to make it more responsive to societal conditions. Such a planning process can seem too difficult to pursue due to political constraints, limited resources, lack of expertise, and the like. The process is flexible, however, and can be adapted to particular contexts with plans developed to a level of detail appropriate to the needs and resources of the situation. In the end, we as conservation professionals must decide whether we will take a leading role in promoting advancement or continue to serve heritage in a reactionary capacity. If we believe in the possibilities heritage conservation provides for reinforcing communities, fostering tolerance, creating meaningful attachment to places, and making us better citizens, we will have to make for ourselves a strong role to ensure that those possibilities can become a reality.

References

Australia ICOMOS
1992 *The Illustrated Burra Charter: Making Good Decisions about the Care of Important Places.* Ed. Peter Marquis-Kyle and Meridith Walker. Sydney: Australia ICOMOS. See also *http://www.icomos.org/australia/burra.html* (24 July 2002).

"The Declaration of San Antonio" (1996)
1999 Cited in Gustavo Araoz, Margaret MacLean, and Lara Day Kozak, eds. *Authenticity in the Conservation and Management of the Cultural Heritage of the Americas.* Washington, D.C., and Los Angeles: US/ICOMOS and the Getty Conservation Institute.

ICOMOS
1964, *International Charter for the Conservation and Restoration of Monuments*
1965 *and Sites (The Venice Charter).* Venice: ICOMOS.

Larsen, Knut Einar, ed.
1994 *Nara Conference on Authenticity.* Paris: ICOMOS.

Mason, Randall, ed.
1998 *Economics and Heritage Conservation.* Los Angeles: The J. Paul Getty Trust.

Throsby, David.
2002 "Cultural Capital and Sustainability Concepts in the Economics of Cultural Heritage." In Marta de la Torre, ed., *Assessing the Values of Cultural Heritage.* Los Angeles: The Getty Conservation Institute.

de la Torre, Marta, ed.
1997 *The Conservation of Archaeological Sites in the Mediterranean Region* (Proceedings of an International Conference Organized by the Getty Conservation Institute and the J. Paul Getty Museum, May 1995). Los Angeles: The Getty Conservation Institute.

Planning for Conservation and Management of Archaeological Sites
A Values-Based Approach

Martha Demas

In recent decades, the need for a planning methodology for the conservation and management of archaeological sites has arisen in response to the rapidly changing world in which we now operate. The extent and pace of change—whether manifest in the physical destruction of sites, in the varied uses of sites, or in our ways of thinking about and valuing the past—pose an enormous challenge for those involved in preserving and interpreting the archaeological record. In the face of such challenges, the planning process described in this paper provides a way of managing change and making decisions about the way in which an archaeological site will be conserved and managed in the future. It is premised on the following three assumptions or convictions that have been explored in previous papers presented at the workshop and in this publication:

1. Many of the problems facing archaeological sites today, as described in Gaetano Palumbo's paper, are rarely capable of being solved definitively, but can be managed; that is, their adverse impacts can be mitigated or controlled.
2. The best or most appropriate decisions for a site are those that will preserve the values of the place and are sustainable; Randall Mason and Erica Avrami have explored the basis for this conviction in their paper.
3. "Good" decisions are the result of careful planning.

Accepting these premises, the planning process will serve as a road map for making good decisions and managing problems. Although this process can be applied to all types of cultural heritage, the emphasis in this workshop and paper is on archaeological sites; in particular, those sites already recognized as having value and, therefore, having been given some form of legal protection and public access.

Why Is There a Need for a Planning Process?

The benefits of engaging in a planning process, which requires a commitment of time and staff, are not always easy to appreciate in the midst of crisis management—the state in which many managing authorities of archaeological sites find themselves. Too frequently, importance is attached to a specific outcome or destination (a "plan"), while the process for achieving that end (the "journey") is undervalued or overlooked. The process in and of itself always yields benefits that go beyond any specific outcome—or, in the words of the Alexandrian poet Constantine Cavafy, the journey makes you "rich with all you have gained on the way."[1] In more prosaic terms, the benefits of engaging in a planning process may be stated as follows:

A planning process is an opportunity to

- create a shared vision among staff responsible for the site and external parties who have an interest in the site;
- involve key players, and thereby strengthen relationships, negotiate conflicts, and form alliances that will benefit the site;
- engage in transparent decision making; that is, to make the decision-making process open and clear to all;
- reassess, evaluate, and synthesize information about a site; and
- take account of the needs of future generations as well as our own.

A planning process is also a powerful tool for

- thinking and making decisions in a logical way;
- sorting through complex issues facing archaeological sites today;
- setting priorities by understanding what is really important about a site;
- explaining and justifying decisions; and
- ensuring that the results of decisions are sustainable.

Finally, where altruism fails, there is always self-interest to help motivate the unconvinced. All the current trends in conservation point to management planning for archaeological sites as the tool of the future. Anyone dealing with international organizations today will have seen that trend—whether it be the European Union, UNESCO (United Nations Educational, Scientific and Cultural Organization), ICCROM (International Centre for the Study of the Preservation and Restoration of Cultural Property), the World Heritage Centre, the World Bank, or granting programs, such as the Getty Grant Program or the Heritage Lottery Fund in England. All of these organizations are engaged in management planning initiatives or require management plans prior to approvals for funding.

Why This Particular Planning Process?

The planning process advocated here has its origins in the Australia ICOMOS (International Council on Monuments and Sites) Burra Charter, which has been used by Australian government agencies and the private sector for over twenty years with a high degree of success and continues to evolve in response to experience and changing values (see Bibliography 2 for references to this and other approaches to management planning).

Since 1989, the Getty Conservation Institute has advocated, adapted, and explored this planning process in training courses and field projects, through research initiatives, and, most recently, in a partnership with the national heritage authority in China and the Australian Heritage Commission to develop guidelines for conservation practice and management planning at a national level in China.

This process places values and the participation of a wide spectrum of interested parties at the core of the decision-making process. This is an adaptable and flexible process: it is culturally adaptable in that it has been adopted and used successfully in many parts of the world and it is flexible in that it can be applied to a site, a region, or an entire country—or even to an individual monument or structure within a site.

Despite all these commendations, however, neither this nor any planning process is a magic formula for making the right decisions; the process is only as good as what one puts into it. Valid data are essential, but so too are the efforts toward building relationships based on trust and mutual understanding.

The Planning Process

The planning process is structured as a logical progression from the collection of information (phase 1), through assessment and analysis of all the factors that influence management of the site (phase 2), to decision making (phase 3). Implicit in this structure is the understanding that decisions cannot be made in a vacuum but are the result of sound information and the careful assessment and analysis of that information. The three major phases of the planning process are as follows:

1. Identification and Description: collecting information;
2. Assessment and Analysis: taking stock; and
3. Response: making decisions.

This structure also implies sequence: a beginning, middle, and end. A common mistake among those professionals with decision-making responsibility has been to begin at the response phase—that is, to make decisions—and then work backward to collect and assess information that is relevant to those decisions. While the integrity of the process rests on following sequence, it is also important to recognize that this is an iterative process; that is, it is not strictly linear in its progression and frequently necessitates looping back to previous steps to check, clarify, and augment information and modify the assessment. Graphic presentation of the process in the flowchart (Fig. 1) shows the logical progression of phases, but the dynamism and feedback loops are more difficult to convey and need to be kept in mind.

The result of the process is a plan that makes clear a strategic vision, while it documents and publicizes the essence of the process's three major phases. It stands as a record of the process and the decisions reached about how the site will be conserved and managed for a defined period of time.

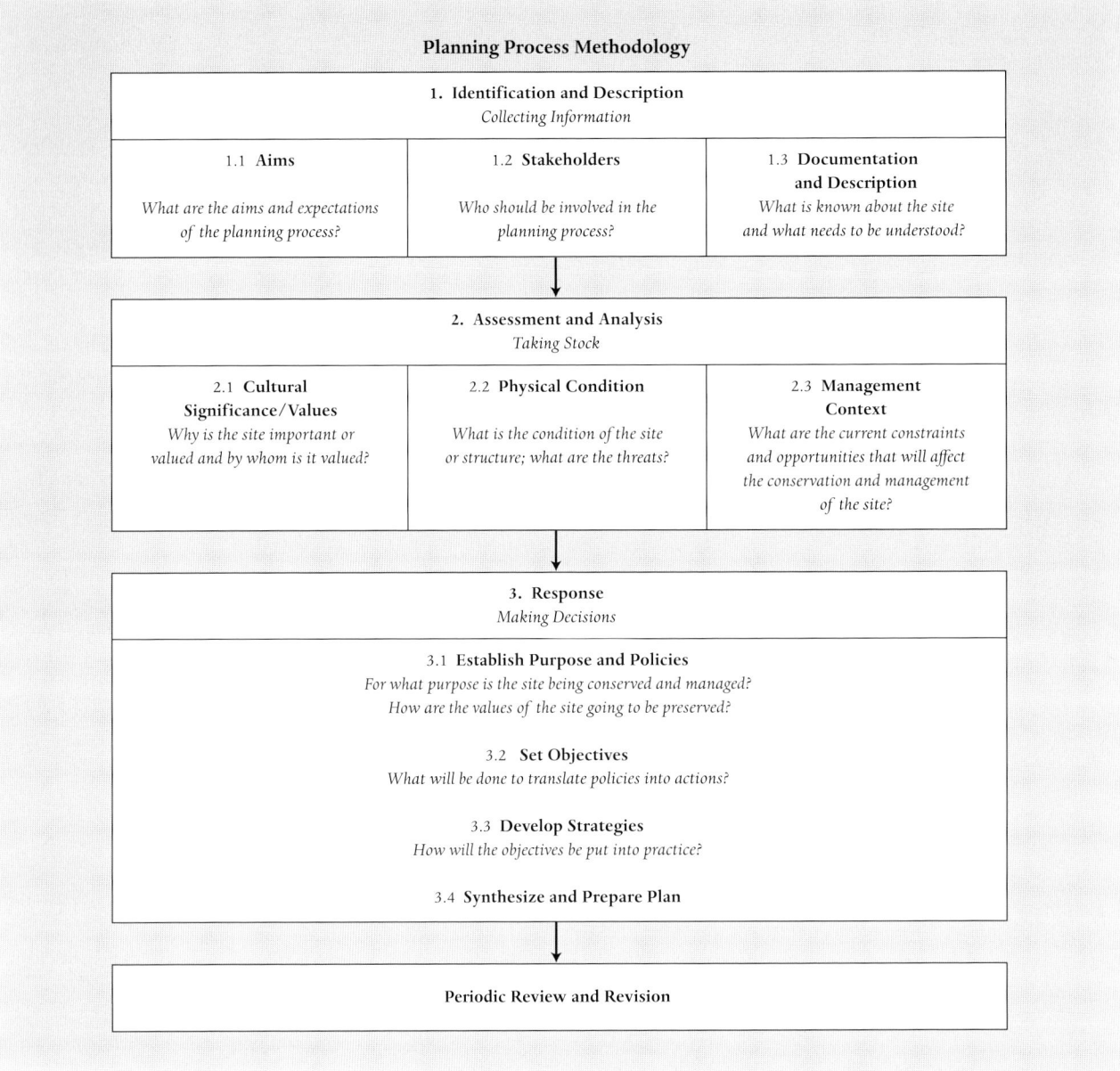

Figure 1
Flowchart showing Planning Process Methodology.

1. Identification and Description

The first phase of the planning process—identification and description—is essentially about gathering background information and laying the groundwork for the assessment and analysis phase to follow. There are three discrete aspects of this phase, which are not necessarily sequential:

1.1 Stating the Aims

During the initial stages of the planning process, the lead organization and those stakeholders who will play a key role should be encouraged to state their motivations for engaging in the process and what it is that they anticipate getting out of it. Each participant will come to the table with preconceived ideas and expectations; therefore, it is important for all involved to hear these expectations and begin to establish common ground, as well as to understand where expectations differ and may be in conflict. This stage of the process is not to be confused with making decisions about a site at the beginning of the process; rather, it is a way of clarifying the planning process itself, its aims, and the eventual outcomes.

1.2 Identifying a Planning Team and Stakeholders

The planning process is in essence about bringing the right people and organizations together with the correct information. Identifying the individuals and organizations to participate in the process is, therefore, critical to success in making good decisions about a site. The managing authority (that is, the principal decision makers of the lead organization), which will lead and guide the planning process, takes on this responsibility.

The selection of a core planning team to oversee and guide the process is the first step in identifying the right people and ensuring continuity throughout the process. Although outside expertise may be required, it is crucial to involve in-house professionals (that is, professionals from the managing authority) so they feel like they are a part of the process (ultimately they will have some level of responsibility to carry out the decisions).

The second critical group to identify are the stakeholders: that is, those who have a special interest or stake in how the site is used, developed, interpreted, or preserved; those who have the potential to impact the site (for better or worse); and those who are themselves impacted by what happens at the site. These are the people who will need to be brought in or consulted as the process unfolds.

Typically, stakeholders include the following:

- Government agencies, such as environmental agencies, tourist agencies, religious authorities, or nongovernmental organizations (NGOs) with an interest in the site;
- Archaeologists and other researchers who have done significant work at the site;
- Groups with an affinity or ancestral relationship to a site, such as Native Americans in the United States;
- Local community members who benefit economically or who want to use the site for commercial or social purposes; or conversely, who may be adversely affected by the site as a result of land disputes or influx of tourists and traffic;
- Private tourist agencies representing the interests of tourists and local or regional business interests; and
- Specialized tourists, such as religious tourists or pilgrims, or groups who come in large numbers and may have special requirements or may impact the site.

The makeup of this diverse group will vary depending on the context of the site. At many archaeological sites in the Americas and Australia, groups claiming an ancestral relationship may play an important role; at other sites, tourism interests may be paramount. Some stakeholders, especially those who exist outside the social and political power structures, may need encouragement to become involved or express their opinions. In these cases, it is important to find culturally appropriate ways to engage them in the process.

Figures 2, 3
The pressures of tourism on archaeological sites such as Tulum in Quintana Roo, Mexico, pose one of the greatest challenges to site managers. Managing the negative impact of visitors, while providing them with a meaningful experience and raising their awareness of the values and fragility of a site, has become a key component of the management planning process at heavily visited sites. Photographer: G. Aldana. © J. Paul Getty Trust, 1991.

These are the people (or their representatives) who should be invited to participate in the process. This is often one of the most difficult steps for the managing authority, who may question the practicality or perhaps the very premise of inviting stakeholders to the table. The reluctance to do so stems from the feeling that we will give away control of our sites to people we may not like—to the very people who cause us sleepless nights and who we believe damage the site, degrade its values, or wish only to exploit the site for economic gain. Against this sense of loss of control should be weighed the pitfall of not inviting others to participate and the benefits of bringing them into the process.

The Pitfall: There is one major pitfall associated with not inviting stakeholders to participate: they will cause you grief later. To adapt an adage from the 1960s, if you do not make these people part of the solution, they will make themselves part of the problem.

The Benefits: Stakeholders can offer resources, knowledge, different perspectives, and a concern for different values that we need to recognize in order to make decisions about the site. If these stakeholders are on our side, or at least engaged in the process, they can become very powerful forces for good. At the very least we will have more opportunity to influence them or mitigate their impact by understanding their intentions and their motivations. Furthermore, this is not a one-way street: it is equally important for stakeholders to understand the perspectives, constraints, and values of the managing authority if the authority hopes to enlist their cooperation for the benefit of the site.

If the practicality of engaging stakeholders is being questioned, the following mechanisms and strategies have been developed to help manage consultation and enhance cooperation:

- Use an external facilitator: a neutral outsider, who is trained in bringing people with diverse interests together, can be helpful in negotiating difficult relationships;

- Convene small workshops to address specific issues: planning is often most efficiently done with relevant stakeholders in small intensive workshops at key points in the process;
- Prepare discussion papers on key issues: a clear exposition of difficult issues for comment by relevant stakeholders is a way of soliciting interest and gauging reactions prior to engaging in face-to-face discussions;
- Undertake a tourism marketing study: determining the site's potential economic benefit to the local community, or ways to ensure that profits from tourism stay in the community, displays a commitment to stakeholders;
- Target the educators: enlisting the support of teachers within a community will bring to the fore stakeholders who have a special interest in the site and are highly regarded by the community; and
- Encourage the development of advocacy groups: community members with interests in the site may be eager to contribute their skills and can be a means of persuading and influencing the larger community for the benefit of the site.

It is undoubtedly easier to write a plan oneself or bring in an expert to do it than to engage in a participatory process, but the end result is always less viable. Participation and consensus-building almost always results in some compromise, which means that values may be affected. The closer one can get to a true participatory process, however, the better the chances to reach realistic decisions that can actually be implemented and sustained over time and will preserve the multiplicity of values of a site.

1.3 Documenting and Describing the Site

The purpose of this step in the process is to delineate the components of the site and to collect and synthesize information and documentation. This involves identifying and inventorying important documents and archives; delineating the boundaries of the site (both legal and cultural); and identifying and naming its specific components for purposes of defining discrete management entities (if appropriate) and for consistent reference throughout the planning process and in the planning documents.

The archaeology and history of sites for which planning is being undertaken is often well known and documented. What this stage in the process offers is an opportunity to identify gaps in knowledge that will influence decisions about the site; this is a time to assimilate and synthesize what is known and identify what is not known. The information that is most important in this synthesis is the history of interventions, both excavation and conservation, and the state of research at the site.

The mistake that can be made with this activity is to see it simply as compiling information for its own sake. Rather, the activity needs to be seen as strategic: the results will inform the assessments and contribute to establishing policies for research and excavation, interpretation, conservation, and use of the site.

To conclude, phases 1 through 3 will provide the necessary background preparation, in terms of clarifying the aims of the process, identifying stakeholders, and collecting and synthesizing data, to move into the next phase.

2. Assessment and Analysis

Assessment and analysis is the core of the planning process. Decisions made about the site will flow directly from this phase, with the implication that much of the burden of work and the integrity of the process reside here.

There are three types of assessment in this phase:

2.1. Significance: establishing why the site is important and to whom;
2.2. Condition: establishing the physical condition and identifying threats; and
2.3. Management: establishing the constraints and opportunities that may affect the ability of management to preserve and protect a site.

The understanding of the site and its management context derived from these three assessments will guide all subsequent decision making. Although an assessment involves collection of information, it is principally a process of evaluation and analysis of information, in which value or worth is revealed, and relationships analyzed—both cause-and-effect relationships and those between people and institutions. In this undertaking, the skills of analysis and synthesis, as well as experience, are important qualities to look for in staff and consultants assigned to carry it out.

2.1 Assessing Significance
Why is this site important or valued and by whom is it valued?
Since archaeological sites have no meaning other than those we give them, one can understand the importance of a place only by defining its values. As discussed in the paper by Randall Mason and Erica Avrami, the multiplicity of values attributed to archaeological sites derives from the varied perspectives and judgments of persons, professional groups, and communities. Within the planning process, the assessment of significance serves to identify the range of values that people have attributed to a site, which, in turn, drives the decisions about why and how to preserve and protect the site.

It is necessary to remember, however, that the idea of conservation as a values-driven process for making decisions is not a new one. A values-based approach to conservation is precisely what lies behind the traditional reliance on conservation guidelines and principles of the type that we are familiar with in the Venice Charter and other national and international guidelines, such as the principles of minimum intervention, reversibility of interventions, compatibility of materials, and distinguishing old from new materials, to name the most prominent. All of these principles derive from the high value we place on authenticity and original fabric, artistry, and design. These are the historic and artistic values that have

Figures 4, 5
The large site of Niuheliang in Liaoning Province, China, has yielded significant new information about the Neolithic period in China. Its research potential is very high but its remains are fragile. The resulting policy has been to limit excavation at the site and emphasize curation of artifacts and protection of the site through stabilization or reburial and sheltering of excavated areas. Photographer: M. Demas. © J. Paul Getty Trust, 1998.

been the foundation of conservation theory for the last century. Principles or guidelines help us translate these values into practice.

With a values-based approach to planning, we are simply expanding on a traditional reliance on values to inform a broader range of decisions. In the last thirty years of conservation practice, society has been transformed through a resurgence of ethnic and racial identity, a concern for the natural environment, increased access to information, global tourism, and many other factors, with the result that there are now many more groups of people (the stakeholders) with a vested interest in archaeological sites, and, therefore, many more values with which to contend. Archaeologists—who were once the sole group with a recognized stake in archaeological sites—are now only one of many constituencies vying to define the significance of archaeological sites.

At its most fundamental level, therefore, the planning process is a means of identifying those diverse values and the constituencies that they represent and integrating these values into decision making about a site.

Values Attributed to Archaeological Sites

Looking briefly at the variety of values attributed to archaeological sites, one can distinguish two broad categories of values. Historical, artistic, and research values are the traditional or core values, as defined by the professionals who have long had an academic or professional stake in sites. Natural, social, spiritual, symbolic, and economic values are championed by a more diverse and recent set of stakeholders, whose claims on archaeological sites are today a reality. It is these latter values (and their varied constituencies) that are often not sufficiently considered when assessing significance.

Historical and artistic values, along with research values discussed below, have been the core values of the stakeholders with the greatest interest in archaeological sites until very recently—namely, the archaeologists, historians, art historians, and other scholars whose professional lives depend on archaeological sites. More than any other category of cultural heritage, archaeological sites are repositories of information and artistic creations essential to understanding the past. For this reason alone, historical and artistic values, which have been central to informing conservation decisions in the past, will continue to be of fundamental importance to guide decision making about archaeological sites.

When it comes to particular buildings or features at a site where intervention is planned, however, frequently we do not consider these values in sufficient detail nor do we articulate them in a way that is meaningful for decision makers and the public in general. The more intervention planned, the greater the need for a clear and detailed understanding of why a site or structure is important: what are the particular features, design elements, materials, technology, and historical associations that give this structure or place historical and artistic values? This point comes up again when strategies are discussed below.

Research value is the potential of a site to yield new information and answer research questions. This is an especially important value for archaeological sites—one that is often not considered adequately when making decisions about the future of a site. We tend to plan for and manage sites based mainly on their revealed or known values, but it is equally if not more important in the case of some sites, to manage them for their future potential to yield information. The implications of identifying and understanding this potential will be seen most clearly when it comes to establishing policies and objectives; for instance, sites with high research potential often need protection against looting, poor excavation strategies, erosion, agricultural activity, and so forth. The relationship between research value and decision making is further explored in the example of policy development at the end of this paper.

Natural values are evident in the survival of habitats or species of flora or fauna, especially at sites that have long been protected but not fully excavated or opened to the public. There may be a conflict of values when excavation or presentation to the public is contemplated. Conversely, of course, many places protected as natural reserves preserve important archaeological remains. Under this same rubric might also be included landscapes and vistas, and more elusive values such as clean air or a clear night sky unimpaired by light pollution.

Social or civic values relate to how people use sites: for recreation (for instance, picnics or social gatherings); for concerts and festivals; for social rituals or ceremonies; or as a focus for regional or national pride or political sentiment. These values can create a very strong bond between the site and its proximate communities, which often makes the site part of the civic activity of a community once again. The ability of a site to impart knowledge and understanding of the past to the public—its educational value—is another important way that it can serve a greater social purpose.

Spiritual or religious values are associated with spiritual or religious aspirations of diverse groups, and may be manifested in a traditional or contemporary manner. New Age spiritual seekers have shown a significant interest in certain archaeological sites, attracted by astronomical events or ancient myths; the gathering of such groups at archaeological sites during the so-called Harmonic Convergence in 1987 is one such example. Christian pilgrimage at many archaeological sites in the eastern Mediterranean has flourished with the increase in international tourism.

Symbolic or identity values are the means by which specific groups claim their place in the world through a spiritual and cultural connection with sites, or these values may assert or symbolize a community's ethnic or cultural identity. The strong links between prehistoric archaeological resources and aboriginal peoples is now a political reality in many countries.

Figures 6, 7
The identification of values and those who hold them is an ongoing process. Some of the values that are attributed to archaeological sites may not be self-evident, leading to uses that were never anticipated by the managing authority. Such was the case with New Age spiritual seekers who converged at Chaco Canyon in New Mexico, among many other sites, during the Harmonic Convergence in 1987. [Fig. 6] Photographer: G. Aldana. © J. Paul Getty Trust, 1993. [Fig. 7] © Chaco Culture National Historic Park, 1987.

Economic values of archaeological sites have lingered for some time in the shadows, a vaguely sinister presence that we would sooner banish from the pure land of culture. Many heritage professionals prefer to exclude economic values from the roster of values, seeing them as secondary to or derived from the primary values. Such exclusion, however, does not reflect the reality of many archaeological sites today. For many major stakeholders—local community, business interests, and government agencies—the question "Why is this site important and to whom is it important," can only be fully answered with reference to its economic value. That this economic value is a reflection of the site's cultural and natural values is key to framing the issue, but it does not diminish the economic value in the eyes of the stakeholder.

Conservation and the derivation of economic benefit from sites are not inherently antithetical but have been too frequently cast as antagonists; clearly it is time for a more productive discourse. As a profession, we need to consider more carefully the fragile but potent relationship between cultural and economic values, broadly speaking, and the relationship between the site as economic benefactor to a local community or the national treasury and the investment required to conserve and maintain that site. We also need to better understand the willingness of the public to sacrifice tangible and quantifiable economic benefit for the "public good" (that is, the less tangible and quantifiable values that society attributes to heritage sites). It is, of course, the tension between that segment of society willing to forego economic benefit to preserve a place and those who hold economic values most dear that must be negotiated at the level of the stakeholder and within the context of values.

How Do We Assess Significance?

Assessment of significance requires a comparative approach. We cannot assess the importance of a site in isolation: one needs to look at a building within the context of other structures and the whole site, and to examine the site within its regional context. Without a comparative approach, it is not possible to say whether a site is unique or rare, representative of a particular period and culture, a well-preserved example, of high or low research potential, and so on.

Significance is multifaceted and, therefore, may require expertise from different professions and input from varied stakeholders. The stakeholders will play one of their most important roles in making clear what it is they value about the site. Attempts to establish methods and criteria for identifying significance abound. While there is no consensus on approach, criteria, or categories of values—nor likely ever to be one—the many models put forward offer insights and ways of thinking about values (see Bibliography 3 in this volume for the literature on this subject).

Who Should Make the Assessment?

An assessment of significance must be done with integrity, empathy, and sincere intent to consult with and understand other people's perspectives. Outside expertise is often required for greater objectivity, but final responsibility falls on the managing authority, which must ensure completeness of information and coverage, and the integrity of the process. The core team is often the most knowledgeable about a site, while stakeholders can provide a broad understanding of the varied meanings associated with a place.

What Is the Outcome?
The assessment results in a clear statement of significance that reflects all the values of a site. It is not at this stage, however, that one resolves conflicts among values; this occurs in the next phase, when formulating policy. All values need to be assessed, recognized, and put into a statement of significance, but potential conflicts need to be identified and acknowledged.

2.2 Assessing Physical Condition
What is the condition of a site or structure; what are the threats?
The purpose of a condition survey is to document and assess the physical state of a site or a structure. The end product of a condition survey is an archive of valuable graphic and written documentation representing baseline data about the site, which can be used to make recommendations for its future use and treatment and to monitor change over time. Assessment of a site's physical condition is viewed by some practitioners as being a part of the management assessment because it involves evaluating strengths and weaknesses of the site. This is a good way of looking at this assessment since the physical condition of a place will have tremendous influence on its use and the level of intervention needed to preserve it.

A condition survey will generally proceed in the following three basic stages:

- Collection of historical documentation relating to past condition, use, and previous interventions to structures or site. Some of this documentation may have already been identified and gathered in phase 1.3.
- Objective recording of the current physical condition. Condition recording, like standard archaeological recording, strives to be an objective record of what exists. It is concerned primarily with effects (with what one sees), rather than causes.
- Diagnosis and prognosis. Diagnosis is concerned with examination and analysis of current condition to determine probable causes of deterioration. It requires an integrated approach through analysis of the whole structure or site, using the knowledge and experience of specialized disciplines such as architectural conservation, engineering, hydrology, and so on, and may also necessitate further research and long-term monitoring. Implicit in diagnosis, but not usually brought forth explicitly, is prognosis. By linking extant conditions with historical documentation and diagnosis, rates of deterioration may be estimated, and thus priorities of intervention are brought to the fore in decision making.

Figures 8, 9
The 3.6-million-year-old hominid trackway at Laetoli, Tanzania, has very high scientific value and great tourism potential. The assessments of condition and management context, however, made clear that the fragile nature of the volcanic tuff, the lack of any infrastructure and trained staff, and the remote location of the site were serious obstacles to keeping the site open for research and visitation purposes. The decision was made, therefore, to rebury the site, while providing scientific documentation and an exhibition to meet the needs of stakeholders. Photographer: N. Agnew. © J. Paul Getty Trust, 1995.

The condition survey is also the time to identify significant threats to a site such as erosion, vegetation, floods, cliff instability, and other external forces; or from human actions such as visitation, looting, inappropriate development near the site, or lack of maintenance. A detailed condition survey of a building or features can be a lengthy undertaking and one needs to decide the level of recording needed for purposes of planning. On a large, complex site, the outcome of a condition survey may simply be prioritization of problem areas or identification of structures that need more detailed condition recording or monitoring. Undertaking of such recording would then be integrated into the plans for the site in the future.

2.3 Assessing Management Context
What are the current constraints and opportunities that will affect the conservation and management of the site?
The management assessment looks at all the relevant factors other than condition that may affect the future conservation and management of the site. Some of these factors involve assessing the sort of information that managers of sites deal with all the time, ranging from financial resources to visitor statistics. Other aspects may benefit from an analysis of the political

and economic context in which the plan will operate. This could mean determining, for instance, the plans for regional development and projections of tourism to the area, and identifying the real power brokers who make decisions that will affect the welfare of the site. The management assessment is in some respects a reality check and needs to be tackled early on in the process. Along with the condition assessment, the results of the management assessment may restrict how values can be preserved and revealed.

Examples of Categories of Management Assessment

Legal and legislative context: Is the legal protection for the site sufficient? Does it have an adequate buffer zone? Is there legislation that needs to be taken into account or that may impose constraints in making decisions for the future, such as land-use or zoning regulations?

Financial base: What financial resources are available? Are there opportunities for securing funds that should be explored?

Power base: Who are the people and institutions that hold decision-making power at the local, regional, or national level? How can the managing authority best leverage this power base for the good of the site?

Infrastructure: This refers to capital development and improvements, often to accommodate visitors, such as roads, parking, amenities, restaurants, and so forth. What is the current situation and what are future needs? Where can development be located and what will be its impact?

Regional and local development context: Are there regional and local development plans that may impact the site? Can the plans for the site be integrated with other, regional plans?

Visitor numbers, profile, and impact: Are visitors a threat to the site? Has a carrying capacity been established, and if not, is it warranted? What is known about visitors to the site? Is more information needed?

Structure of organization: Is the management organization adequate to meet current and likely future needs? Can it be changed or augmented within the existing legal and financial context?

Staff resources and expertise: Is there sufficient staff with the appropriate expertise? Do the staff need training in particular areas of expertise?

Monitoring and maintenance systems: Are the existing systems adequate? Is maintenance receiving priority before any new interventions, such as restoration of a building or new excavation? Can the resource be adequately maintained in the future?

Research assessment: What are the research needs of the site? What are the gaps in knowledge, as identified in the synthesis of background information in the first phase?

This type of assessment—sometimes called a SWOT analysis, since it looks at Strengths, Weaknesses, Opportunities, and Threats—is mainly the responsibility of the managing authority, which generally deals with it in isolation; however, it benefits greatly from consulting with relevant stakeholders for two reasons: first, stakeholders have information the managing authority needs and may well have resources it could use, and second, stakeholders are more likely to be cooperative or understanding if they realize the constraints under which the managing authority is operating.

Some aspects of a management assessment may be highly political and beyond the control of the managing authority. This is all the more reason to assess what we can control, and therefore where we can be most effective.

Achieving a global view of the main values, issues, conditions, threats, and opportunities that arise out of the assessments is essential to understanding how the condition and management assessments may impact the values of a place. This will require a concise summary of the main values, issues, conditions, and so on, so that they are readily understandable and accessible for the purpose of making decisions in the next phase.

3. Response

The response phase is in many respects the moment of truth in the planning process. This is when decisions are made resulting from the assessments of significance, condition, and management context. This is also the time when any conflict of values is resolved or a compromise found, and when the preservation of values must be balanced against existing constraints of condition and management context. In this difficult process of balancing values, stakeholders' interests, and existing constraints, the sustainability principles outlined in the paper by Randall Mason and Erica Avrami can serve as a useful guide to making decisions.

The overarching guiding principle, however, for determining whether decisions are appropriate is that they preserve the values of the site. If, as a result of decisions taken, values will be destroyed or compromised, this is where we make clear why and what steps will be taken to mitigate or compensate for loss. This balancing of the results of the assessment phase is elaborated further in the example of the development of policy, objectives, and strategies at the end of this paper.

There are three levels of response, which can be seen as a hierarchy of decisions progressing from the general to the specific:

3.1. Establishing Purpose and Policies: deciding the overall vision and guiding principles;
3.2. Setting Objectives: deciding what will be done; and
3.3. Developing Strategies: deciding how it will be done.

3.1 Establishing the Purpose and Policies

For what purpose is the site being conserved and managed? How are the values of the site going to be preserved?

Policies, or guiding principles, as they are sometimes known, are the critical link between the assessments of values, condition, and management context on the one hand, and the objectives and strategies on the other. Policies identify the most appropriate ways of preserving the values of a site and serve to guide its future care and development. In establishing policies, it is necessary to ask the following questions: is this a policy that will preserve and reveal the identified values? Does it conflict with other values? Is it technically and financially feasible? If all the values of a site cannot be fully preserved, policies will address how to reduce adverse impact or compensate for loss of value and will explain why a particular value cannot be preserved.

It is useful to establish policies in terms of programmatic or activity areas—examples of which are given below—since most, if not all, of these categories will be carried through the rest of the process; that is, through to establishing objectives and the strategies needed to achieve the objectives. Nevertheless, it is equally important that policies for programmatic areas add up to a unified vision for the site. A broad statement of purpose in managing the site is, therefore, a necessary prelude to ensure that the overall vision does not become fragmented in multiple policy statements.

Examples of Typical Policy Categories

The following examples of policy categories reflect typical programmatic or activity areas that are applicable to most archaeological sites, but additional or different categories can be defined to better suit a particular site and its management needs.

Appropriate Use

Appropriate use is a broad and very important policy category. It can govern use of a site for research and excavation purposes; for access by the public and interpretation to visitors; for entertainment, recreation, or other social purposes; for religious pursuits; for commercial gain; and so forth. One sees most clearly here the connection with value assessment and stakeholders, since stakeholders often want to use the site in a particular way. Thus archaeologists are major stakeholders who want to use the site for excavation and research purposes; tourist authorities or agencies may have a strong interest in the use of a site that draws large numbers of visitors; and community leaders or special-interest groups may claim a stake in the use of a site for recreational or other social purposes. If any of these uses will have a significant impact on the site and its resources (such as the use of an ancient theater for performances) or if any use is of particular relevance to an archaeological site (for instance, a policy on research and excavation, as described below), these can be discussed in separate policy statements. It is helpful, however, to have a general statement on appropriate use that puts specific uses in the context of the overall vision for the site.

Figures 10, 11
The ruins of the Hellenistic-Roman monuments at Ephesus, Turkey, including the Fountain of Trajan (top) and the Monument to Gaius Memmius (bottom), have been subject to various restoration approaches over the years. This has resulted in an inconsistent and sometimes incomprehensible presentation of the site for visitors. Policies that place limits on the type or extent of restoration and put forth a clear approach to how and why a site will be presented are a means of controlling excessive interventions and contributing to a coherent vision. Photographer: G. Aldana. © J. Paul Getty Trust, 1993.

Conservation Intervention

In this category typically are policies that define a philosophy of intervention or establish limits to intervention. Such policies may require that interventions be governed by existing international or national charters, guidelines, or laws. These are important from both a legal and professional perspective, but they cover fairly general ground. In addition to these general policies, it is always good to try to spell out what is special about the site. So, for instance, for sites with monumental classical buildings, where restoration, anastylosis, and reconstruction are often practiced, one might want a specific policy addressing those types of interventions; or on a multiperiod site, there might be a policy that refers to conserving all periods or favoring one period by removal of later buildings or deposits, or by reburial of earlier remains. All policies, but especially controversial ones such as allowing removal of later deposits or buildings or reconstruction of a building, must be justified in terms of the significance assigned to the site.

Visitation and Interpretation

Closely linked with conservation and use policies are those policies related to visitation and interpretation: what will the visitor see; where will access be denied; will there be limits on visitor numbers or an attempt to increase visitation or attract a particular type of visitor; is a policy needed on differential fees for local versus foreign tourism? A policy could also relate to interpretation—whether it is the language of interpretation or the need to interpret a site in a sensitive manner to a particular constituency; here again the relationship between stakeholders and values is obvious.

Interventions such as restoration or reconstruction often have their rationale in the desire to interpret a site to the public, rather than in the need to conserve a building. In this case it is the educational value of the place that is being promoted, and this should be made clear in the policy statement.

Research and Excavation

Research and excavation policies, which may also include curation of artifacts, are clearly among the most relevant for archaeological sites. Typically, policies will state the general conditions under which research and excavation can take place, and set limits on the extent and nature of excavation, or forbid any excavation. Policies may also address such issues as ensuring adequate integration of conservation during and after excavation, and the protection of archaeological resources that have not been excavated.

Maintenance and Monitoring

A policy statement is an opportunity to establish the critical importance that the managing authority places on maintenance and monitoring. A policy, for instance, might make clear the role that is played by maintenance as a preventive measure in slowing damage at a site. Even where maintenance practices are routine, they should be given high priority and emphasis within the formulation of policies. Since most maintenance regimes are repetitive and interventionist, however, they can lead to loss of fabric (for example, continuous repointing). Thus, depending on the maintenance needed, some caveats or limits may be in order.

Facilities and Infrastructure

Policies under this category may address ensuring standards for design and construction and placing limits on the extent and location of facilities for touristic and commercial development, interpretive exhibits or displays, water and utilities, transportation and parking, and so on. A policy might also refer to the need for archaeological clearance prior to any subsurface disturbance for construction of facilities or infrastructure.

Consultation

There may be a need for a policy to ensure ongoing consultation with and involvement of the stakeholders in situations where stakeholders hold opposing views, where they need to be reassured that their views are being taken into consideration, or where regular input would be of value to the managing authority.

To summarize, the statement of purpose and policies defines the broad framework and limits within which specific actions will take place. Taken together, they provide the big-picture thinking about the site. The picture that emerges may reveal, for example, a site where research and excavation are paramount while visitation and interpretation to the public is restricted or even prohibited; a site where use for social and tourist purposes is balanced with research and excavation; or a site where tourism prevails, infrastructure development is extensive, and excavation is forbidden.

Whatever the picture is, there should be a demonstrable correspondence between it and the values identified in the assessment of significance; that is, the picture should reflect what is valued at the site. If it does not reflect this, it needs to be stated why not. In writing policy statements, therefore, it is important that context is conveyed by indicating what values are being preserved or what constraints or conditions prevail that make preservation of a value difficult or impossible.

Policies, therefore, set the stage for *why* the managing authority is following a particular trajectory for a site. What will be done and how it will be achieved are the actions that come later with the development of objectives and strategies.

3.2 Setting Objectives
What will be done to translate policies into actions?
At this stage it is necessary to identify specific objectives related to the policies defined for each programmatic area or activity. Objectives are clear targets with measurable results. The distinction between objectives and strategies is not always clear and even the most experienced practitioner can become confused. Some practitioners prefer to go directly to strategies from policies. One way to think about the distinction is to see objectives as destinations and strategies as the road map to the destination. Mastering the distinction, however, is not nearly as important as simply setting clear targets for achieving the purpose for which the site is being managed, whether those targets are framed as objectives or strategies.

One method used by practitioners to clarify objectives and to make them more targeted and measurable, is to state what will have been achieved within a specific time frame (for instance, by the end of five years we will have achieved these specific objectives), then list them. In this way the objective can be formulated more concretely, since its results are envisioned. An example of an objective related to tourism and interpretation could be to have undertaken a visitor survey (within a specified period of time) in order to better understand the types of visitors and their motivations and interests in visiting the site. This is a clear target whose completion can be easily verified.

3. 3 Developing Strategies
How will the objectives be put into practice?
Strategies are the most detailed level of planning, specifying how the objective will be achieved and establishing resources required and time frames and responsibilities to get the work done. If an objective is to undertake a visitor survey—to continue with the example used above—the strategy will state how and by whom that targeted goal will be achieved; it may be accompanied by a detailed plan, which in this case might specify the methodology to be followed, the questions to be asked, and the personnel and budget required.

Figures 12, 13
Interventions often focus on a part or component of a site. This is the case, for instance, of sites with mosaics, which are sometimes treated as a "site within a site" with the result that they are decontextualized. The individually designed protective structures over the mosaics at Zippori in Israel respond only to the mosaics they are protecting without reference to any overarching vision for the site. [Fig. 12] Photographer: M. Demas. © J. Paul Getty Trust, 1997. [Fig. 13] Photographer: C. Godlewski. © J. Paul Getty Trust, 1997.

Unfortunately, the development of strategies for intervention is too often the stage at which we begin when responding to the challenges of conserving and managing a site, since action is equated with progress and detailed planning is perceived as time not well spent. What typically happens when strategies are allowed to become the starting point at a site is an "organic" proliferation of independent "strategy projects"; that is, projects carried out independently by different institutions, organizations, or individuals and without reference to the objectives and priorities established in the plan. The individual projects (for example, excavation, documentation, or conservation projects, or a tourism initiative) may have their own justification, but too often they fulfill the needs of the institution or individual who is carrying them out rather than the needs of the site and the managing authority.

In the development of strategies, separate, detailed plans for complex undertakings are necessary. These strategy plans must begin, however, with a clear link to the general plan, repeating the relevant policies and objectives of the appropriate programmatic area so that there is a clear continuity of purpose. This becomes especially important if a strategy plan is being developed by an organization other than the managing authority.

When it comes to physical intervention, it is in the development of strategies that we often need a deeper understanding of what is really important about a site's structures or features, as was touched on in the discussion of values. Having made the decision that a certain structure, for instance, requires restoration, stabilization, or protective sheltering, it may be necessary to revisit the assessment stage to establish more detail about significance, past interventions, and present condition. This process of returning to the assessment stage is inevitable for any complex site or component of a site, since the level of detail required for a major intervention is impossible to achieve when planning long-term for the whole site. The level of detail required for full development of many strategies would, in fact, only weigh the general planning process down with data not pertinent to establishing the big picture for the site.

3.4 Preparing the Plan

The emphasis in this paper has been on the planning process, but obviously there is an end product, a plan that may variously be referred to as a management, conservation, or even a master plan, depending on local usage and the ambition and scope of the undertaking. During the course of the process and after completion, the information collected and decisions reached must be documented and written down in a plan; however, there are differing opinions about what level of information should be included in the final plan. A few remarks will suffice about the "product," which espouse a minimalist approach based on wise advice from practitioners who have written and implemented many plans. The general plan—whatever it is called—should be

Holistic and integrated: Examples of fragmented authority, differing visions, and multiple implementors working at cross-purposes abound at complex archaeological sites. While it is useful and frequently necessary to bring in consultants, partners, or collaborators to develop and implement aspects of the plan, there must be one lead authority that coordinates all efforts and one plan that articulates the importance of the place and the goals for its conservation and development in the future.

Short, concise, and accessible: A plan that can be understood by all the stakeholders allows everyone to easily grasp the vision and overall goals and the reasoning behind decisions, which means a plan that is short, concise, and written with a broad audience in mind. Background information—whether it be interviews conducted to work out significance, detailed condition surveys, or historic documentation—is vital to preserve, but can be included in reference binders. Detailed strategy plans can and often should be separate and, in fact, are frequently developed later as the plan is implemented. As mentioned earlier, these should begin with the policy statements and objectives for the relevant category to provide the link with the general plan.

Legally binding: Not all or even most plans are statutory plans in nature, but if a system exists for legal approval and ratification by the national authority, this will allow the plan to have not just moral weight but legal clout as well.

Comparable and compatible with other plans: If it is possible to achieve a national approach to management planning, this will simplify evaluation of plans for approval purposes, allow comparability of management plans among sites of similar character, and promote an integrated vision for cultural resources at the regional level.

Ultimately, the plan is a vehicle for communicating a message to a potentially diverse audience of professionals, government bureaucrats, business interests, and, in some instances, even the general public. The essence of that message needs to be: this is why the site is important and this is what is planned to preserve that importance. The more clearly the message can be formulated and the more widely it can be disseminated, the better the chances for it to become an effective tool to protect the site and its values.

It is equally beneficial, once the planning process is complete, to keep the lines of communication with stakeholders open and active. Periodic review of the plan can be one opportunity to reinforce these relationships. Furthermore, since there is no such thing as a perfect plan and circumstances are sure to change, periodic review allows for regular fine-tuning and revision of the plan.

Conclusion

Like most challenges in life, the first time one works through a planning process is always the most difficult. Subsequent reviews and updates will build on the foundation of the first plan, so the better the foundation, the easier it will be next time around and the more sustainable will be the outcomes. One of the most common responses to planning is the assertion of "no money, no time, no staff to do it or implement it." Good planning does require a commitment of time, staff, and money. Increasingly, funding is available for planning, as organizations recognize the importance of planning before implementation. While strategizing to increase resources is certainly part of planning, the decisions that are made must be commensurate with the resources available. The aim of planning is not to decide how to spend a pot of money but to make decisions about what to do within the constraints and resources at hand. Nor is the aim of planning to solve all the problems of a site; it is more satisfying and more sustainable to aim for small incremental changes from present conditions to better conditions than risk being thwarted by unrealistic expectations of achieving major changes.

Perhaps the greatest challenge to pursuing a values-based approach to planning is acknowledging that values are mutable and there are few absolutes in terms of what is right or wrong. As social, political, and economic conditions change, interest of the stakeholders waxes and wanes, and research goals and strategies evolve, so too will the values that we attribute to sites. Values-based planning is an approach capable of being manipulated, or, for the faint of heart, of being turned into formulas or rules. It needs honesty, integrity, and dedicated practice, but the reward is a far more intellectually engaging process, yielding a deeper, broader, and more intimate understanding of what gives a site relevance and meaning to society.

Given the focus of this workshop on conservation and management of archaeological sites, it is fitting to end this paper with a challenge to the archaeological and conservation professions. Almost thirty years ago, when William Lipe issued his prescient call for archaeologists to adopt a conservation ethic,[2] both the archaeological and conservation professions were still too preoccupied and vested in excavation and technical interventions, respectively, to respond in an integrated way to the challenges facing archaeological sites. More recently, developments in archaeological theory (postprocessual archaeology) have called for archaeologists to become more engaged in the world beyond the academy, and to recognize other values, voices, and perspectives in the practice and interpretation of archaeology. Since the early 1980s the conservation profession has been moving in much the same direction in developing and advocating a values-based approach to the conservation and management of archaeological heritage.

These two conceptual movements have thus far developed largely on parallel tracks, with very little convergence. And yet they have their essential starting point in common—the archaeological heritage—and much to gain from one another. Archaeology will benefit from the conservation profession's more practiced engagement with the world; conservation can find much of value from an understanding of archaeology's theoretical framework. At a time when the archaeological heritage is recognized as so necessary to our quest for a past, and yet is so threatened, it is hard to imagine a more natural and productive alliance among professions.

Acknowledgments

This paper is a summary of an approach to planning advocated by the Getty Conservation Institute for many years and as such it reflects the thinking of many colleagues, both within and outside the Conservation Institute. The author gratefully acknowledges the advice and wisdom that she has received over the years from Sharon Sullivan on the theory and practice of management planning, much of which has found expression in this paper. Special thanks are due to Neville Agnew and Marta de la Torre for their insightful comments and critique of drafts of this paper, and to fellow authors and colleagues, Erica Avrami, Randall Mason, and Gaetano Palumbo, for their input before and after the workshop.

Notes

1 The complete text of the poem entitled "Ithaca" (1911) by Constantine Cavafy is found in *The Complete Poems of Cavafy*, trans. Rae Dalven (New York Harcourt Brace, 1961).

2 See William D. Lipe, "A Conservation Model for American Archaeology," *The Kiva* 39 (1974): nos. 3–4, 213–45. See, however, Laurajane Smith, "Heritage Management as Postprocessual Archaeology?" *Antiquity* 68 (1994): 300–309, for an attempt to bridge the gap.

Linking Assessments with Decisions: The Development of Policy, Objectives, and Strategies

The following example of the development of policy, objectives, and strategies uses a hypothetical site called Rongovia, which is based on actual conditions and policies from real sites. It focuses on a single value—research—to illustrate the impact of assessments on decisions and the relationship between policies, objectives, and strategies.

Research Value as Established by the Assessment of Significance

Rongovia has been a rich source of information about the complex culture of the prehistoric inhabitants of the Rongovian Basin. Based on the evidence of previous excavations and numerous surveys of unexcavated sites throughout the basin, Rongovia has demonstrated significant potential to yield important new information in the future about the way of life, political organization, and architecture of its inhabitants.

Commentary

The assessment of significance involved archaeologists familiar with the site and utilized the results of the phase 1 collection and synthesis of information. The importance of Rongovia as the administrative, economic, and ritual center of an ancient culture had long been recognized. From the assessment, however, it was clear that despite extensive exploration and excavation in the past, there were still many outstanding research questions. Most of the previous excavations had been undertaken in the late nineteenth and early twentieth century, when excavation techniques and methods of analysis were not well developed or were poorly practiced. Extensive unexcavated deposits found throughout the basin, as well as more thorough study of previously excavated remains, could provide important new data to answer these questions.

Results of Condition and Management Assessment Relevant to Decision Making about Research and Excavation

- Exposure of structures through excavation requires continuous maintenance that cannot be sustained with current and projected funding levels;
- Routine maintenance of existing structures (such as repointing, stabilization, and capping of walls) has led to gradual loss of the original fabric of these structures over time;
- Previously excavated buildings and artifacts have not been adequately documented, studied, or published; and
- Unexcavated sites in the outlying areas are subject to natural erosion and looting, while unexcavated deposits in the visited areas are subject to erosion and casual removal of artifacts by visitors.

Commentary

The condition and management assessments revealed significant conservation and maintenance problems related to previously excavated structures and artifacts, which would only be exacerbated if new excavations were undertaken. Furthermore, it became clear that these previous excavations had been poorly published and documented, and that the unexcavated deposits, which were a principal source of the site's research value, were being threatened by erosion and looting. In making decisions about future research and excavation, the constraints to undertaking further excavation and the threats to unexcavated deposits were of paramount importance in establishing the resulting policies.

Research and Excavation Policy

Rongovia has been a rich source of information about the complex culture of the prehistoric inhabitants of the Rongovian Basin and has high potential for yielding new information through study of existing collections and excavated remains, which have been poorly published, and from new excavation of undisturbed sites. Excavated structures are subject, however, to decay and constant cycles of maintenance, which cannot be sustained, while unexcavated sites within the basin area are being threatened by erosion and occasional looting.

Unexcavated archaeological sites will be left undisturbed, therefore, in order to preserve them for the future when methods of excavation and analysis will have improved and to reduce the amount of exposed fabric and artifacts that must be conserved and maintained. Research that is nondestructive to artifacts or sites and provides for an enriched interpretive program will be encouraged. Small-scale testing may be allowed in the context of specific research questions, but test excavations must be reburied after completion of the study. Research proposals that address the needs of study and documentation of previously excavated structures and existing collections will receive priority for approval over those requiring excavation or disturbance to intact archaeological deposits.

Commentary

The first paragraph establishes the context to understand the policy that follows in the second paragraph. The policy sets forth the conditions under which research and excavation will be allowed and establishes priorities for research. Any proposal for research would be evaluated with these conditions and priorities in mind. The policy preserves the research potential of the site by encouraging research that is nondestructive and by protecting unexcavated deposits for the future; however, it severely limits excavation—which is the most common way of actualizing the research value—because of the constraints of maintenance and resources, and the recognition that previously excavated material has yet to be adequately studied and original fabric and unexcavated sites are being lost and must have first priority. Although the archaeologist-stakeholders, who very much want to excavate at the site, may not be happy with this policy, their response will be tempered by understanding why excavation is limited and through being encouraged and assisted in undertaking nondestructive types of research.

> ### Research and Excavation Objectives
>
> At the end of five years, we will have achieved the following:
>
> - Made significant progress in publishing the existing collection;
> - Completed the documentation (plans, elevations, and sections) of three major structures (structures X, Y, and Z);
> - Completed the dendrochronological analysis of wood in structures X, Y, and Z; and
> - Reduced the looting and erosion of unexcavated deposits in the visited areas and outlying archaeological sites by at least fifty percent.

Commentary

The objectives are measurable to the extent that they establish a time limit and largely quantifiable goals that will be achieved. These are objectives that were established as clear priorities in the course of the planning process. This does not preclude the possibility for independent proposals to be submitted and accepted by the managing authority in the future, as long as those proposals are compatible with the stated policies for research and excavation.

As part of the conservation intervention policies and objectives for the site, it was decided to rebury parts of structures X, Y, and Z as a method of conserving original fabric, which was being lost not only through natural causes of deterioration but also from constant cycles of maintenance. The conservation and research objectives were linked by focusing the documentation on structures X, Y, and Z, so that these structures would be fully documented prior to reburial.

The original proposal submitted by the archaeologist was to undertake the dendrochronological analysis for structures A, B, and C. The proposal was accepted by the managing authority because it fit well with the policy to encourage study of structures already exposed through excavation in the past. In light of the priorities established for documentation and conservation, however, the archaeologist was requested to do his study on structures X, Y, and Z. In this way the research will be fully coordinated and integrated with conservation policies.

> ### Research and Excavation Strategies
>
> - Apply for a grant from the Rongovia Foundation to study existing collections;
> - Create a collaboration with the local university for students to carry out documentation of exposed structures;
> - Carry out the proposal with the University of Rongovia to date structures X, Y, and Z using dendrochronology; and
> - Hire two additional law-enforcement staff and create a public-awareness campaign to discourage removal of artifacts and walking off trails.

Commentary

The strategies specify how the objectives will be achieved. Most of these strategies will not require detailed strategy plans, but staff, budget, and a timeline will need to be established to carry them out. The proposal for dendrochronological analysis is a detailed plan submitted by the archaeologist. This strategy plan does not become part of the general management plan for broad dissemination; it is supplementary information that can be kept in a separate reference binder.

PART TWO

Case Studies

Introduction to the Case Studies

The Corinth Workshop extended over four days during which the discussion progressed from the presentation of a theoretical model for site management planning to the consideration of a number of case studies in which theoretical principles could be examined in the light of practical constraints and complex realities.

The first two case studies report on experiences at sites outside the Mediterranean region, specifically at Hadrian's Wall in the United Kingdom and Chan Chan in Peru. In each of these cases, a values-driven planning model advocating the active participation of stakeholders and an assessment of values and significance as central elements of the process (see Demas, in this volume) has been utilized to develop and implement a site management plan. Both sites are inscribed on the World Heritage List and, in different ways, both represent complex physical, social, and political environments. These cases were meant to illustrate diverse situations in which the proposed planning model has been successfully implemented in practice.

The second group of case studies includes three major archaeological sites in the eastern Mediterranean—Masada in Israel, Petra in Jordan, and Corinth in Greece. All are complex sites that represent a multiplicity of values and face serious challenges related to physical conservation, competing interest groups, tourism pressure, funding, and management structure. These cases were chosen as illustrative of the many issues facing those charged with the conservation and management of such sites in the region and because they have had varied management histories. All three cases were used as catalysts for discussion and to consider the role that a values-based approach to site management planning might play in the future stewardship of archaeological sites in the region.

Experiences from Europe and Latin America

As a linear site extending over a large geographic area, Hadrian's Wall is challenged by its size, the range of conditions present on the site, a large number of stakeholders with often conflicting interests, multiple ownership, and intense tourism pressure. In general, the site management plan adopted in 1996 is seen to have been effective in promoting a more integrated and holistic approach to site management. Work has just been completed on a review and revision of the plan that has allowed for evaluation of previous experience and subtle changes in the new plan in what is always an iterative process.

Chan Chan is another vast site with its own set of challenges. Built entirely of earth, it is subject to continued physical deterioration from the environment, especially in the face of phenomena like El Niño. Like Hadrian's Wall, Chan Chan represents a range of values from aesthetic and historical to social and economic. The site remains extremely important as a symbol of cultural identity but faces numerous threats from urban encroachment, competing agricultural and industrial use, and an emerging tourism market. The site management plan developed in 1998 and officially approved by the Peruvian government in 2000 has attempted to reconcile competing interests through the creation of use zones and the inclusion of proposals for community development and education in the plan. In this case, too, a clear understanding of the site's significance and broad participation in the planning process are seen as critical to the successful implementation of the plan.

Three Sites in the Region

Masada is a site with strong political and symbolic value, which also presents extraordinary conservation and access challenges due to its daunting physical location. It has become an important tourist destination for both national and foreign visitors with the concomitant pressures for improved access and better tourist facilities. In the period immediately following the site's declaration as a national park, conservation and management tended to be incremental, responding to needs as they presented themselves. With increasing tourism pressure, a strategic development project was carried out from 1995 to 2000, driven largely by the desire to enhance the visitor experience. The case discusses the way that decisions have been made in light of the site's values and the management structure that has been created to coordinate the various components of the plan.

Petra in Jordan is another complex geographical, social, and cultural environment with a long history, many and varied stakeholder groups including a local Bedouin population, and ever increasing tourism pressure. Different from Masada, it has a complex management history involving the preparation of three different management plans or studies over a roughly thirty-year period, each carried out by a different foreign agency using a different approach. The resultant management structure is somewhat fragmented and faces difficulties arising from a lack of coordinated activity as well as from multiple and often competing relationships with various government agencies. In addition, the site's complex social environment has not been sufficiently addressed, and local communities need to be more engaged in the planning and management process. The case elucidates the lessons learned and recommends a more integrated approach to the future conservation and management of the site.

Introduction to Case Studies 59

Corinth, the final case, represents another large and complicated site with a long history of excavation. Unlike Masada and Petra, the site has not been the subject of strategic planning efforts; attention has largely focused on the site's historical and research values with only limited concern for conservation and interpretation for the public. Due to increasing tourism pressure and a desire to reap more economic benefit from the site, however, the time is ripe to consider a more integrated planning effort that would seek to understand and conserve the many values of the site. Corinth actually served as the focus of a group exercise at the workshop regarding the identification of stakeholders and the role of values in management decisions. Thus, unlike the other cases, the Corinth case study is more a presentation of background information on the site that served to inform the exercise (and an eventual management planning process) rather than a discussion of the site's values and its past or current management strategy.

Hadrian's Wall, United Kingdom

Christopher Young

THE WORLD HERITAGE COMMITTEE inscribes places that are of outstanding universal value as World Heritage Sites. Equally, it requires that these sites should have adequate legal and management arrangements in place to protect that significance. In the United Kingdom, the government has maintained since it ratified the World Heritage Convention in 1984 that existing conservation legislation gives adequate legal protection to British World Heritage Sites through national and local systems of designation and control. A series of decisions on planning applications in the early 1990s supported this contention. In 1994 the government formally recognized World Heritage Sites and their settings to be "key material considerations" in determining applications for consent for development (Department of the Environment 1994). The same Planning Policy Guidance Note recognized the importance of proper arrangements for site management by recommending the preparation of management plans for World Heritage Sites.

Since that time, the United Kingdom has made considerable progress in developing such plans. World Heritage management plans have been completed for twelve of the twenty-one World Heritage Sites in the mainland United Kingdom and Northern Ireland. Consultation is in progress on one more site, and work has started or is about to start on all except one of those remaining. Plans are prepared as an integral part of the process of nomination for sites now being put forward for inscription as World Heritage Sites. The purpose of all such plans is to achieve an integrated and holistic approach to site management.

Initially the principal guidance used in preparation of management plans was the seminal work of Bernard Feilden and Jukka Jokilehto, published by ICCROM (International Centre for the Study of the Preservation and Restoration of Cultural Property; Feilden and Jokilehto 1993). Since then plans in the United Kingdom have been strongly influenced by the similar methodology of the conservation plan. These broadly follow the model developed by James Semple Kerr in Australia (Kerr 1996).

Central to this model and to the management plans now being developed is the use of a logical approach based on the significance of the site concerned. The process starts with a full description of the site, covering not just its archaeological or historical aspects but any other interesting features. From this the site's significance can be defined and a statement of significance can be detailed. The next stage is to assess the site for what may threaten those values and then to examine the options for dealing with those threats. After this stage, it is possible to set out policies for dealing with such pressures and also for enhancing the site's positive aspects.

Following this approach should mean that all actions affecting the site are based on an assessment of their impact on the site's significance. Defining the site's significance correctly, therefore, becomes central to the whole planning process. It is important too that the statement of significance is not confined solely to its archaeological value but looks more widely at other ways in which a site is important. The range of values within a site can vary widely and are not necessarily confined to the field of either cultural or natural conservation; other values can be economic or social. Different people and sectors of society may see entirely different types of significance within the same site, and, therefore, at the least will rank perceived values in a different order.

It is vital, therefore, that there should be as full as possible an involvement of all those in a position to influence the treatment of the site or those who are affected by what is done to it. Only by doing so is it possible to deal with a wide and complex ranges of values and to achieve a satisfactory outcome in deciding how the site should be treated.

Given the size and complexity of most World Heritage Sites, the number of stakeholders involved can be considerable. Involving them and developing an acceptable consensus on what should happen can be complicated, time-consuming, and difficult. The first World Heritage Site in the United Kingdom for which such an approach was adopted was Hadrian's Wall. Inscribed in 1987, the wall is, in fact, one of the largest sites in the United Kingdom and probably the most complex because of its size, the wide range of conditions within the wall, and the high number of potentially conflicting interests. The management plan was begun in 1993 and adopted in 1996.

The Hadrian's Wall World Heritage Site

Hadrian's Wall was the northernmost frontier of the Roman Empire for nearly three centuries; it was also the most complex in design. Centered on the wall itself, the complex included turrets, milecastles, forts, and other installations. The forts in particular attracted civilian settlements while further back were two towns supplying other needs. The wall itself stretched from sea to sea across the waist of Britain. The World Heritage Site includes known surviving remains above or below ground along the whole line of the wall (72 miles or 120 kilometers), plus the defenses that stretched down the Cumbrian coast and a number of outlying sites. There is a very wide buffer zone, or setting, around the site itself (Fig. 1).

About 10 percent of the site now lies under modern towns, while much of the remainder can be found in wild and beautiful uplands (Fig. 2). Parts of it have been excavated and conserved as standing masonry, but most of it survives as earthworks or as totally buried archaeology. Due to its size, the site has many different owners, most of whom are private. Only about 10 percent of this site is conserved and managed for public

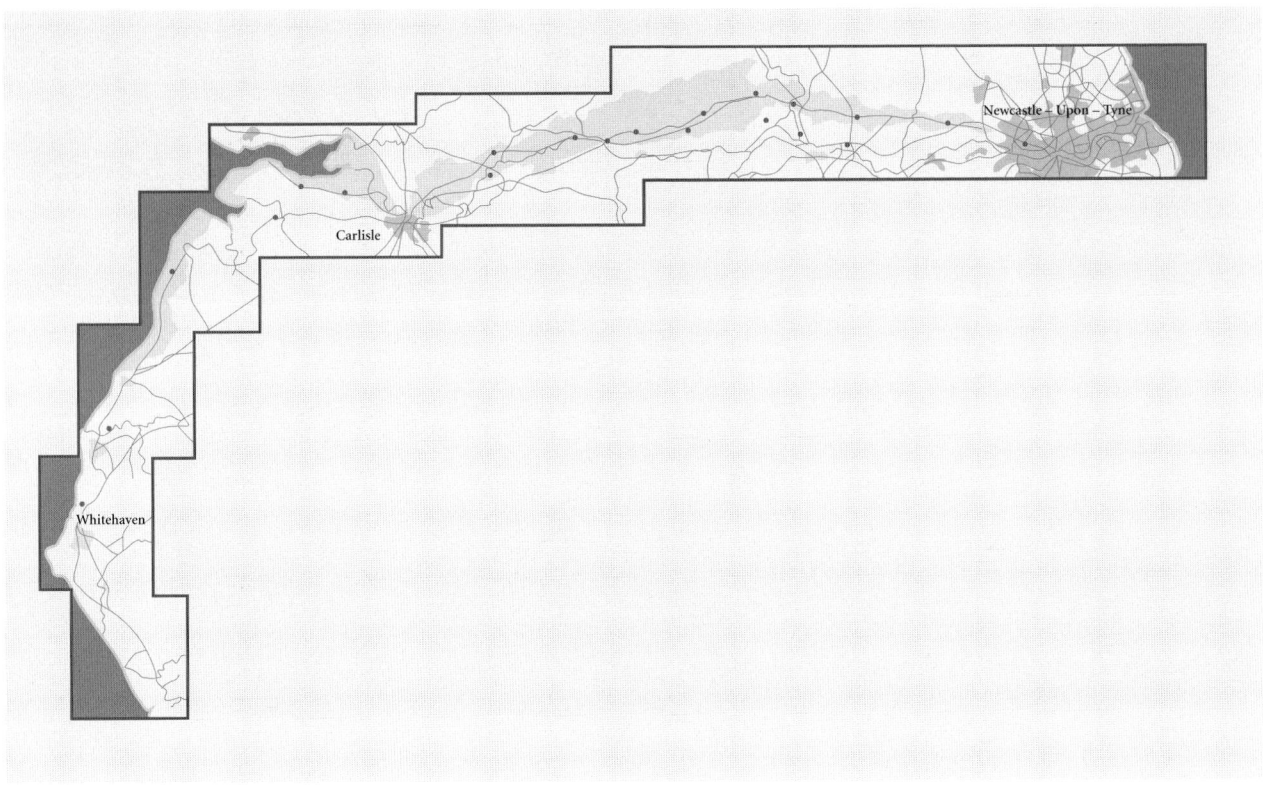

Figure 1
Map of Hadrian's Wall World Heritage Site in England and its setting. © English Heritage.

access. Ownership of this part of the site is divided among English Heritage, two charitable trusts, and a number of local authorities. The remainder of the World Heritage Site is in a variety of uses, partly urban but mainly agricultural, both pastoral and arable. Approximately 1.25 million people visit the accessible parts of the site each year.

Large numbers of public bodies are also involved, with about twelve national ministries or agencies and twelve local authorities all having some role. These roles vary considerably but include regulation of various aspects of the environment and also economic assistance and development. Only a few of these bodies have conservation of the environment

Figure 2
Hadrian's Wall looking east in the central sector along the Whin Sill. © C. Young.

as their primary function. Some have dual roles; local authorities, for example, may be dealing with both development control and tourism promotion. In addition, some are also site managers, responsible for conservation and public access, and needing to earn revenue while managing their holdings sustainably, in order to meet the costs of conservation and management.

The one body with a remit for the conservation of the whole site is English Heritage, which is a NDPB (Non-Departmental Public Body), largely funded by the government and recognized as the leading official body for the historic environment. It exercises this role through a mix of statutory control, advice, assistance, and direct management. Its role is, therefore, a multifaceted one. It too has the need to earn revenue sustainably from the sites it manages within the World Heritage Site.

Apart from responsible management by its owners, there is a range of controls and incentives available for the conservation and sustainable use of the wall. Most new buildings, alterations to existing structures, and new land uses will require planning consent from the relevant local authority under English development control legislation. Contentious cases may also involve central government through a public inquiry. Any intervention to a protected archaeological site requires consent from the government, advised by English Heritage. One exception to this system of control is that much agricultural activity, including some new building, requires no consent. A system of development control is also of little use in promoting positive conservation such as regular maintenance. There are a number of incentive schemes available, including an increasing amount of support for conservation-sensitive farming.

The values of the World Heritage Site and its setting are not just archaeological and historical. Parts of the site also have high natural or scenic value; in fact, the central sector is particularly valued for informal recreation. There is high agricultural value in much of the area, and the wall is one of the major tourism destinations in northern England. It has almost iconic recognition as a symbol of the north and is being used as such in efforts to develop sustainable economic growth. Because of these potentially conflicting factors, as well as its size, the site is subject to a considerable number of pressures, including development and the impact of plowing and overgrazing that leads to erosion. Another pressure is the impact of tourism. Highly desirable as a means of providing access to the world's heritage and also as a stimulus to the local economy, tourism has also led to erosion in some small parts of the site. There are also occasional clashes of interest between public access and other land uses such as grazing.

The Management Plan

The World Heritage Site Management Plan was developed as a response to these pressures and the need to coordinate management of the wall. It was started in 1993 under the leadership of English Heritage, the government's principal advisor on the historic environment. From the start, the plan was perceived as a cooperative exercise produced for a partnership of all the different interests, public and private, involved with the wall.

As such, the end result represents a consensus. Like all such documents, it is to some extent a compromise. It was also a high-level statement rather than a detailed prescription for management. The plan was published in 1996 after one year of public consultation (English Heritage 1996).

The plan followed the basic model recommended by ICOMOS (International Council on Monuments and Sites) and UNESCO (United Nations Educational, Scientific and Cultural Organization). Following a statement of significance, it proposed boundaries for the World Heritage Site and discussed pressures affecting it, then proposed a vision, aims, and more specific policies for protecting the wall within its modern context. It also recommended the establishment of a Committee and a Co-Ordination Unit to oversee its implementation. The role of the unit was not to do everything but to facilitate the work of others and develop partnerships to achieve particular objectives. The plan had a limited lifespan of five years and provided for its revision at the end of that time.

Central to the whole plan was an understanding of the significance of the World Heritage Site and the use of that comprehension to develop policies for its management. Also crucial to the plan was the recognition that it had to encompass the aspirations and needs of not just the archaeologists but also those who lived and worked in or around the World Heritage Site and those who visited it. The plan was not a statutory document backed by the force of law; therefore, it could only work with at least the tacit support of those affected by it and of the bodies in a position to implement its policies.

Figure 3
Hadrian's Wall looking west at Walltown Craggs. © English Heritage Photo Library.

Figure 4
The new museum at Segedunum located at the eastern terminal of Hadrian's Wall. The museum provides a focus for visitors to the World Heritage Site within urban Tyneside.
© C. Young.

We are now five years into the life of the management plan and work has just been completed on its review and revision. This revision has taken account of what has been achieved and what has not happened, as well as of changes elsewhere in the approach to site management. Within the site itself, the major change has been the development of sustainable access, achieved through the work of the Hadrian's Wall Tourism Partnership and the establishment of a National Trail. In addition to investment in this Hadrian's Wall path, there have also been major developments at a number of sites along the wall, most notably at the eastern terminal of the wall at Wallsend. Here, in urban Tyneside, the fort of Segedunum has been reexcavated and displayed with a new museum (Fig. 4). This will provide a clear focal point for the World Heritage Site in the middle of the main center of population.

There has also been work conducted to understand better how the World Heritage Site is used for tourism. This has demonstrated that visitor figures to the managed sites have not increased greatly in recent years. In the open countryside, the pressure from visitors through erosion of sensitive sites is also less intense than suspected in 1996.[1]

Progress has also been made on the conservation of remains. A major three-year project is under way to establish policies, guidelines, and techniques for the management of earthworks under pressure. Major gaps are the failure to develop research and conservation strategies not just for the World Heritage Site but also for its setting. It is important that any research strategy deals with how the site is currently being used as well as with its history and development.

The need to implement the plan has helped to develop the consensus and systems necessary for doing so. There is a committee created to oversee the implementation of the management plan. This is supported by a Co-Ordination Unit, whose role it is to facilitate action by others as well as to carry out specific projects. The unit is very small but essential if the plan is to be put into effect. Parallel to these bodies and working closely with them is the Hadrian's Wall Tourism Partnership, which has the role of developing sustainable tourism while working within the guidance of the management plan; this, too, has been generally effective.

The plan has also provided comfort to potential funding bodies by providing an overall structure within which individual projects can be bedded. In the early years of the plan of 1996, this was reflected in a number of major grants for capital schemes. More recently, the Tourism Partnership has received major revenue funding for various schemes to increase the sustainable contribution made by the World Heritage Site to the regional economy.

Finally, communication of the plan's objectives and work in progress has been important. Various means have been tried. For dealing with specific issues or the development of policies for specific areas, involvement of stakeholders through meetings, consultation, and discussion has been effective. More generally it has been found that public meetings are not effective unless there is a specific issue for discussion. Probably the most effective means of communication has been the site's newsletter, *News from Hadrian's Wall*, produced three times each year. This is available free on all the managed sites and is sent to a mailing list of twenty-three hundred people.

The Revision of the Plan

The management plan for Hadrian's Wall has been revised in the light both of these general developments and of our experience on the wall. It was issued for consultation in June 2001 (English Heritage 2001) and was adopted in its final version by the Management Plan Committee in December 2001. The new draft shows several changes from the plan of 1996. Since the plan is based on four years' experience of the implementation of the previous plan, it has been possible to make it more detailed with thirteen specific policies and consequential action points to be achieved over the next six years. These have been grouped under the four headings of Protecting, Conserving, Using, and Managing the World Heritage Site. It has also been possible to include a Project Register of specific tasks to be undertaken during that period. These policies are based on revised thirty-year "Aims," intended to fulfill an overall vision. The Aims are a revised version of those contained in the plan of 1996; in fact, many of the policies also reflect back to that plan.

Nonetheless, the new plan reflects changes in emphasis, with more concern with sustainable economic regeneration and a holistic approach to the landscape and historic environment as a whole. This includes emphasis on the development of a research strategy to provide the knowledge base essential to proper management of the site's significance, as well as on certain specific pieces of conservation work. There is also recognition of the need to use the World Heritage Site sustainably to repair the damage of the recent outbreak of foot-and-mouth disease to the rural economy as a whole.

The plan follows more explicitly the conservation plan model referred to above, with a full description serving as the basis for a revised statement of significance. Significant additions this time have been appendixes on the geology and natural environment of the area. This is in recognition of the fact that while the World Heritage Site was inscribed for its archaeological and historical value, it has other values of at least national, and in some cases international, significance. As noted above, it is important that management policies for the World Heritage Site are based on an understanding of all its values.

One result of this is that the revised draft plan is considerably longer than its predecessor. The main tool for consultation, therefore, was a 24-page illustrated summary written and published in more accessible language for all those affected by the World Heritage Site. A 4-page summary was published in *News from Hadrian's Wall* as a signpost to the consultation. The full draft has gone to all the significant stakeholders and is available on request. Both the summary and the full plan are also available on the World Wide Web (*www.hadrians-wall.org*). It is anticipated that the same approach will be used for the publication of the final plan later in 2002. It is likely that for many readers, the 24-page popular version of the plan will be the only one that they consult.

Conclusion

The United Kingdom has made considerable progress in recent years in the development of management planning for historic places. Hadrian's Wall is one of the sites with the longest experience of this, so it is now possible to begin to assess the results and to plan for the next cycle of what must always be an iterative process. Crucial to the whole approach is the definition of the values of the site, based on a full description of it. If this is not done, it is not possible to produce appropriate policies. Also crucial are the consent of all the stakeholders involved and a mechanism for implementation of the plan. If these requirements can be achieved, the process of management planning is a powerful and effective technique for the management of change and the conservation of the essential value of a site.

Note

1 The outbreak of foot-and-mouth disease in early 2001 has had a major impact on visitor numbers, with most managed sites closed for several weeks at least, and access to footpaths in the open countryside barred for several months. The long-term impact on tourism is unclear, but it is likely to take some years for visitor numbers to recover.

References

Department of the Environment
1994 *Planning Policy Guidance Note 15: Planning and the Historic Environment*. London: DOE.

English Heritage
1996 *Hadrian's Wall World Heritage Site Management Plan*. Hexham: English Heritage.

2001 *Hadrian's Wall World Heritage Site Management Plan, 2001–2007: Consultation Draft*. Hexham: English Heritage.

Feilden, B., and J. Jokilehto
1993 *Management Guidelines for World Cultural Heritage Sites*. Rome: ICCROM.

Kerr, J. Semple
1996 *The Conservation Plan: A Guide to the Preparation of Conservation Plans for Places of European Cultural Significance*. 4th ed. Sydney: Australia ICOMOS.

Chan Chan, Peru

Carolina Castellanos

Conservation of archaeological sites is faced with significant challenges that range from fabric deterioration in diverse environmental conditions to context-related issues, such as the availability of human, financial, and material resources; legislation; and administrative and social issues. These challenges are often increased by the lack of planning; interventions at sites are frequently undertaken without a clear analysis or understanding of how different factors interrelate and the potential consequences of proposed actions. In this respect, comprehensive planning for the conservation and management of a site provides an essential framework not only to better respond to these conditions but also to better conserve and promote the cultural significance of these places for present and future generations. This paper is meant to illustrate the case study of the Archaeological Complex of Chan Chan, where a participatory, value-driven process was implemented in 1998 for the development of the site's management plan.

The Site and Its Significance

Chan Chan, capital of what was known as the Chimú Kingdom between the ninth and thirteenth century A.D., is one of the largest earthen architecture cities in the Americas. It is located on the north margin of the Moche or Chimor Valley, 5 kilometers from the city of Trujillo on the northern coast of Peru. The Archaeological Complex of Chan Chan extended for 20 square kilometers during its maximum development during pre-Hispanic times, out of which only 14 square kilometers have been preserved. Of the latter, 6 square kilometers belong to the central urban zone, where nine palaces were built as independent units; the other 8 square kilometers include the agricultural and rural zone (Fig. 1).

The cultural history of Chan Chan encompasses a period of six hundred and fifty years, and has been reconstructed and interpreted from archaeological data and ethnohistoric studies, such as administrative and judicial documents from the sixteenth century and myths regarding the Chimor dynasties recorded in the seventeenth century (Fig. 2).

Based on this information, it is assumed that in A.D. 850, the Chimú political organization was similar to a local chiefdom with an

Figure 1
General view of Chan Chan, Peru, showing the extent of the archaeological remains as well as the contemporary surrounding agricultural fields.

	Topic (1980)		Kolata (1982)	
A.D. 850	Local	Chayhuac	Early Chimú	Chayhuac
		Tello (NW)		Uhle
				Tello
	Early Imperial Phase	Uhle		Laberinto
		Laberinto		
A.D. 1100	Middle Imperial Phase	Gran Chimú	Middle Chimú	Laberinto
		Bandelier		Gran Chimú
				Squier
A.D. 1400	Late Imperial Phase	Tschudi	Late Chimú	Velarde
		Rivero		Bandelier
				Tschudi
				Rivero
A.D. 1470	Inca Chimú		Inca Chimú	
A.D. 1532	Colonial		Colonial	

Figure 2
Chart showing the cultural history of Chan Chan as compiled from Topic (1980) and Kolata (1982).

economy based on agriculture. Catastrophic rains related to the El Niño phenomenon, as well as several tectonic movements, produced an economic and social crisis in approximately A.D. 1100, which led to significant ideological, social, and religious changes, including an increase in military activities to conquer neighboring valleys, reflected in the city's urban and spatial distribution and in other cultural expressions. The integration of large provincial territories, the increase in tribute, and the large production of goods at Chan Chan resulted in the diversification and refinement of the administrative functions, and the massive development of intermediate architecture for the state bureaucracy and popular neighborhoods around the palaces. At this point the Chimú State reached its maximum development and territorial expansion, consolidating a vast coastal empire, from Tumbes in the north to Lima in the south. After the Inca conquest in 1470, the city was abandoned, and the powerful Chimú Empire was reduced to a local chiefdom that provided specialized goods for the Inca.

Chan Chan, therefore, represents the synthesis and culmination of the cultural evolution of the Central Andes, particularly at the northern coast of Peru. It reflects the most significant aspects of the Chimú society, such as the social, ideological, political, and economic organization. The interpretation of the site allows us to understand the evolution of the city and the cultural processes of the Moche Valley and the surrounding region, since it was the dominant center of an extended state that exerted a powerful influence. This is revealed in the architectural and cultural vestiges of its subject cities and territories.

On an aesthetic level, Chan Chan reflects the management and organization of space that integrates architecture with decorated surfaces. The constructive order, design, form, and architectural features at Chan Chan reflect a harmonious relationship with the environment. Earthen architecture was adapted to fit diverse needs and emphasized the vastness of space, elevated constructions, and use of decorated surfaces (Figs. 3, 4).

On a scientific level, Chan Chan is an important reserve for the understanding of the evolution and history of the societies of the northern coast of Peru. Studies on pre-Hispanic agricultural development and earthen architecture technology provide data that is still useful for contemporary

Figure 3
Outer sectors of Tschudi Palaces at Chan Chan exemplify construction order, design, form, and characteristic architectural features, such as the use of elevated constructions.

Figure 4
Detail of decorated surfaces at Velarde Palace at Chan Chan, where the Chimú cosmology and craftsmanship are represented. These sectors were partially excavated for monitoring purposes within a training initiative. Like most decorated surfaces at the site, they were later reburied for conservation purposes.

application. On a social level, Chan Chan represents for different local and regional cultural groups a sense of identity, continuity, and a direct link between the past and the present. Its significance survives in the construction techniques, the use of materials, and the use of land and water; economic activities; and customs and beliefs. Also, Chan Chan serves as a symbol of identity on the local, regional, and national levels, and it has a prime economic potential for the sociocultural development of the region. Likewise, the site presents an enormous educational value for archaeology and earthen architecture conservation.

Archaeological Research and Prior Conservation Interventions

Although formal archaeological research at Chan Chan is a very recent development, the settlement has been known largely from references made first by Hispanic chroniclers and later by other European travelers who were interested in the Chimú Kingdom. The earliest attempts to understand the Chimú culture date to the nineteenth century and consist of the review of historical archives, descriptions of the monuments, architectural surveys, and some isolated excavations. In the twentieth century, systematic and scientific archaeological investigation was begun, focused basically on the relative chronology for the site and settlement pattern studies, with the most extensive research at the site undertaken by a team from Harvard University between 1970 and 1980. This sustained research program led to a better understanding of the site and the Chimú culture, including its regional development and influence. Likewise, all palaces and architecture were surveyed; to date, this still constitutes the site's main source of documentation.

The history of interventions at the site can be divided into two phases with reference to conservation. During the first phase, from the early 1960s to the early 1970s, interventions were largely oriented toward reconstruction for formal presentation, which is well illustrated by the case of Tschudi Palace (Fig. 5). Beginning in 1974, a stronger emphasis was placed on conservation of existing material remains, with no extensive restoration. To date, interventions focus on the stabilization of structures, through the application of sacrificial renders and capping, and most of

Figure 5
General view of the Tschudi Palace at Chan Chan, from the Audiencias sector, which was reconstructed in the late 1960s.

Figure 6
Shelters erected at Tschudi Palace to protect decorated surfaces and original construction materials from the effects of the El Niño phenomenon in 1998. The protective shelters, made of canes and woven thatch, provided a low-cost alternative to mitigate the extensive damage that has historically occurred as a result of this climatic phenomenon.

the decorated surfaces have been reburied. Similarly, there is a stronger emphasis on preventive conservation, as illustrated by the building of protective temporary shelters during the events of El Niño in 1998 (Fig. 6).

Conditions Preceding the Management Plan

The Archaeological Complex of Chan Chan is subject to environmental conditions that cause the continuous deterioration of structures and decorated surfaces and the progressive loss of construction materials. Among these, the influence of wind and sun are relevant; however, it is perhaps the periodic phenomenon of El Niño that causes the most extensive deterioration at the site (Fig. 7).

Conservation and maintenance of Chan Chan's palaces and *huacas*, the monumental truncated pyramidal structures associated with ritual and ceremonial functions in pre-Hispanic times, have been constant and frequently carried out in collaboration with international and national

Figure 7
Perimeter wall of the Laberinto Palace at Chan Chan. Once standing six meters high, this wall has suffered severe deterioration and significant loss of construction materials due to years of exposure to environmental conditions.

entities. The scarcity of financial, human, and economic resources has, however, impacted the effectiveness of actions taken to halt deterioration. In addition to conditions related to the environment, deterioration of the archaeological heritage of Chan Chan is also caused by factors related to its management and social context, particularly in the periphery of the site. Urban encroachment and invasion, as well as agricultural and industrial production, have generated pressure from the adjacent communities and have led to the destruction of archaeological remains. In addition, soil is constantly extracted for the manufacturing of adobes, which adversely affects the landscape as well (Fig. 8).

The low-income levels of the adjacent communities promote looting and deterioration of the site's structures, which are also increased by uncontrolled access to the site. The area is known for the high quality of its ceramics and textiles, which unfortunately are highly valued in the strong external and private markets. Also, new settlements in the area tend to use the construction materials, particularly adobes, from the site, which leads to structural problems and the eventual collapse or loss of structures (Fig. 9). Finally, uncontrolled tourism with no visitor management strategies in place has also played a large part in the deterioration of the site.

To address these conditions, some specific measures were implemented, including the drafting of legislation for the protection of the site and the recovery of illegally occupied sectors used for agricultural and industrial activities. Nonetheless, these actions did not result in greater social or political support and commitment to conservation endeavors and did not have a long-term impact. In 1996, the INC-DRLL (Instituto Nacional de Cultura—Dirección Regional La Libertad) developed and presented to the Ministry of Education a plan that integrated the needs for conservation, research, presentation, dissemination, education, and

Figure 8
Deterioration and loss of construction materials in the periphery of Chan Chan due to social conditions including urban encroachment, invasion of protected areas, and destruction of archaeological remains.

Figure 9
Perimeter walls of Rivero Palace at Chan Chan, where significant portions of the original constructed areas have been lost not only due to the exposure to environmental conditions but also as a result of social issues, particularly the extraction of soils and removal of adobes for contemporary construction.

protection, among other actions at the site. The project was not implemented, however, and actions continued to be carried out basically on an emergency basis.

It was not until 1997, when UNESCO's World Heritage Committee met in Naples, Italy, and recommended to the Peruvian government that a management plan be created for Chan Chan, as a requirement of its status as World Heritage and World Heritage in Danger, that activities were formalized to prepare such a plan. The project was deemed to be one of the priorities in the Peruvian government's cultural policy; thus, between January and December 1998, the planning process was begun by the INC-DRLL, with the collaboration of the World Heritage Center, UNESCO, ICCROM (International Centre for the Study of the Preservation and Restoration of Cultural Property), and the Getty Conservation Institute.

The Planning Process

The planning process for Chan Chan consisted of three phases: study and documentation, analysis, and response. The methodological approach was derived mainly from the didactic materials and methodology developed for PAT 96, a Pan-American course on the conservation and management of earthen architecture and archaeological sites.[1] It is essentially the same

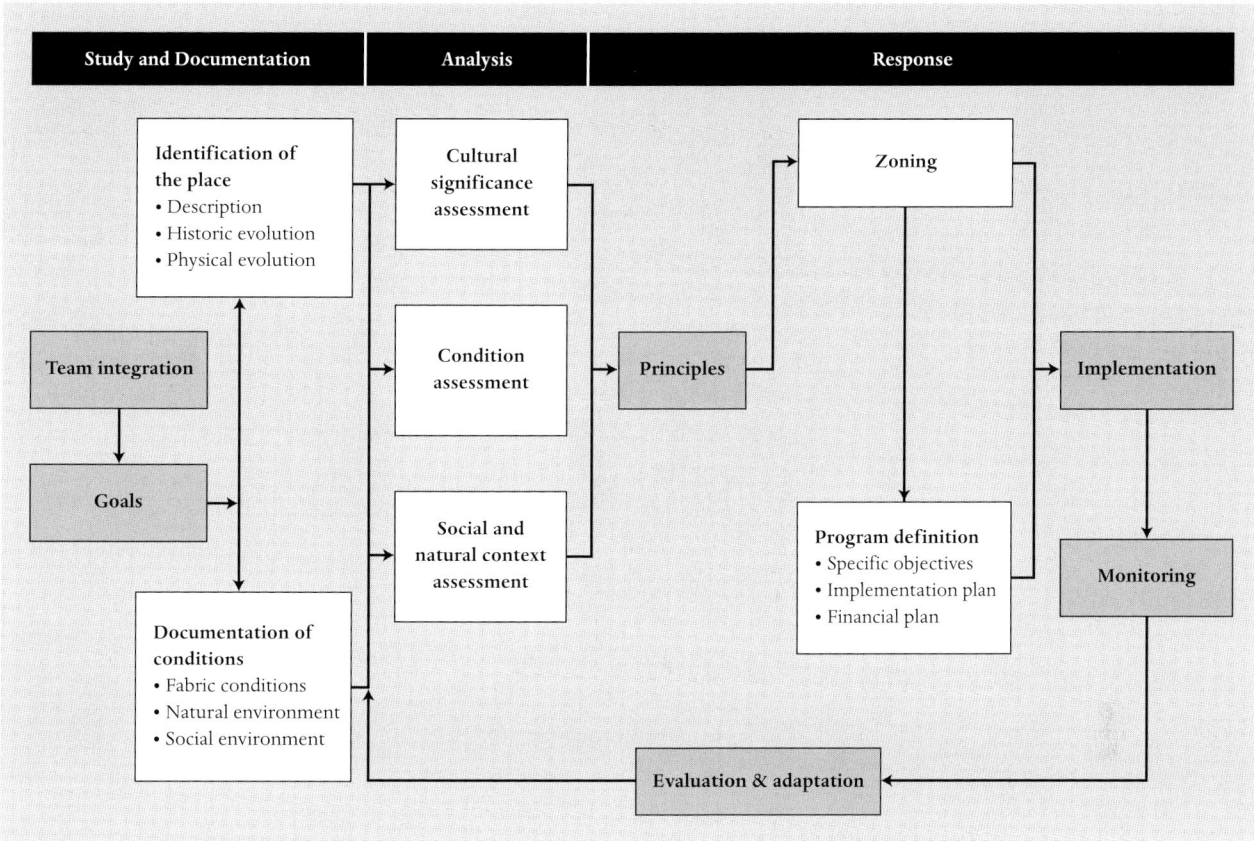

Figure 10
Planning process for the development of the management plan for Chan Chan.

process as that described in the paper by Martha Demas in this volume, with minor adaptations made for the Peruvian context (see page 30; Fig. 1).

The main purpose of preparing the plan was to integrate, with an interdisciplinary and participatory approach, every action that is carried out at the site and to develop a phased action plan that sought to conserve and promote the values that make Chan Chan a significant place. It was assumed that a series of programmed actions ranging from archaeological research and conservation to *mise en valeur*,[2] education, administration, and promotion would also help to optimize the limited financial, material, and human resources, by investing them in priority needs.

The goal was to respond holistically to the conditions that existed at the site, while considering the site's cultural significance as the driving force in the decision-making process. By employing a value-driven process, the proposed plan was not limited to the fabric of the site but also addressed other social and economic issues that influence the sense and meaning of heritage in the lives of different social groups in the area, thus making them direct beneficiaries of its conservation. Given the complex issues related to the conservation and management of the site, the planning process promoted the active involvement of different stakeholders, which would lead to broader commitment and support for both conservation endeavors and the overall implementation of the plan.

Preliminary Work

The first sessions of the process were meant to introduce and reach a consensus on the proposal for the development of the plan and to create a planning team that shared a common vision and methodological approach. Given the recognized importance of an interdisciplinary approach in management planning, it was decided that the following areas of expertise would be needed to develop the plan: archaeology, architecture, conservation, social anthropology, ecology, administration, education, tourism promotion, legislation, and planning, among others. Specialists were selected according to their knowledge in the particular field of expertise; besides the core planning team, there was technical support for logistics and organization from the INC-DRLL and the participation of several university students, who undertook different tasks such as interviews and surveys with visitors, field condition reporting, data processing, and so forth.

Creating a team with local experience was important in order to guarantee the long-term multiplying effect of the initiative and also to design a plan appropriate to the social, economic, and political context of Peru, as well as the existing technical capabilities for its implementation. In addition to the definition of the planning team, public and private institutions—as well as other stakeholders—were identified so that they could be integrated during different phases of the planning process.

Besides these issues, the first phase of the plan focused on identifying the reasons why a management plan needed to be developed. Some of the issues that were raised include the following:

- Integration and programming of actions to use available resources more efficiently;
- Participation of the community in heritage endeavors by defining shared tasks;
- Addressing social and economic problems with alternative means derived from the site; and
- Strengthening identity and social cohesion through conservation.

Given that the next phase would focus on study and documentation, information was reviewed to provide an idea of what existed, what needed to be updated, and what needed to be produced for the planning process. Many documents and data had been completed or compiled at different times, but without a clear idea of the purpose or intended use of the information and without a systematic analysis. Consequently, appropriate tools and methods were identified in order to provide coherent and systematic information. It was emphasized that not only did fabric-related issues need to be considered but also that the social and natural environments played an essential role in understanding the place and were thus determining issues in developing a holistic response. Collaboration mechanisms for effective communication, both within the planning team and with other interest groups, were identified. Some of these included the creation of inter-institutional agreements and committees, the assignment of institutional counterparts to collaborate in the compilation of information, as well as meeting schemes to evaluate progress.

Study and Documentation

The planning phase focused on the documentation of the physical and historical evolution of the Archaeological Complex as well as the recording of conservation conditions with direct or indirect impact on the site, considering both the natural and social environment. Lastly, issues pertaining to the management framework were addressed, such as the legal, administrative, and social situations that influenced the site. The bibliographic compilation and the condition recording were carried out under the premise that thorough and specific data would allow a precise analysis and consequently the design of programs that responded to conditions and could be effectively implemented.

The planning team, led by the project's coordinators according to their particular areas of expertise, ensured the fulfillment of all tasks. The most complex part of this phase involved recording the site's condition. Since resources were very limited, a specific methodology was developed and areas were prioritized; thus, a more detailed survey was carried out in areas with exposed decorated surfaces while only a general inspection was done where they were not present. A group of over fifteen conservators, archaeologists, and architects was put together to comply with the objectives and guidelines set forth during the first phase of the process. Despite the large amount of resources devoted to this task, it took twice the time originally planned to accomplish this phase.

Analysis

The purpose of the planning phase was to assess the cultural significance of the site in terms of historic, scientific, aesthetic, and social values that could be ascribed to the site. Likewise, the physical condition of the site was analyzed, as well as social, legal, administrative, educational, and promotional issues, because of their relationship to the conservation and management of the site. All of these elements were essential in determining the objectives and priorities for the response phase.

Given the participatory approach to the planning process, all of the aforementioned issues were presented in plenary sessions attended by representatives from public and private entities that presented their views. With objective and simple presentations, and broad discussion on the specific themes presented, a commitment to the conservation and management of the site was initially attained from several representatives of different interest groups.

Cultural significance assessment was widely discussed; issues regarding the nature of values and their attribution were brought up during the meetings. An initial proposal of values,[3] as seen from the planning team's perspective, was presented during the plenary meetings. All of the issues were examined in light of existing documentation to determine if they were, in effect, values, and who considered them to be values. This was essential because the defined values were the driving forces behind the decision-making process for the site's management. As anticipated, some of the audience's comments were not related to values per se but rather to desired projects and objectives. It was important, therefore, to facilitate and guide the meetings so that values and interests could be differentiated.

It was particularly relevant to have values ascribed to the site within the framework of economy, education, and local and national history, which is ultimately shown in the final significance statement. As in other planning initiatives, values seemed to be easily identified from the perspective of the archaeological and conservation communities. Nonetheless, the strong participatory nature of the process led to a realization that values are relative and in need of prioritization in accordance with different perspectives, including those held by other interest groups. The prioritization of values took place within the framework of these discussions. The guiding criteria in this process were to create a balance within the overall context of the place but also to build toward the long-term vision for the site. It is evident that the existing and potential economic values were significant issues, particularly in regard to the development of the area. These were thoroughly "argued" to reach a consensus by all groups involved, attempting to create a balance among their interests and perspectives.

Through a holistic discussion, all of the varied issues that affected the site were addressed, and there was an initial consensus on priorities, related directly both to the fabric and to social conditions such as awareness, education, and outreach. The open collaborative approach created an environment that fostered a more direct participation of stakeholders and their involvement in the development of the plan's programs.

Response

This phase encompassed the definition of principles, as a reference for all actions prescribed for the conservation and management of the site. Additionally, different use zones were determined and specific objectives for each were defined so as to design targeted programs.

The first step, then, was to define the general policies for the management of the site. These were established based on the values ascribed to the site, balanced by recognition of the realities imposed by the multiple conditions that influenced the site's conservation and management. With these policies in place, values could be prioritized and cultural significance conserved, but in ways compatible with the restrictions imposed by the physical, social, and economic context. All of these general policies were also agreed on during the plenary meetings. Obviously, reaching a consensus on them was difficult as it entailed conflicting perspectives and reconciling the needs of different stakeholders with those of conservation. Summary examples of the policies that illustrate this process include such issues as the integration of the Archaeological Complex within the economic activities of the adjacent areas, including industrial and agricultural development; the respect and promotion of traditional practices and knowledge of cultural development; the fostering of educational and outreach activities; the promotion of the Archaeological Complex as a means of socioeconomic development of the region; the emphasis on minimum intervention in conservation; and the prioritization of conservation activities in the intensive and extensive use zones so that more areas would be presented and opened to the public.

Another key issue was zoning. Different interest groups that would be affected by it examined an initial proposal made by the INC-DRLL. The ultimate zoning plan for the site was agreed on with the municipality of Trujillo, in accordance with its Metropolitan Development Plan, in order to make certain proposed uses feasible. The premise was that the definition of different zones would guarantee that the management actions prescribed in the plan would respond to overall function. Established zones were not only related to uses of the physical space, therefore, but also to the way in which actions and interventions were prioritized.

Criteria for the determination of use zones included the characteristics and conservation conditions of each zone, the type of existing infrastructure, the types of uses compatible with conservation, the protection and facility needs for visitor use, and the feasibility of establishing additional areas for public use. Ultimately, the established use zones included the following: restricted, intensive, extensive, and special uses, and a buffer zone. The latter two were particularly relevant to Chan Chan. In the special use zone, it was agreed that uses could include the agricultural revival of *totorales* (rush species that grows in soils with a high concentration of salts and is characteristic of Peru's northern coast), which would balance the subsistence needs of the agricultural communities with the conservation of the site. These proposals were regulated by the INC-DRLL, and their implementation will be monitored by several entities. The establishment of the buffer zone proved to be the first step in the commitment of Trujillo's municipality to the future of the site; the city both accepted the buffer zone and reconciled it with their existing development plan.

Once the zoning was finalized, programs were developed for each of the zones, concentrating on priority issues and building on the long-term vision for the site. Each program was structured to fulfill specific objectives in terms of research, conservation, presentation, and education, among others. The contents of each project were defined jointly by the planning team and other parties, maintaining an interdisciplinary collaboration and close relationship with entities that would be responsible for project implementation. Ultimately, seven programs with twenty-four subprograms and one hundred and forty projects were defined for the management and conservation of Chan Chan. Among other issues, projects addressed future scientific investigation, conservation of architecture and decorated surfaces, emergency preparedness, presentation, visitor management, museum and education, outreach, alternative uses, and sustainable development for adjacent communities.

During the response phase of the planning process, particular attention was focused on abiding by established policies in all actions prescribed. Indicators and monitoring issues were agreed on in order to provide methods for evaluating the success of each project while recognizing the importance of continued review and adaptation of the prescribed programs. Likewise, such review also identified projects that were not priorities but that could be implemented through public and private support, without endangering future actions. All actions were ultimately weighed against the reality of the limited government resources available for cultural heritage in Peru. Certain projects were deemed priorities inasmuch as they affected the whole implementation of the plan, such as protection and legal measures. Part of the discussions were then centered on conditions for the implementation of the plan; diverse strategies were examined and set forth in the plan to support the administrative, technical, financial, and political framework. A more active participation in the implementation and monitoring of the plan was assured through a revised administrative set-up.

At the beginning of the process, the principal objective was not only to develop a management plan for Chan Chan but also to build on existing capabilities so as both to implement the plan and to carry out further planning initiatives in the region. As a pilot experience in the region, the methodological approach can be considered successful, in that it allowed these objectives to be fulfilled. It provided an organized framework and a logical sequence of steps in the decision-making process, during which very precise objectives were met and tasks accomplished. The model demanded that every proposed action respond to a thorough understanding of conditions; all proposals were evaluated in terms of prioritized values and potential impact on significance, not as defined by specialists but as understood by the diverse groups related to the site.

Interdisciplinary participation was essential throughout the development of the project in order to achieve a comprehensive approach to the conservation and management of the Archaeological Complex of Chan Chan. Although nothing new in the field of conservation and management planning, such an interdisciplinary approach provided an opportunity to collaborate with colleagues having different perspectives, who ultimately shared the goal of conserving the site's significance. In this way, each team member played an essential role in the planning process, and his or her contributions were related not only to the information produced by specialized surveys but also to the views of different stakeholders. A strong emphasis was placed on cultural processes, identity, and fostering a continued sense of well-being, which is reflected in the inclusion of programs related to sustainable community development and education. Similarly, the conservation and archaeology programs were revised to accept innovative uses of the site, such as the revival of agricultural use in sectors that originally functioned that way. Through dissemination and outreach strategies, archaeology fostered a stronger valuing of the site, leading to greater reflection on why heritage is conserved and, most importantly, for whom.

As a result of this continuous interdisciplinary and participatory process, proposals for the improved use and enjoyment of Chan Chan were examined and included in the plan, always taking into account the conservation of its significance. Thus, proposed projects go beyond the mere design of sound strategies for the conservation of physical fabric; they also attempt to bring meaning to heritage in the lives of different social groups, attempting to make them direct beneficiaries of the site's conservation.

Implementation of the Plan: Challenges and Solutions

A participatory approach was an essential tenet of the planning process. Involving stakeholders in the initiative created a framework in which the needs of conservation could be reconciled with the needs of different social groups. This broad-based type of participation advanced collaboration, which is reflected in the current implementation of specific projects. By making various social groups feel like owners of the process, a stronger commitment to the site was achieved; in the long run, this should guarantee the successful implementation of the plan.

Given the above, it became clear that the future of the site cannot rest solely on institutions such as the INC-DRLL; a stronger commitment is needed from society at large. Chan Chan can be the focus of diverse projects, which through adequate conservation and management will bring both economic and social benefits to many segments of society. Important progress has been made regarding the establishment of the buffer zone, the norms for certain sustainable land uses, and the regulation of development around the site; tourism and education are particularly promoted, but in accordance with the site's significance.

Although longer than initially planned, the ultimate success of the project led to official approval of the management plan by Peru's government in early 2000; hopefully, this should ensure full support for continued implementation. Recent political and social crises in Peru have slowed the scheduled implementation of the plan. Nonetheless, limited actions have been undertaken on prioritized projects.

In summary, a value-driven participatory management planning approach could play a significant role in the region for the development of plans that provide comprehensive and sustainable responses to the needs of different places. Success will rest largely on the ability to adapt the methodological framework to specific conditions. Successful implementation depends on broad participation and reconciling the needs of different stakeholders; in the end, so does conservation of cultural heritage.

Acknowledgments

The author wishes to specially thank all the institutions and individuals that have contributed to and supported this project. Among these are the following: Instituto Nacional de Cultura de Perú, World Heritage Centre, UNESCO's office in Peru, ICCROM, CRATerre-EAG, and the Getty Conservation Institute.

Notes

1   Curso Panamericano sobre la Conservación y el Manejo del Patrimonio Arquitectónico Histórico—Arqueológico de Tierra, Trujillo, Peru, 1996. This six-week course was carried out as a collaborative project of the INC-DRLL (Instituto Nacional de Cultura—Dirección Regional La Libertad), CRATerre-EAG (International Center for Earth Construction—School of Architecture of Grenoble), ICCROM (International Centre for the Study of the Preservation and Restoration of Cultural Property), and the Getty Conservation Institute. The course was given for the first time in 1996 (PAT 96) and subsequently, in revised form, in 1999 (PAT 99).

2   The term *mise en valeur* is used in this context to indicate those activities focused on the presentation and "enhancement" of the site's values for the better use and understanding of the public, and, potentially, for additional economic benefits.

3   The planning team decided the typology of values after evaluating the existing literature on the subject of values. Terms were reviewed, taking into account what would be most appropriate for the Peruvian context and what was most likely to be understood by the different members of the interest groups.

References

Castellanos, C.

1999 *Complejo Arqueológico de Chan Chan: Proceso de Planificación para el Desarrollo del Plan de Manejo.* Unpublished report. Los Angeles: Getty Conservation Institute.

Castellanos, C., and A. M. Hoyle

1998 *Complejo Arqueológico de Chan Chan: Proyecto Plan de Manejo. Primer Informe de Trabajo a UNESCO.* Unpublished report. Peru: INC-DRLL.

1998 *Complejo Arqueológico de Chan Chan: Proyecto Plan de Manejo. Segundo Informe de Trabajo a UNESCO.* Unpublished report. Peru: INC-DRLL.

Getty Conservation Institute

1996 *El Enfoque de Manejo.* Unpublished report. Los Angeles: Getty Conservation Institute.

Hoyle, A. M.

1999 *Complejo Arqueológico de Chan Chan. Plan Maestro de Conservación y Manejo. Tercer Informe de Trabajo a UNESCO.* Unpublished report. Peru: INC-DRLL.

Kolata, Alan L.

1982 "Chronology and Settlement Growth at Chan Chan." In *Chan Chan: Andean Desert City*, 67–85. Ed. Michael E. Moseley and Kent C. Day. School of American Research Advanced Seminar Series, Albuquerque: University of New Mexico Press.

Topic, John R.

1980 "Excavaciones en los Barrios Populares de Chan Chan." In *Chan Chan Metrópoli Chimor*. Lima: IEP.

Masada, Israel

Esti Ben Haim

Historical and Archaeological Background of Masada, Israel

Historical Background

Masada is a unique location in that it is possible to compare actual archaeological discoveries with an historical source. Flavius Josephus, a Jewish Roman historian of the first century C.E., is our sole source of information on the history of Masada, and much of the information he imparted in his works such as *The Jewish War* and *Jewish Antiquities* has been confirmed by archaeological finds. According to Josephus, the first to fortify Masada—an area that provides the perfect natural defensive position—was Jonathan the High Priest (Hasmonean). Until now, there have been no finds unearthed from the Hasmonean period.

The most prominent construction work in the rather isolated Masada was that of King Herod the Great (reigned 37–4 B.C.E.), who built a king's citadel as a refuge for troubled times. When Herod died, a Roman garrison held the place. In 66 C.E., at the beginning of the revolt of the Jews, a group of Jewish zealots surprised and destroyed the Roman garrison, controlling Masada throughout the war. Jewish rebels from different political groups settled in Masada, particularly following the destruction of Jerusalem and the second temple by Titus in 70 C.E..

In 72 C.E., the Roman governor Flavius Silva decided it was in his best interest to destroy this outpost of resistance. He led the Tenth Legion into Masada, its auxiliary troops and thousands of prisoners of war carrying the equipment. The Jews on top of the mountain, commanded by Eleazar Ben Yair, prepared themselves for defense.

Silva's troops prepared for a long siege, building camps at the base of the rock and a siege wall around the fortress. On a rocky site near the western approach to Masada, Silva's troops constructed a ramp on which they moved a siege tower with a battering ram. Directing it at the fortress wall, they succeeded in making a breach in it. There was no hope for relief or escape for the besieged Jews. In fact, they had only two alternatives: surrender or death. Ben Yair resolved that "a death of glory was preferable to a life of infamy," and persuaded the nine hundred and sixty men, women, and children of Masada to kill themselves.

When the Romans reached the top of Masada the following morning, they were met with complete silence. According to Josephus's account, "And so met (the Romans) with the multitude of the slain, but could take no pleasure in the fact, though it were done to their enemies. Nor could they do other than wonder at the courage of their resolution."[1] This story became the myth of Masada.

After several hundred years of abandonment, a small settlement of Byzantine monks settled on the site in the fifth and sixth centuries C.E. They built a modest chapel and lived in miserable dwellings and caves.

Archaeological Excavations

The first excavations carried out in Masada in the twentieth century were part of a survey set out in 1955–56 on behalf of the Israel Exploration Society, the Hebrew University, and the Department of Antiquities of the

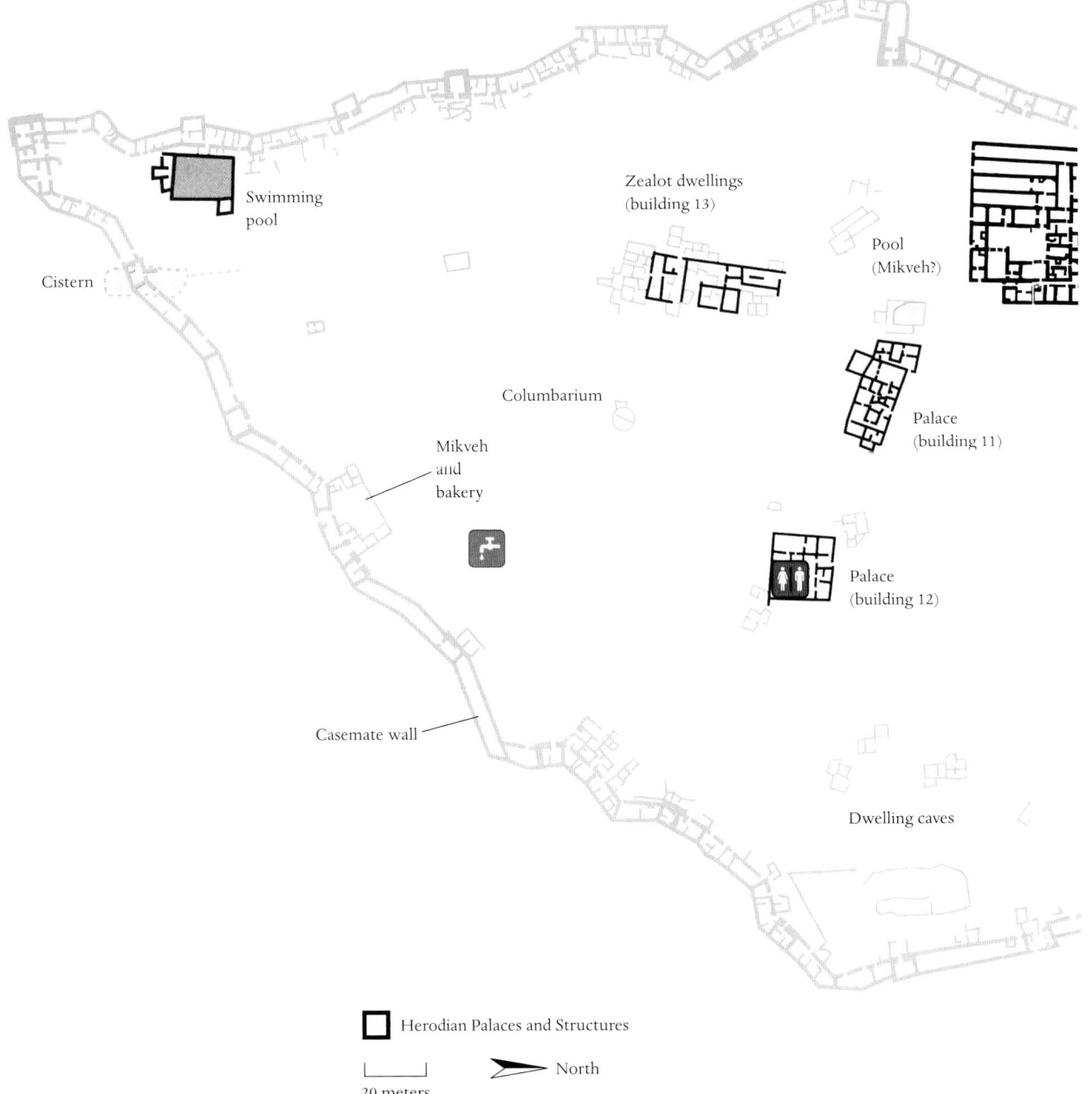

Figure 1
General Plan of the Masada mountaintop. Plan courtesy of The Israel Nature and National Parks Protection Authority.

Ministry of Education, headed by N. Avigad, M. Avi Yonah, Dr. Y. Aharoni, I. Dunayevski, and S. Guttman. The main excavations of the site were carried out during an expedition led by Professor Y. Yadin of the Hebrew University in Jerusalem from 1963 to 1965. These excavations were carried out on behalf of the Hebrew University with the aid of the Department of Antiquities and the Israel Exploration Society, in conjunction with conservation and reconstruction works by the National Parks Authority (NPA), which at the time was called the Department for Landscaping and the Preservation of Historical Sites. During the excavations, and for one year following their completion in 1966, large-scale reconstruction and development work was carried out.

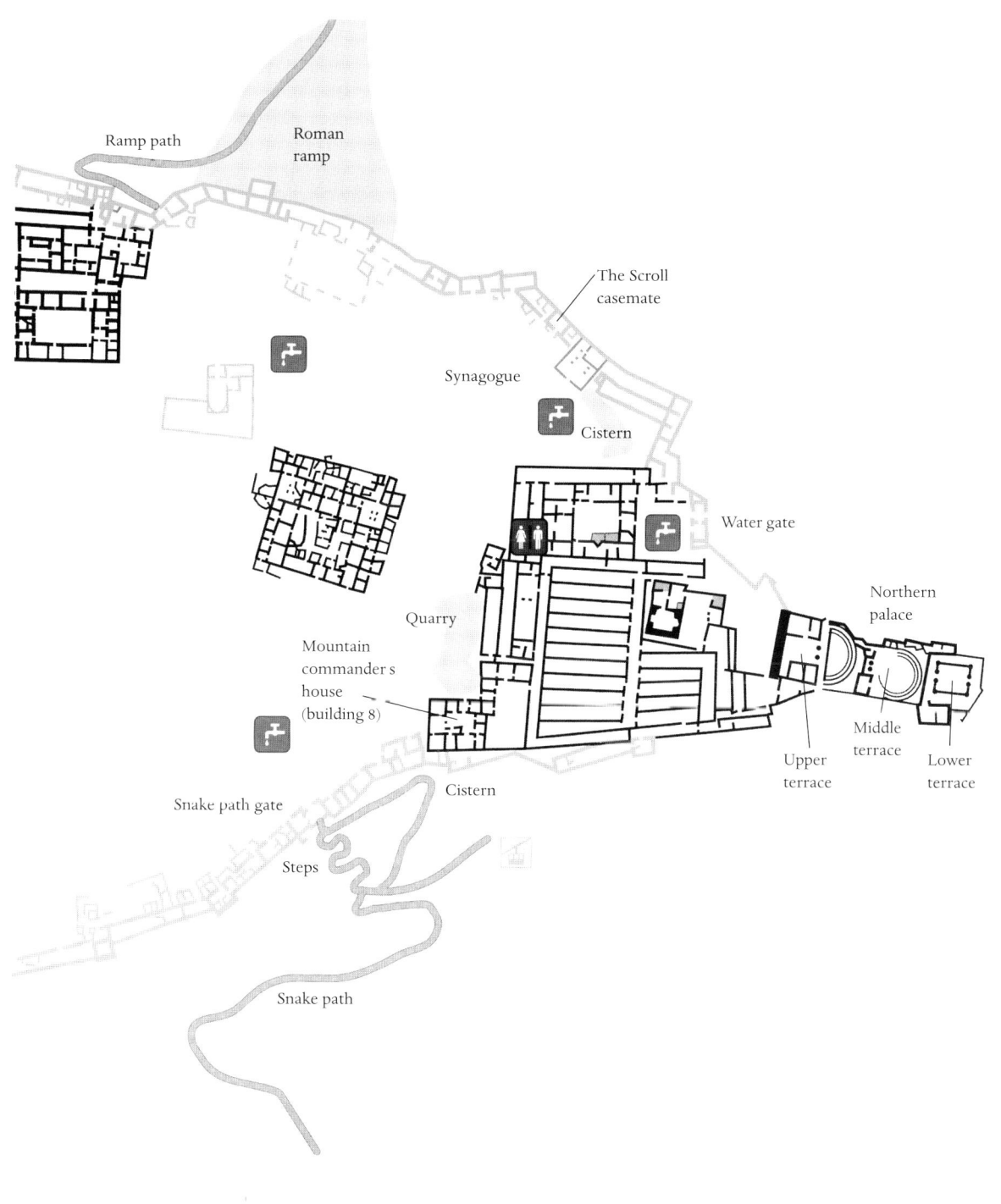

Yadin's excavation was the largest and most challenging archaeological project ever carried out in Israel. The project was made possible due to Yadin's rather special personality. Considering the conditions of those days, it was a complicated campaign in every respect and the Israeli army was extremely helpful in the endeavor. Yadin inspired thousands of volunteers from many countries, who dug in difficult conditions with great enthusiasm. Yadin's expedition revealed spectacular remains and quite interesting finds.

Additional excavations on the summit were carried out by Professor E. Netzer of the Hebrew University in 1989, and within the framework of the development project in Masada National Park between the years 1995 and 2000. Another excavation, headed by Professor G. Foerster of the Hebrew University, was carried out in 1995, in Camp F. and the Roman ramp, at the west foot of Masada Mountain.

Statement of Significance

Masada is an isolated rock in the far corner of the Judean Desert. Its archaeological remains relate to three periods of human habitation of the site, periods chronologically separated and different in character from one another. Each period of habitation in Masada reflects, on the one hand, a certain uniqueness; and on the other hand, a fabric of intertwined cultural contexts of its period.

Masada's Values

Archaeological/Scientific/Cultural Values

The three main periods represented at Masada are as follows:

1. The period of King Herod the Great (reigned 37–4 B.C.E.);
2. The period of the Great Revolt (66–73 C.E.); and
3. The early Christian period, the Byzantine period (fifth and sixth centuries C.E.).

Most of the Masada site has already been excavated. The buildings that have been uncovered, as well as many additional finds, have provided considerable scientific information on the relevant periods. They have confirmed information from the historical sources as reported by Flavius Josephus regarding the story of Masada from the period of the Second Temple and the Great Revolt. In addition, the excavations enabled the study of Herod's architecture, the Roman military system, survival methods used in the desert, and much more.

Trials of conservation methods specific to the unique conditions of Masada are being implemented at the site according to accepted principles of conservation theory and practice.

It is worth expanding a bit on Herod's construction works and architecture, as well as the Roman military works, as each of them is considered to be a unique feature of Masada. Herod built Masada in three phases during the time of his reign, and most of the archaeological remains of the mountaintop are from his period. King of Judea, Herod was of Edomite origin and was referred to—among other things—as the

Figure 2
General view of Masada, aerial photograph. The three terraces of the Northern Palace are seen in front. Photo courtesy of The Israel Nature and National Parks Protection Authority.

Builder King. He left his mark on many places in Israel, and it would appear that he reached the pinnacle of his building at Masada, with its great heights of vision, daring, and genius. Herod brought to this remote, harsh place the best of the skill of Roman construction and culture. Thoroughly familiar with Roman culture, Herod admired it and wanted to have the final word in Roman architecture and ornamentation, the customs of the Roman court, and the consumption of goods and tools used by the Romans. Since bringing authentic building materials from abroad was costly, Herod found local solutions that looked like the genuine article.

Herod's daring and the skills of his artisans succeeded in turning Masada into a king's fortress, which could serve, if necessary, as a place of protection but also as a pleasure palace where the king could indulge in the hedonistic delights he loved so much. In any event, it was a place where solutions could be found to all the necessities of a man's existence. The following are among the many important elements in Masada.

The Water System

Water is the source of life, and its importance in an isolated desert location is great. In addition to the cisterns dug out of the mountaintop, the solution that Herod found for providing water to Masada was to dig twelve cisterns on two levels of the northwestern slope of the mountain, to which two aqueducts brought the flood waters of two wadis in the region. One flood in the winter could provide enough water to fill the cisterns and ensure an abundant water supply for the entire year, not only for drinking and washing but also for the pleasures of the swimming pools and the bathhouse.

The Northern Palace

The private palace of King Herod, located on the coolest and most shaded spot on Masada, overlooks breathtaking landscape. The palace's problematic location, a narrow place on a steep slope that drops down into an abyss, did not deter Herod. He knew where to find the rock that was geologically most solid, to carve and fashion it according to his will into three terraces, and to place on it a palace with columns decorated in stucco; Pompeii-style frescoes, which were popular at the time; mosaics; and more. The palace was built of soft limestone, which was not locally available. On its eastern side, the king's private bathhouse was built on a slope, while on its western side, steps were built reaching all the terraces of the palace. A number of sections were built on the palace's southern side, which made access difficult for anyone who was out of favor with the king.

The Roman Siege System

There is an excellent view of this system from the mountain. The only complete system of its kind that survived from the Roman period, it is made up of eight Roman camps, a siege wall (circumvallation, or a low wall that connects the camps to one another), and a ramp, on which (according to Josephus) the battering ram that breached the wall was carried. The point where the breach was made is clearly seen today.

Natural/Aesthetic Values

Masada is an isolated cliff, part of the Judean fault scarp that lies between the low area of the Dead Sea and the Judean Desert edge platform. Masada is incised by wadis that separate it from the sequence of rock to the west, leaving it an isolated mountain. This isolation resulted in its being highly sought after as a place of refuge and protection. The area of the national park with its surrounding buffer zone forms a unique landscape and ecosystem of many components. The Judean Desert is a local desert caused by the Judean mountain ridge that prevents precipitation in the

Figure 3
General view of the western side of Masada Mountain with the Roman siege rampart (and the three terraces of the Northern Palace) on the left. Photo courtesy of The Israel Nature and National Parks Protection Authority.

Figure 4
Herodian mosaic from the Western Palace, Masada. Photo courtesy of The Israel Nature and National Parks Protection Authority.

area. On the other side lies the Dead Sea, the lowest point in the world, and the oases that act as refuges for wild animals and plants. The whole area is a meeting point for different types of flora and fauna between the extreme desert, the steppe, and the Mediterranean biogeographical sources. The result of this is a unique ecosystem that contains a very special expression of cultures.

Masada Mountain towers over its surroundings, and anyone standing on it is provided with a glimpse of the primeval and untamed landscape of the Judean Desert and the Dead Sea. Considerable efforts have been invested by various groups to prevent construction on the periphery viewed from Masada, and to leave the primeval landscape untouched.

Social/National-Political/Religious/Symbolic Values

In the twentieth century, Flavius Josephus's account of the end of the Jews in Masada became the myth of Masada. The myth was one of the cornerstones of the Zionist Movement, in which a desire to renew the Jewish life in Zion, the land of Israel, was pursued. The pinnacle of the identification with the Masada myth, as an example of valor and sacrifice, was during World War II. At that time, the Jewish population in the country was threatened from the north and south by Nazi and pro-Nazi forces, and a plan—"Masada on Mount Carmel"—was formulated, along the lines of the ancient model of Masada. According to this plan, the Jewish population would be gathered together on Mount Carmel, to defend itself against the enemy—the few against the many, liberty or death.

In the end, there was no need to implement this plan; however, its implications were preserved in the national consciousness for many years to come. The plan undoubtedly contributed to the advent of Masada as a pilgrimage site for youth movements and members of pre-Israeli State underground movements, soldiers, and school pupils after the foundation of the state of Israel in 1948.

Religious Value

While Masada is not considered a sacred place, the archaeological finds indicating that religious rites took place at the site have granted it religious significance. The synagogue of Masada is one of the few that existed at the time when the Second Temple stood in Jerusalem. In modern times, Jews from all over the world flock to Masada to celebrate their children's bar or bat mitzvahs, ceremonies accompanied by prayers and great emotion. In addition, the Byzantine Church on Masada is one of the first churches of early Christianity, and it is the southernmost church in the Judean Desert. The church attracts many visitors and groups of Christian pilgrims who hold religious and spiritual ceremonies there.

Economic Value

With its magical landscape, archaeological relics, historical background, and religious and national significance, Masada is a magnet for visitors, many of whom are foreign tourists whose numbers are constantly on the increase. The quantity of visitors and the expected increase in tourism require that improvements be made in the site's visitor services and management to enhance the experience of the visit on the one hand, and to make sure that the conservation of the site is not compromised, on the other hand. The movement of tourists and visitors to the site is of economic value: a source of income for the local population and a source of foreign currency for the state of Israel.

Masada in Our Era: Management History and the Development of the Management Plan

The Masada National Park: 1965–1995

The first management decision regarding Masada took place following the completion of the archaeological excavations carried out by Yadin's expedition. Toward the end of the excavation, the Department for Landscaping and the Preservation of Historical Sites, a part of the Prime Minister's office, decided to open the site to the public as a national park. Consequently, immediately after excavation was concluded, conservation and reconstruction works began. These works were undertaken according to a plan made by a special committee of experts in related fields and were carried out according to the best knowledge that existed in 1966. The first stage of the works began during the excavations and was combined with them. First aid treatment was given to more delicate elements, including frescoes, stucco, and mosaics. Although it is not recommended today, the use of Portland cement for mortar prevailed, as it was considered to represent the most advanced technology of the time. Professional conservators from abroad were employed to work side by side with local people who showed talent for conservation, gaining most of their experience from fieldwork. The excavation's surveyor, a young architect named Ehud Netzer, was in charge of the reconstruction works. Decisions such as where to conserve, where to reconstruct, and where to add architectural elements like pergolas, steps, handrails, and so on, were made by individuals who were in charge of the works and knew how to preserve the remains. In this way, for example, the decision was made to mark the reconstruction by using a black line that separated the original wall from the reconstructed one. From 1965 to 1995, routine conservation maintenance was carried out at Masada when the need arose.

Masada Is Declared a National Park

In the early 1960s, the planning process to prepare Masada to become a national park began. The park area covered 2,300 dunams (230 hectares), including within its boundaries the Masada mountain, the Roman siege system, and the area beyond the siege system and close to it. The first to deal with the declaration of the place as a national park was the Prime Minister's office of the Department for Landscaping and the Preservation of Historical Sites. Later, the site was handed over to the care of the National Parks Authority (NPA), which was founded by law in 1963.

In 1966, Masada was declared to be a national park by Israel's Minister of Interior Affairs. In the same year, the Masada National Park was opened to the public. The large extent of the archaeological excavations—the quantity of the finds and the publicity given to the site's finds by the media—attracted many visitors to Masada, especially walkers who climbed up through the Snake Path. In 1967, the park's area was enlarged to 3,400 dunams (340 hectares), and it included part of the road connecting the town of Arad to Masada, in the western area of the park. Since that year, tourism in Israel has increased. The road from Jerusalem to the Dead Sea, which was built at that time, made access to the site shorter and easier from the east side. The Hollywood production of the movie *Masada* contributed worldwide publicity to the site, and people from all over the world wanted to see the scene of the original events.

Thus Masada became an important tourist attraction, with the number of visitors increasing on a fairly gradual basis.

The Cable Car

It became clear that something needed to be done in order to make the journey to the mountaintop easier for the average visitor. Officials of the NPA decided that a cable car would be the best method to transport visitors. This method met with great objection from those who wished to leave the site as it existed—an isolated mountain cliff—in its natural wild desert landscape.

Members of the NPA argued about this issue among themselves. After the decision was made in the NPA, the NPA had to persuade others who objected to the idea, including the Nature Reserves Authority and other "Green" supporters (those who objected to changing the site's appearance). Since the cable car began operating in 1972, there has been a great increase of visitors to the site.

The Masada Project: 1995–2000

Background—The Need for a Development Plan

Management of the NPA made a major decision in the early 1980s to improve Masada's facilities in order to adapt it to the needs of an ever-increasing number of visitors and to upgrade the experience of visiting the site to the standards of the twenty-first century. Masada National Park was developed in the 1960s according to the criteria and forecasts of an increasing tourism movement; however, the increase in visitors to Masada has exceeded all expectations. According to estimates by tourism economists, 1.25 million visitors are expected to visit the site during the year 2010, compared to the 700,000 visitors who currently make the journey.

Over the course of several years, the different infrastructures of the site have been worn out, causing Masada to be unable to function effectively as a major tourist site adapted to modern tourism needs. The most crucial problem involved lines to the cable car, which, at times, caused visitors to wait up to two hours in unbearable heat. The NPA came to the conclusion that the waiting lines had to be eliminated and that the site had to be developed and adapted to accommodate the influx of visitors and the needs of modern tourism.

Together with the Israeli government's Ministry of Tourism, the NPA reached a decision to address the need for further development of Masada. The outcome of this decision is the Masada Project, financed mainly by the Israeli government. Most of the funding was allocated for modern construction; however, assistance is still required to carry out the planning of the mountaintop.

The Masada Project

Overall planning of the project is based on a survey carried out among visitors to Masada, as well as specific research on general trends and characteristics of foreign tourism to Israel. The combined data pointed to the need for improvement both in the site's general tourist services and in its presentation to the public. Background work designed to obtain exact data for the preparation of the various plans included the following:

- A survey of archaeological components and potential;
- A conservation survey carried out by the Antiquities Authority that documents the physical condition of the remains;
- A forecast of the number of visitors to the site up to the year 2010;
- A survey and mapping of visitor movement at the site;
- A quantitative and qualitative survey of the satisfaction and expectations of the visitors to the site;
- A forecast of the number of cable car users;
- A forecast and program for the commercial areas;
- Proposals and ideas for presenting and imparting the Masada story;
- A survey and mapping of the physical infrastructure; and
- A definition of infrastructure needs at the site.

The following are several objectives defined for the development project:

- To foster and emphasize the values associated with the site as well as its historical and cultural significance, much of which is done through conservation and restoration works;
- To enhance and enrich the visitors' experience through the emphasis on cultural and historical values of the site;
- To improve the site's capability to handle a large number of visitors, with 1.25 million visitors expected in the year 2010. The admittance capacity of the site is a problem common to the mountain base as well as to the top, places where a bottleneck situation often occurs; and
- To improve visitor services and facilities, and to create a smooth flow of visitors.

Value decisions were defined along with the project objectives, with the approach being to leave the appearance of the ancient remains as they exist. In this regard, decisions included avoiding modern construction on the top of or within the Roman siege boundaries; camouflaging the new construction as much as possible from view of the mountain (the plan unfortunately could not include essential elements such as the cable car station, the cliff bridge, or light pergolas); and disallowing any commercial activity on the mountaintop.

A master plan made for the development program included a few planning components, such as the eastern entrance complex, a new cable car, landscape rehabilitation, archaeological excavations, and conservation and development of the mountaintop. The long-range plan includes long-term programs related to the development of the western entrance complex, the development of tracks on the mountain's slopes, and night activity in Masada.

A New Cable Car. The first part of the development program took place over six years (from 1995 to 2000), with a cost of over $40 million (U.S.),

Figure 5
Modern development at Masada: the cliff bridge and the upper cable car station. Photo courtesy of The Israel Nature and National Parks Protection Authority.

Figure 6
Modern development at Masada: the Exhibition Hall in the Eastern Complex. Photo courtesy of The Israel Nature and National Parks Protection Authority.

and includes a new cable car, which hopefully will eliminate the waiting lines. The new cable car, which began operating in May 1999, has twice the capacity that the former one had. From the upper station, people walk over the cliff bridge to the Snake Path Gate, the historical gate that leads to Masada. The bridge enables disabled visitors, including those in wheelchairs, to access the mountaintop.

The NPA held a public hearing to ask the public and professionals their opinion on what they believe is the best way to enter the mountaintop from the cable car's upper station: by bridge or tunnel. The public, in harmony with the planners, was divided into two more or less equal camps. After long discussions, the NPA decided to build a bridge, because it is reversible and it enables visitors to see the landscape and enter Masada through its historical gate.

A Modern Entrance Complex. The modern entrance complex on the east side with visitor services available, including presentation elements, was the second part of the development program. This complex has been in operation since September 2000.

Mountaintop Conservation and Development. The third part of the project involved a mountaintop development highlighting the location of ancient remains, the scene of the historical events and the primary purpose that visitors come to Masada. The leading principle in the treatment of the mountaintop is to leave the original arrangement of the place as it was first found. The necessary additional elements such as toilets, pergolas, and models of monuments are installed inside the ancient buildings in order to avoid changing the original appearance of the site.

The mountaintop is the core of a visit to Masada, with its archaeological remains (together with the Roman siege systems at the mountain's base). Its development is adapted both to groups who come to the site with a guide (about 80 percent of the visitors) and to individuals.

In the first years of the Masada project, efforts were focused on conservation. This enabled the team to gain important time for planning the presentation of the project. Simultaneously, a concept-design team worked on the interpretation and presentation of the story of Masada to the public. The team put forward the concept of an open-air museum, where the ancient monuments could speak for themselves.

To realize this concept, a visitors' route was planned to enable people to view and walk among the conserved buildings, mostly in the northern part of the mountaintop. The buildings tell the historical story and emphasize the strong contrast between the luxurious palaces of Herod and the miserable dwellings of the zealots. Along this route, there are signs, models (three-dimensional models of parts of the site with detailed description), and theme centers to explain the site.

In addition to the presentation elements, developments have been made to add to the public's convenience and to make the site accessible to the disabled. The different elements are built with great attention paid to the general appearance of the site, and all the elements are reversible and can be easily removed.

The approved planning decisions are implemented in part by the site development and conservation team, and in part by external contractors. As part of the development project, a Masada Conservation Team underwent a six-month training period by experts of the Israeli Antiquities Authority. The team became familiar with modern conservation techniques, and among its tasks was to remove the cement-pointed joints that were placed in the 1960s and replace them with lime-based mortar, similar to that used in the original construction. This team became expert in conservation problems typical to Masada, and now enjoy the appreciation of all professionals in this field.

The team works according to a conservation master plan devised by the mountaintop planning team and the conservation planning architect. This plan integrated conservation needs—with priority given to the more urgent ones (partly based on the conservation survey made at the beginning of the project)—with tourism needs. The project is financed by the Ministry of Tourism, whose priorities do not necessarily match those of the conservation community. The conservation master plan is updated from time to time according to progress made, or to attend to urgent conservation needs that appear on occasion.

Once the project is completed, part of the team will remain at the site as a permanent conservation maintenance team. The implementation of the mountaintop plan was expected to end due to budget shortages during the year 2001. A five-year continuance program for the mountaintop has been prepared according to the approved master plan.

The conservation and reconstruction work has been upgraded and the site's appearance has improved since the establishment of this conservation team specializing in problems unique to Masada. The team is knowledgeable regarding the ancient construction traditions at the site, placing emphasis on professional conservation work and the preservation of the site's authenticity.

Overall Coordination among the Various Plan Components

The Masada project is a large, complicated undertaking with many components. This type of project cannot be managed and implemented without major coordination among its different components. The project includes dozens of consultants, planners, contractors, and workers (in addition to government and NPA officials). The eastern entrance complex is managed by an external company called Tik Projects. Authority and management responsibility for the project rests with a steering committee, which is composed of NPA and governmental officials and contains a number of subcommittees (planning, budgeting and implementation, evaluation and development, bids). The principal decisions of the planning and development team are approved by the steering committee, which is composed of officials of the Tourism and Treasury ministries and the NPA.

The mountaintop planning team's principal plans are approved by the steering committee. The plans are prepared according to the guidelines of the master plan. Each planning phase is presented to the steering committee by the team that dealt specifically with the subproject, and the committee approves it (or asks for revisions or other options). The fieldwork is done strictly according to the plans approved by the steering committee.

The Influence of the Site's Values on the Creation and Implementation of Present Management Decisions

Masada could be just another archaeological site, among the many others scattered throughout Israel. The values of this site and its unique features had an effect on the public and, in turn, caused Masada to become a central site of tourist attraction in Israel and throughout the world.

The excavations in Masada—even those performed for scientific reasons (scientific/cultural values)—were motivated also by the Masada myth (political-national/social values). Great interest from the media and the public accompanied these excavations, reminding the public once again of the story of Masada. Following the production of the movie *Masada,* even more publicity was brought to the site, bringing tourists from all over the world there.

This increase in tourist activity was the purpose for building the first cable car that led to the mountaintop and was among the reasons to improve the roads to the Dead Sea region. Other natural and geographical values regarding the vicinity of the site, such as the landscape, the desert, the Dead Sea, the hotels and spas in the region, the nearby site of Qumran, the location on the way both to Jerusalem and to Eilat, contributed greatly to the site's attractiveness.

The consistent increase in tourist visitation led to the decision to upgrade the site, its archaeological remains, and its tourist facilities. The goal of the development project to preserve the site and to improve visitors' experience embodies, in a way, the economic value. This decision had to be followed by governmental assistance. The Israeli government chose to finance a large part of the project's costs, as Masada is considered a national asset and an important tourism center with economic advantages.

Unfortunately, government funds cannot finance the entire project. While the lion's share of funding was provided for the modern infrastructure, the mountaintop, with its cultural/historical/scientific values, suffers from a lack of financing. Fund-raising material is under preparation for presentation to potential donors—private and institutional—with the hope of obtaining funds to complete the implementation of mountaintop plans as well.

Postscript

Masada was declared a World Heritage Site by UNESCO in December 2001.

Note

1 Yoram Tsafrir, "Masada and Its Warriors: The Rise and Fall of a Fortress of the Second Temple Period," in *The Story of Masada—Discoveries from the Excavations*, ed. Gila Hurvitz (Provo, Utah: Brigham Young University Studies, 1997).

Petra, Jordan

Aysar Akrawi

The PNT (Petra National Trust), a nonprofit and nongovernmental organization (NGO), is one of the associations responsible for the preservation of the cultural and natural heritage of Petra, Jordan. PNT does not set policy; rather, it works with the policy makers in Jordan's government and other NGOs to reach its goals. As the executive director of PNT, the author is a member of the Petra Regional Planning Council (PRPC); therefore, the PNT is an integral part of the decision-making process for the site.

Site History

Located in southwestern Jordan, Petra can be found halfway between the Red Sea and the Dead Sea in the region of the Shera' mountains (Fig. 1). These mountains dominate the Wadi 'Araba to the west. For over two hundred thousand years, Petra has been a place for human habitation: the prehistoric periods are well documented, as are the later Islamic periods. Today, people living in the Petra area live in modern stone- and concrete-constructed hillside villages and Bedouin encampments. Remains of Paleolithic campsites, together with flint artifacts that are some forty to eighty thousand years old, have been found in the surrounding hills. About thirteen thousand years ago, an early seasonal village was established at Beidha, just north of Petra. The site was rebuilt and occupied year-round by a group of Neolithic farmers in about 7,000 B.C. In addition, the presence of mineral resources made the region important. Both bitumen and copper, the first metal introduced to humankind, have been mined and marketed since the earliest times.

In the first millennium B.C., the Edomites rose to prominence. During the seventh century B.C., they built settlements, some of which were fortified, in the mountains. Most notable of these are Umm al-Biyara and Tawilan, high above the Petra basin. Subject to Assyria, Babylonia, and then Persia, Edom became the nucleus of an Arab state, the Nabataean Kingdom, in the third century B.C. The Nabataeans made Petra the capital of their rich and powerful kingdom, filling it with spectacular buildings and carved facades, and making water flow to every corner of the kingdom. In A.D. 106, the Nabataeans acquiesced to Trajan, the Roman general;

Figure 1
Map of Jordan, identifying Petra in the southwestern region.

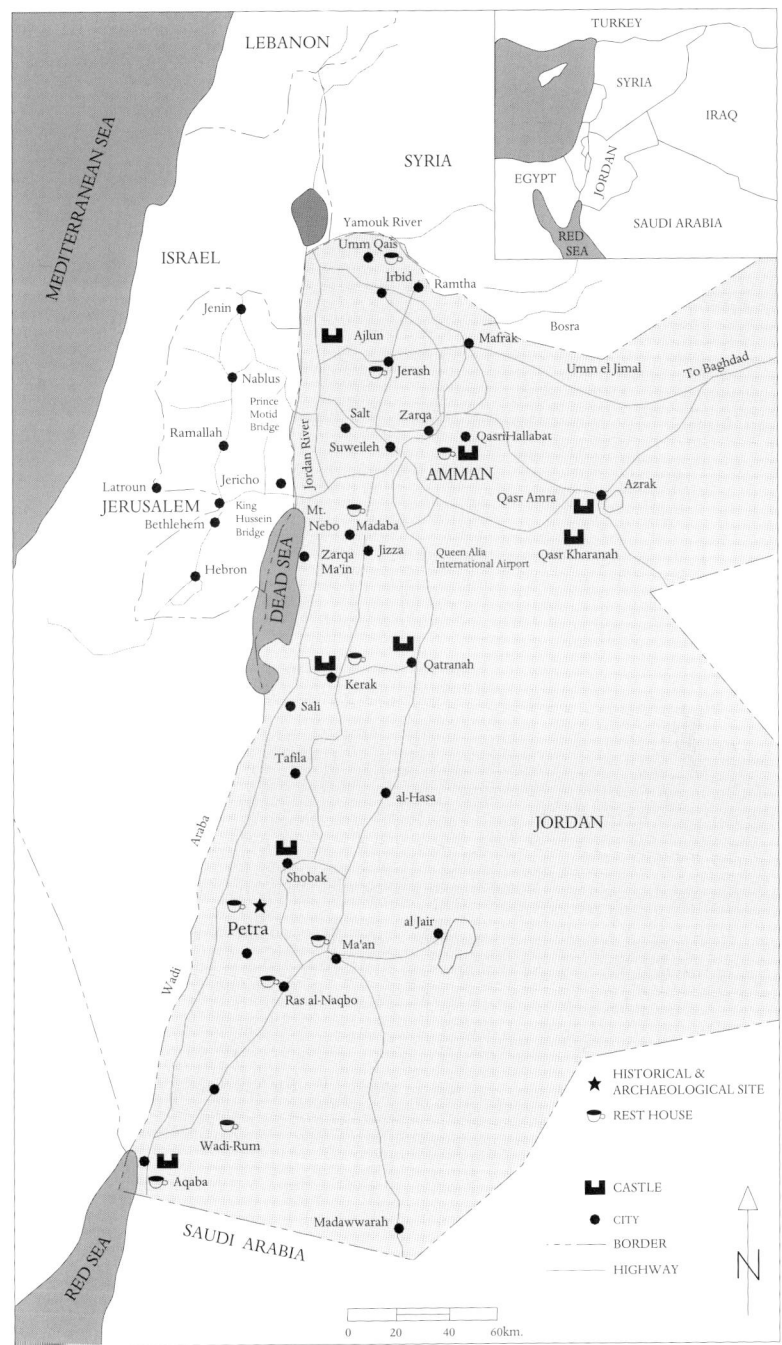

at this time, Petra became part of the Roman Province of Arabia. After the transfer of the capital of the Roman Empire to Byzantium in A.D. 330 under Constantine, Petra became the seat of a bishopric. By the fifth century A.D., Petra was the administrative center of the Byzantine province of Palaestina Tertia. Although Petra's wealth had gradually declined because of the redirection of trading goods via sea routes and the greater traffic on the northern land routes that passed through Palmyra, it remained a prosperous and important center and a provincial capital. The papyrus scrolls recently found in the Petra Church show a flourishing economic and social life there throughout the sixth century A.D. It was not until the next century, in the years following the Islamic takeover, that trade routes were redirected and Petra declined even further.

In the early twelfth century, the Crusaders first ventured across the rift valley from their capital of Jerusalem to Petra, recognizing its strategic advantage and establishing an outpost to defend their eastern border. The fortress they built in this area known as Moses's Valley, now Wu'eira, was the last of all the eastern fortresses to be abandoned when the Crusaders withdrew to the Mediterranean in 1189. Under the leadership of Salahedin al-Ayoubi, a Moslem of Kurdish descent, the Ayoubids drove the Crusaders out of Jerusalem in the twelfth century A.D., and from this time on, Petra dropped out of Western consciousness. When the site of Petra was abandoned and the water collecting and supply systems that made it possible to live further down the valley were destroyed, the stable settlement remained in the mountainous areas. This was found along the circle of springs in the traditional villages of Wādī Mūsa, Bedebedeh, Beidha, al-Hay, Nawafleh, and Taybeh. For many years, and even today in several areas, people continued to use the traditional stone Arab houses, to cultivate the land on terraces, and to keep the water supply system working. It was not until 1812 that Petra was visited once again by a Westerner, Swiss explorer Johann Ludwig Burckhardt (1784–1817). Travelers that followed gave vivid descriptions of its monuments and the conditions of the country during the Ottoman rule. They describe the Huwaitat tribes and their roles in ensuring the security of the caravans and the protection of the pilgrims. Under the Huwaitat, a Bedouin confederacy, fell the Bdul, Layathneh, and 'Alaween tribes. Traditionally, the tribes in the Petra area tended to their animals—flocks of sheep, goats, and camels—and undertook the seasonal planting of grains. Later, with the arrival of tourism, they moved closer to the archaeological site and sustained a living by tilling the land, working on archaeological excavations, and guiding tourists through the site.

Resources

Several resources have conditioned the life of Petra's inhabitants throughout the centuries. Water is the most important natural resource, one that was and continues to be an essential factor governing their day-to-day survival. In addition to domestic uses, an intricate irrigation system allowed for agricultural uses. Water also had a ritual and spiritual value, and was used aesthetically to decorate the famed gardens of Petra. Main

Figure 2
Water channels located on both sides of the Siq.

watersheds found in the region are Wādī Mūsa, Wadi Mataha, Wadi Turkomania, Kharrobit al-Fajja, and Wadi Beidha. The Nabataeans developed an elaborate and well-regulated water supply (Fig. 2), as well as a conservation system displaying outstanding ingenuity and skill. They developed complex hydrological and diversion systems to protect their sandstone monuments and inhabitants from flash floods.

Archaeological Investigations and Conservation Interventions

As one of the most spectacular sites in the Near East, Petra has long attracted travelers and explorers. Archaeological investigations have been carried out in Petra and surrounding areas since the 1950s, with excavations at the theater, colonnaded street, the Temenos Gate, and other monuments, as well as at Beidha, Umm al-Biyara, and Tawilan (the last two are Iron Age Edomite sites). Some of the more recent projects executed by international teams include the following: the excavations and restoration at Petra Church, a papyrus archive found in the church, the mapping project of the Petra basin, the Great Temple excavations, the survey and excavation of Petra's Lower Market, the Zantur excavations, the Siq excavations, the water survey, the excavations at Ba'ja, the excavations at Harun, the stone preservation project, the excavations at Wu'eira, the presentation of the shops along the colonnaded street, and the excavation and consolidation at the Temple of Winged Lions.

Ecology

Petra has strategic ecological importance because of its location at the meeting point of three zoogeographic realms (Palearctic, Afrotropical, and Saharo-Arabian), which has resulted in the heterogeneity of the fauna in this area. Petra is also the southernmost limit for many indigenous reptiles and mammals, and is an important site for vultures and migratory birds (Fig. 3). The Petra region is also significant because of its unique and diverse ecosystem. The variety and richness of plant life in the area is exceptional. The Hisha forest is

Figure 3
The endemic *Agama sinaita*, a lizard indigenous to Petra.

the southernmost vestige of an ancient oak tree forest in Jordan, while the juniper forest represents the northernmost end of its distribution. One of man's earliest settlements was in Beidha, where animals were domesticated and agricultural plants, mainly wheat, were produced for the first time.

Geology

The geographical formations located in the Petra region are renowned throughout the world. Inside Petra, the sandstone is formed at the upper level of its stratigraphy of white Ordovician sandstone and a

Figure 4
Sandstone carving of a cameliere pulling four camels.

Disi sandstone formation. To the west, at the lower level, the characteristic striated Cambrian sandstone and Um Ishrin sandstone formation create the greater part of the massif (Fig. 4). Toward the western limits of the massif, at the level of the eastern escarpment of the rift, the crystalline substratum appears from below the Cambrian sandstone.

Modern Villages

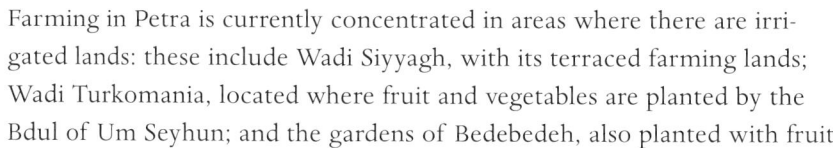

Farming in Petra is currently concentrated in areas where there are irrigated lands: these include Wadi Siyyagh, with its terraced farming lands; Wadi Turkomania, located where fruit and vegetables are planted by the Bdul of Um Seyhun; and the gardens of Bedebedeh, also planted with fruit

Figure 5
Petra region and the protected area surrounding the Petra Archaeological Park in Jordan, 1995.

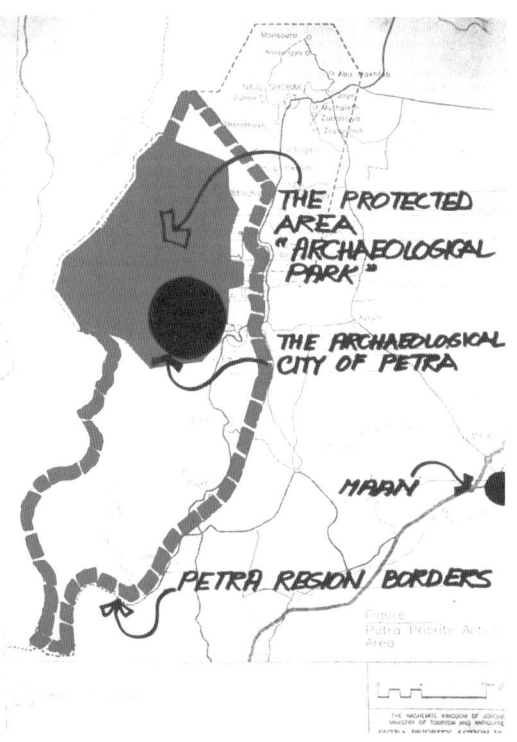

and vegetables. Petra is surrounded by six main villages (Fig. 5). From south to north these villages are Dlagha, Rajef, Taybeh, Wādī Mūsa, Um Seyhun, and Beidha, with a total population of around 25,000. The two main entrances to Petra are through Wādī Mūsa and Um Seyhun. Both overlook the site and have a direct impact on its archaeological heritage. For the most part, the land surrounding the park is owned by the state and is referred to as "Mirri" lands. In the past, these Mirri lands were leased to individuals for agricultural and pastoral use. Many of these Mirri, or state-owned, lands have traditionally been inhabited by the local tribes, and fall under the category of tribal and customary law, which means that the tribes consider this land to be their territory. These and other privately owned lands are quickly changing ownership due to land speculation relating to tourism.

Stakeholders

The main stakeholders in Petra can be identified as the following:

- Local inhabitants belonging not only to different village communities but also to different tribes, who relate to the site in very different ways; for example, consider the Bdul, who used to live in the rock-cut tombs and structures surrounding the site;
- Government, also in this case represented by various entities, such as the Department of Antiquities, which views its responsibility as the preservation and further study and management of the site; the Ministry of Tourism, mostly interested in tourist development; and other ministries that are more interested in the upgrading of living conditions in the area;
- Archaeologists from Jordanian and international institutions, with a scientific interest in the site;
- Conservation professionals, with an interest in solving mostly problems of material decay at the site;
- International schools and aid agencies that are anxious to contribute to research at the site as well as to the preservation of the site through conscious and well-developed tourist access plans;
- Tour operators, tourism investors, hotel owners, and souvenir vendors, all of whom have an economic interest in the site;
- Tourists; and
- NGOs, which are also stakeholders; some work to develop the small-business skills of the local tribes people and villagers, while others, like the PNT, work toward fulfilling their mandate for the protection and preservation of the antiquities, the cultural heritage, and the environment of Petra.

The interests of these groups are often incompatible and frequently competitive, thus generating discord and unease among the stakeholders that must be managed to avoid open friction.

Statement of Significance

All management plans proposed for Petra (see following section) have laid out in more or less explicit manner the values of the site. For the UNESCO (United Nations Educational, Scientific, and Cultural Organization) plan of 1994, the Petra National Park is valued because it conserves outstanding and representative examples of the cultural heritage of the nation and the world. These values stem from the site's historical significance. The density and monumental character of the rock-carved and stone-built temples and tombs as well as the traditional villages and stone-built houses of its Arab owners; the extensive network of hydrological systems; and its art make Petra unique and give it the potential to attract, entertain, inspire, and educate.

- Petra conserves valuable natural assets, grandiose scenic values, striking geological values (Fig. 6), ecological and biological values, and life-conditioning water-related values.
- It encompasses socioanthropological values. Once an important meeting point for the caravans of Arabia, Petra is currently a focal point for tourist itineraries. Then, as well as now, Petra was protected by the tribes of the area.
- It provides economic value both to the country and the community through the adoption of specialized approaches to tourism that incorporate its historical, artistic, ecological, geological, anthropological, hydrological, and ritual values.
- It provides opportunities to sustain natural ecosystem processes through the conservation of resources on which they depend.

While maintaining and protecting its biodiversity and environment, Petra can generate economic benefits through the rational use of marginal lands and support of traditional tribal farming systems. Such processes are essential for human survival and sustainable development.

The 1996 plan by US/ICOMOS (International Council on Monuments and Sites, United States Committee) builds on the cultural and contemporary socioeconomic values identified by UNESCO. It

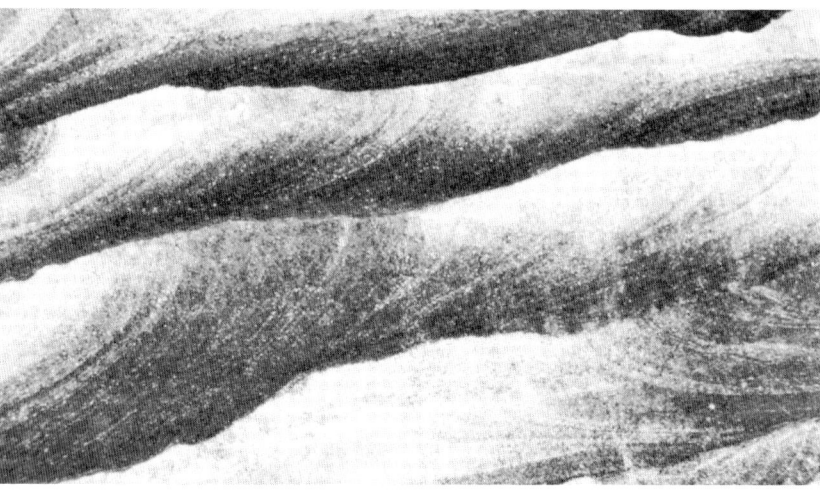

Figure 6
Striations, mineral formations or color banding found in the Um Ishrin sandstone.

emphasizes that such values are not only related to histories of specific groups, like the Nabataeans and the Romans, but also to broad historical and cultural developments. Petra contains material pertinent to several threshold developments in human society, and the plan adds religious and political values to those already mentioned in the previous study.

Impact of Growth

In 1985, Petra became recognized as a UNESCO World Heritage Site for its unique cultural and natural heritage, rendering it incumbent on Jordan to protect and preserve it for the enjoyment, scholarship, and pride of future generations. Much prior to that date, in 1968, Petra had been recognized by government and donor agencies as an outstanding example of national heritage, and the United States NPS (National Park Service) was invited to prepare a management plan. This plan was to be used as a guide for the use, development, interpretation, protection, and general administration of what came to be known as the Petra National Park, a name that was later adopted to describe the protected area within the Petra region.

Many of the issues identified in the National Park Service plan of 1968 have now multiplied; not least of these is the population explosion. In Wādī Mūsa, the population has increased from 7,000 to 15,000, and in Um Seyhun it has increased from a few hundred to almost 1,500. In the absence of zoning and land use plans, uncontrolled construction development encroached visibly on the area. The NPS plan of 1968 described Wādī Mūsa, saying "at present time a drive through the village of Wādī Mūsa constitutes an important bonus for Petra visitors. A view of this unusually attractive terraced and well-watered oasis and its village life is a scene of Jordan that should be kept." This land is now completely under construction. Tourism figures have increased from 31,800 in 1966 to 430,000 in 1999. Instead of the Forum, the lone hotel that previously existed, five large hotels on the scenic Taybeh Wādī Mūsa road directly overlooking Petra were licensed with economic gains in mind, and without regard to the negative visual impact on the site and their location in the catchment area above the line of natural springs. At the time, this was considered a compromise to avert the construction of hotels within the sanctuary itself. In addition to these five hotels, forty-five additional hotels are now licensed and operational in Wādī Mūsa. In 1997 the Minister of Tourism and Antiquities finally declared a moratorium on hotel building. With the increase of tourism came the spread of unregulated commercial activities within and outside the park. That, too, has had a negative impact on both the cultural and natural values of the site.

Management Plans

In response to the impact of growth, the government invited international institutions to prepare management plans for Petra on three occasions. These are as follows:

- The United States National Park Service's "Master Plan for the Protection and Use of the Petra National Park" (1968);

- UNESCO's Petra National Park Management Plan (1994); and
- US/ICOMOS's "The Study on the Management Analysis and Recommendations for the Petra World Heritage Site" (1996).

There is no institutional memory of the procedure that was followed, especially in the first study. Although the plans included some participation of Jordanian counterparts, it is clear that there was no systematic participation of the stakeholders in the identification of the values, the major issues, and thereafter in the formulation or follow-up of the recommendations they presented. It is best to keep in mind, however, that in 1968 no stakeholder (dare I say, throughout the world) was asked what his or her values were.

The first two studies analyzed the management structure at a time when the Ministry of Tourism and Antiquities managed Petra from its headquarters in Amman. While the Ministry of Tourism was responsible for issuing development licenses, the Department of Antiquities was responsible for the management of the archaeological resources since, by law, it is the government body whose mandate is the management and preservation of all archaeological sites in Jordan. The staff was limited, and responsibilities were distributed between several government departments. Coordination was sometimes inadequate, and integrated management of the entire area was not implemented. Most of the problems then and now are a result of this circumstance. On the basis of their findings, the NPS and, later, UNESCO stressed the need to create an independent single authority that would manage and coordinate all aspects of park management. They differed in their approach as to whom this new body should report. While the NPS thought it should report to the Ministry of Tourism and Antiquities, the UNESCO team recommended that it report directly to the Royal Court or, alternatively, to the Prime Minister's office. The outcome was the Petra Regional Planning Council (PRPC), which was established in 1995 by decision of the Council of Ministers. The charter gave the council the mandate to manage comprehensively an area of 1,000-square kilometers inclusive of the protected area of 264 kilometers at Petra. The charter clearly states that the responsibilities given to the PRPC supersede previous laws issued by decree, despite the fact that the Law of Antiquities (number 21) gives the Department of Antiquities (DOA) full authority to manage all aspects of the park. Herein lies one of the underlying issues affecting the efficient management of the park, that of the responsibilities and appropriate location within the government of this body.

The third study (US/ICOMOS) examined this issue and evaluated the functioning of the PRPC. It reported that the establishment of the council was a good first step toward decentralization of the management of Petra away from Amman. It reviewed the major responsibilities of the council, in attending to zoning, land use regulations, licensing of construction, development of infrastructure, and community issues, in addition to those it may have for Petra. The study concluded that although related to the protection and management of Petra, the PRPC would spend much of its time in the immediate future dealing with the pressures of Wādī

Mūsa and other villages, as well as communities. In addition to the PRPC, therefore, the US/ICOMOS study recommended the introduction of a separate authority—that of the Petra National Park Agency (PNPA, now being referred to as the Petra Archaeological Park, or PAP), which would be solely dedicated to the management of all the functions related to archaeological resources preservation, including physical conservation and development; visitor information and education; and visitor services and safety within the protected area only. Nevertheless, this new body would coordinate very closely with the PRPC in view of the common issues that they share. Regarding its location within the government structure, the study saw the affiliation of the PNPA with the Department of Antiquities (DOA) to be the most logical since the mission of the Department is the protection of the archaeological resources within Jordan and it has the legislation to perform this function. The final location of this new structure was discussed at a workshop organized by the Ministry of Tourism and Antiquities in collaboration with the National Park Service: the unanimous recommendation was that the PAP report directly to the DOA.

It is important to note that the concept of the establishment of protected areas and authorities to manage cultural heritage sites in Jordan is still under consideration. This requires thorough investigation and needs further scrutiny of the legislative aspects and deliberation on organizational considerations, to avoid overlapping responsibility and authority with the interest of the park in mind. To date Jordan has identified twelve significant natural areas, six of which are currently managed by the Royal Society for the Conservation of Nature, an NGO established in 1964 in Jordan. A USAID study of 1996 entitled "Jordan Parks Policy Project," under the management of Dr. Cherie Lenzen, acknowledges the need to improve management of protected areas to ensure the sustainability of the cultural and natural resources. The article identified important park policy issues and provided recommendations for a protected area policy and integrated management system. The project investigated several options but fell short of recommending a specific organizational structure. It favored, however, options that do not add more bureaucracy or create another organization to be absorbed into government. It also supported options that would operate within the existing legal framework or at least those that necessitate only minor legislative changes.

For Petra, despite the creation of the PRPC, there remain several organizations often operating independently and frequently with overlapping responsibilities, and each having its own direct line of authority in Amman. There is a definite need to revisit the objectives of all the organizations—governmental and nongovernmental—involved in the Petra area, and to align their roles within the management system.

Plans in Detail

The management structure of sites such as Petra should grow from and strengthen the qualities that make a cultural site valuable and significant, and in the case of Petra, unique. Each of the management plans has addressed the values and significance of Petra, starting with the plan by the NPS and, in more detail, those by UNESCO and US/ICOMOS. All three plans have served as guiding documents for decision makers in the planning and implementation process.

First Plan

The NPS study maintains that Petra's historical "scene" is the site's primary resource, and that the sustenance of natural resources is vital in protecting this primary resource. As such, and in recognition of the significance of the site and its environs, the NPS team took the lead in recommending the establishment of a National Park, an independent park division, and zoning within the park. It addressed other issues through specific project proposals in the fields of tourism development, archaeological protection and preservation, and social and administrative issues. In the 1960s, the intention was to prepare the site for visitors. Toward that end, the plan's proposed projects involve everything from roads, electricity, water, hotels, visitor centers, parking lots, and vendor activities, to special uses. The majority of these projects were realized, and those that were not continue to pose nagging problems, as in the case of vendor activities and special park uses. Some of the building developments proposed at the park's entrance have resulted in congestion of that area, triggering the construction of large hotels in sensitive areas that affect the natural landscape and scenic views.

In the field of conservation and preservation, the NPS study recommended the restriction of excavations until such time as exposed ruins were consolidated, an inventory of historic structures established, and a historic base map developed. Although excavations were never stopped, consolidation and protective measures are being implemented in earnest as of late. Some good examples of excavation and restoration projects are the Petra Church located in central Petra, north of the colonnaded street, by ACOR (the American Center for Oriental Research); the Great Temple, located south of the colonnaded street, by the Brown University team; and the Zantur in Nabataen, dwellings located on a hilltop south of the colonnaded street, by the Basel University team. The inventory was established through the JADIS (Jordanian Antiquities Database and Information System) project between 1989 and 1995, and a base map of the city center was produced by ACOR in 1999. ACOR hopes to expand the map to include the entire protected area. The NPS plan also addresses the issue of watershed management and recommends the rehabilitation of the Nabataean hydraulic network in order to protect the antiquities, to guard against flash floods, and to conserve water that is vital to the maintenance of biodiversity. Although the network was not rehabilitated to the extent recommended, it was partially reinstated by PNT in a project in the area of the Siq with wadis (valleys or gorges) flanking it, an area covering approximately 1 square kilometer (Fig. 7).

The social dimension concerning the peoples inhabiting the region is addressed by the NPS plan in as much as it affects the antiquities. The plan recommended the relocation of the Bdul tribe, mentioned earlier in this paper, to a location outside the archaeological site. The reason given was the need for "preservation of the resources of Petra from the

Figure 7
The Wadi Madrass Dam, which flanks the Siq in Petra.

destructive effects of human habitation." Both this plan and a later study of 1978 conducted by UNESCO consultant Sherif al-Hakim stress the necessity to precede any relocation by studying the socioeconomic dimension and by providing the community with agricultural lands in order to maintain their livelihood. In his recommendations, Hakim emphasized the importance for the design of new housing to be compatible with the lifestyles of the inhabitants, and for the architecture to be in harmony with the archaeological park in view of its proximity to it. Neither of these recommendations was implemented, and their neglect has had a negative effect on several parameters, including social, economic, and visual.

Second Plan

The second management plan was created by UNESCO, and was assisted by and presented in coordination with the Petra National Trust in 1994. This plan, devised some twenty-six years after the NPS plan, addresses many of the same issues. The values of the site are clearly laid out and expanded. This plan bases its recommendations and proposals on the impact of the management at the time on these values. The UNESCO plan identifies the major issues threatening the integrity of the park from a combination of cultural, socioeconomic, and environmental factors, and presents recommendations and proposals to remedy these threats. The proposals are comprehensive and cover zoning, archaeological conservation,

conservation of biodiversity, park infrastructure and personnel, tourism, physical planning, sustainable rural development, mitigation measures, training and communication, research and monitoring, and finally, the implementation of the management plan. In its opening page, the plan states that, prior to its implementation, governmental approval is required of the plan in its entirety since it involves policy decisions. Although official governmental approval was not granted, the plan has and continues to serve as a guiding document for all projects and activities since then, and a large number of the project proposals have been executed.

The plan attempts to present the criteria for the choice of project sites and some of the conservation works being undertaken. It should be noted, however, that there is no formal strategy to date set by the Department of Antiquities for excavation. The criteria for selection, which are generally determined by the applicant and his or her field of interest, range from research interests to providing baseline data, and from the enhancement of sites for tourist presentation to the protection and preservation of monuments. The numerous aspects of this subject have been addressed in all the management plans, and await implementation and integration into the site management and monitoring procedures. A project covering zoning and land use, although lacking building regulations, has more or less been completed. Land use on the scenic road covering the span between Wādī Mūsa and Beidha has yet to be finalized. Although the recommendations of this study serve to control construction development in the areas with immediate impact on the site, these conflict with the interests of owners in several sensitive locations. Some of these lands are privately owned, while others are Mirri lands that fall under tribal or customary law. The restriction of development by traditional owners is not easy to implement.

Recommendations to retain the traditional Arab stone-built houses have fallen on deaf ears; as a result, these traditional dwellings are almost totally lost to pink concrete structures. There are a few exceptions, however, due in part to the fact that current structures are perceived to be modern, in addition to the fact that the value of these lands has risen, especially after the signing of the peace agreement with Israel in 1994. Infrastructure projects such as roads, water supply and treatment, and electricity are under way, as are tourism-related projects. Under the heading of conservation of biodiversity, a survey of the flora and fauna of Petra has been conducted and some reforestation undertaken. This now urgently needs to be followed by a study for the integration of nature conservation and nature-based tourism in Petra into the overall management. The demarcation within the park of areas for grazing and cropping, to reduce their continued effect on the vegetation cover, must also be addressed. Other projects include flood control measures and stone preservation.

Left untouched is the social dimension despite the cautionary signals among the host communities. At the time of the establishment of the PRPC, it was felt that board membership of two mayors of the six main villages surrounding Petra was sufficient. It has become evident since that it is necessary to have representation from all six villages to ensure a better understanding of the objectives of the council and their cooperation as stakeholders. Local awareness programs and community participation and integration in the economic development and protection of Petra need to be addressed. The fast pace of change currently taking place in Petra adds pressure and urgency to the need to address this vital human dimension and essential value.

Third Plan

The third set of plans, entitled "The Study on the Management Analysis and Recommendations for the Petra World Heritage Site," was prepared by a site management team from US/ICOMOS. It was a direct output of a USAID-funded project, the Jordan Sustainable Tourism Development Project (USAID/JSTD/SITES), originally named CERM (Cultural and Environmental Resources Management), and came into effect in 1996. It maintains that management values, in technical terms, are those things that must be preserved in order to retain the essential character of the site. In addition, these values must be closely monitored by site management. The management structures should grow from and should strengthen the qualities that make a cultural site valuable, in this case being the necessity to identify and recognize the reasons that set Petra apart as a unique place. The recommendations it puts forward are based on the maintenance of the values that ensure the retention of the essential character of the site.

"The Study on the Management Analysis and Recommendations for the Petra World Heritage Site" provided the basic framework for a management infrastructure at Petra. This included a statement of significance for Petra, along with management values and objectives. It also included draft text for the authorization of a Petra National Park.

The carrying capacity study conducted by the same project maintains that after a complete management infrastructure has been put into place and perfected over a number of years, as many as seven hundred and fifty thousand visitors per year might be accommodated, which is double the current figure. The number of visitors at any given time would, however, be determined by evidence showing how well the management infrastructure of the site could accommodate visitors without degrading cultural or natural resources, the satisfaction of local communities within the park, or the quality of the experience of visitors to the park.

The authors of the study are currently engaged as principal authors of an operating plan for a Petra Archaeological Park, which is based on the management analysis and is the first such plan to date. The operating plan will provide management policies and detailed operating procedures and standards, a training plan, and the recommended position of Petra Archaeological Park within the organization of MOTA (Ministry of Tourism and Antiquities).

Analysis and Conclusion

Site management has been a concern in Petra for at least the last thirty-two years. In the beginning, tourism was minimal and, in general, limited to the most adventurous souls. As the region became more integrated, policy makers understood the importance of the site for economic advancement. The number of studies conducted and the projects that ensued were evidence of this. There is a basic consensus among the three plans on the type of management structures and interventions needed for Petra. The approach toward the implementation of the recommendations proposed, however, has been fragmented over the years.

Instead of adopting a holistic approach to the plan in its entirety, subprojects were selected for implementation, leading to the imbalance we are witnessing today. This could be due to a number of reasons, which include inadequate participation by related organizations and stakeholders in the planning process resulting in a lack of commitment and follow-up; an insufficient understanding and appreciation of the site values and their potential, which leads to an unbalanced approach to development; inexperience in the management of cultural heritage sites; and frequent changes in government management. For Petra to be preserved, it must be understood in its totality. A clear-cut strategy for the conservation and management of the site must be developed. The impacts of management decisions on the site's values must be clearly identified and appreciated by the decision makers and stakeholders working together as one team. Only in this way will a viable site management plan that is relevant to local conditions be adhered to and implemented with success. Petra is a result of many layers of accumulated historical heritage that needs to be managed and presented in a manner that does not encourage further deterioration. Consolidation of the studies and their recommendations with emphasis on the values that set Petra apart from any other heritage site, using an integrated approach with the participation of those having a stake in Petra, is the shortest and most effective way to achieve this objective.

Recently, in the spirit of cross-cultural cooperation to preserve this rich cultural heritage and in recognition of the urgent need for sustainable development measures, the WMF (World Monuments Fund) has chosen Petra as one of the world's one hundred most endangered sites. The nomination serves as a practical reminder of both the important value and fragility of Petra, and the need for a concerted effort to protect it for future generations.

References

UNESCO
1964 "Petra National Park Management Plan."

United States National Park Service
1968 "Master Plan for the Protection and Use of the Petra National Park."

US/AID
1996 "Jordan Parks Policy Project"

US/ICOMOS
1996 "The Study on the Management Analysis and Recommendations for the Petra World Heritage Site."

Corinth, Greece

Guy Sanders

ANCIENT CORINTH is a multiperiod site with evidence of occupation in all periods from circa 3000 B.C.E. to the present. From the eighth century B.C.E., Corinth was an entrepôt for commerce moving between the western Mediterranean and the Aegean and Black Seas. For fifteen hundred years, from the late fourth century B.C.E. to 1210 C.E., with an interlude of 102 years following the sack of Roman general Lucius Mummius in 146 B.C.E., Corinth was the regional capital of a political entity encompassing the Peloponnese and Sterea Ellada. It was the seat of the Roman governor and later of the Byzantine *strategos* (military commander) and the senior Orthodox archbishop in the region. During this same timespan Athens, by contrast, was degraded from the city of a former regional superpower to a university town, and finally, after the mid–sixth century C.E., to a provincial town of little importance. As such, Corinth was for much of its history seldom less than one of the principal settlements of the eastern Mediterranean. Its history and archaeology are thus authoritative diachronic documents of Hellenic culture.

Corinth is located 80 kilometers west of Athens on the south side of the Isthmus, a narrow neck of land connecting the Peloponnese to mainland Greece, and separating the Corinthian Gulf from the Saronic Gulf, and ultimately, the Ionian Sea from the Aegean Sea (Fig. 1). Corinth is situated on two terraces—one about 60 meters and the other about 90 meters above sea level, 3 kilometers from the Corinthian Gulf coast and 6 kilometers southwest of the Isthmus (Fig. 2). The local geology of Corinth is dominated by marine and lacustrine sediments laid horizontally in bands of porous sandy limestone. These are interbedded with impervious marl clays and older limestone entities, such as Mount Oneion and Acrocorinth, extruding to heights over 570 meters. Local uplift of the land has created a series of raised beaches and broad terraces. At the exposure of the interfaces of the limestone and underlying marl below Acrocorinth are several natural springs that are notably absent from the region of the Isthmus to the east. With water, an imposing acropolis, and large fertile plains to the north and northwest, along with its position between two seas, Corinth commanded the principal nodal point in the land and sea communications of southern Greece. Its strategic and commercial position was supplemented by valuable natural resources for

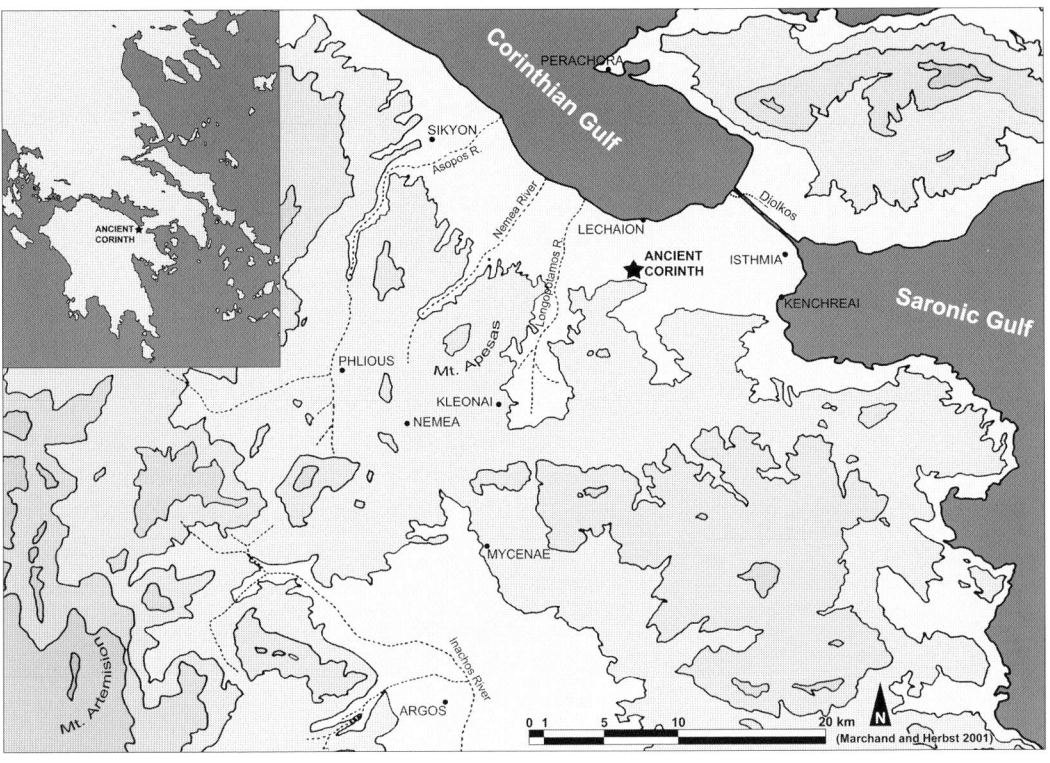

Figure 1
Map of Greece and Corinth showing the Isthmus.

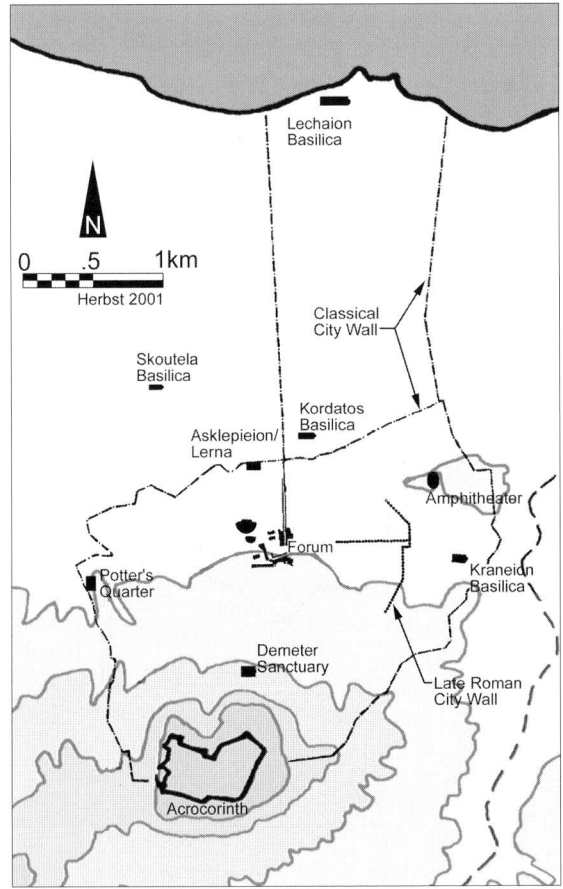

Figure 2
Map of Corinth from Acrocorinth to the sea illustrating principal excavation site.

export including building materials, excellent clays for ceramics and mortars, wood, and agricultural produce.

Research and Education

The American School of Classical Studies in Athens was founded in 1881 and now serves about four hundred graduate students and scholars from over 160 affiliated North American colleges and universities each year. In its regular program, up to twenty-five students per year, many of whom are supported by American School fellowships, are given an intensive introduction to the monuments and topography of Greece. In the spring, students are given the opportunity to learn excavation techniques at Corinth; over the past twenty-five years, about four hundred doctoral students have passed through the Corinth training excavations. The American School at Corinth maintains a year-round presence consisting of the director, two collections curators, two conservators, three conservation technicians, two laborers, and three other domestic workers. A hostel provides catered accommodation for staff, visiting researchers, and students of all nationalities, in addition to a small library and office space.

The American School's remit at Corinth is entirely due to the offices of the Greek Archaeological Service, who approve excavation, survey, and research plans, and oversee their execution. The two local offices of the Archaeological Service, one dealing with Prehistoric and Classical Antiquity and the other with medieval monuments, also make very significant contributions to research at Corinth by undertaking rescue excavation in advance of the granting or denial of building permits.

The school has been excavating at Corinth since 1896, and the interests of its scholars have changed considerably since the time excavation began. The earliest excavators were concerned with ancient topography and planned to reveal much of the center of a Classical city identifying monuments mentioned by the second-century Greek traveler and geographer Pausanias. They also hoped to find inscriptions recording Corinth's laws, personalities, and major events, and to recover examples of the renowned bronze, terracotta, and ceramic art of Corinth, and evidence of her international trade. In all these objectives the school was foiled. As a tyranny and then an oligarchy, Corinth had a different constitution from democracies such as Athens; one that did not require the laws, decrees, and public accounts to be inscribed and set up in public places. In 146 B.C.E., the Roman general Mummius thoroughly sacked Corinth, carrying off much of significance to Rome. The city lapsed into economic and civic obscurity for one hundred years, until its refoundation as a Roman colony by Julius Caesar in 44 B.C.E. The new colonists reengineered the city plan to fit its new needs. New construction tore out the core of the Classical city. The monuments described by Pausanias were not Greek but Roman monuments.

Between the years of 1930 and 1950, there was continued but more systematic and better documented clearance of the Forum area. After this time, interest shifted to taxonomic and chronological concerns, and large numbers of books and articles appeared on buildings, sculpture, ceramics, and minor objects. Many of these set the standards on which archaeologists working in Greece still rely. In the case of medieval Corinth, the three important volumes that appeared at the end of this period made Corinth arguably the single most important Byzantine site for archaeology, notwithstanding the architectural remains of Constantinople and Thessalonike.

From the 1960s, interests underwent a long period of continuous evolution and tended to embracing the human rather than the monumental side of antiquity yet retaining an awareness of and sympathy for post-Classical archaeology. These concerns are reflected in the way in which the excavations have embraced scientific applications to understand the past in collaboration with the Greek National Center for Scientific Research 'Demokritos,' the Wiener laboratory, and the Fitch laboratory in Athens.

Present research is concentrating on poorly understood phases of Greek history such as the Late Roman Period from about 300 C.E. and the transformation from this period to the medieval Dark Ages between about 600 and 800 C.E. Since 1996, several old but tenacious historical precepts and long-accepted chronologies have been abandoned, with new models being embraced as a result of recent excavations. A program of remote sensing of undeveloped land around the present village is helping to identify areas of archaeological interest for future protection.

Ancient Corinth alone consists of several separately excavated locations in addition to the main site. The fenced zone open to the public is the area including and around the Roman forum, theater, and odeion (a small theater for musical performances). This area has been cleared to at least Roman levels and, in places, to Prehistoric and Geometric levels. The main features of the pre-Roman city are the Archaic Temple of Apollo, the Sacred Spring complex with its triglyph and metope wall, a heroon (a temple erected in honor of a hero), baths, a racetrack, and the south *stoa,* or roofed colonnade (Fig. 3). In the Roman period the city was

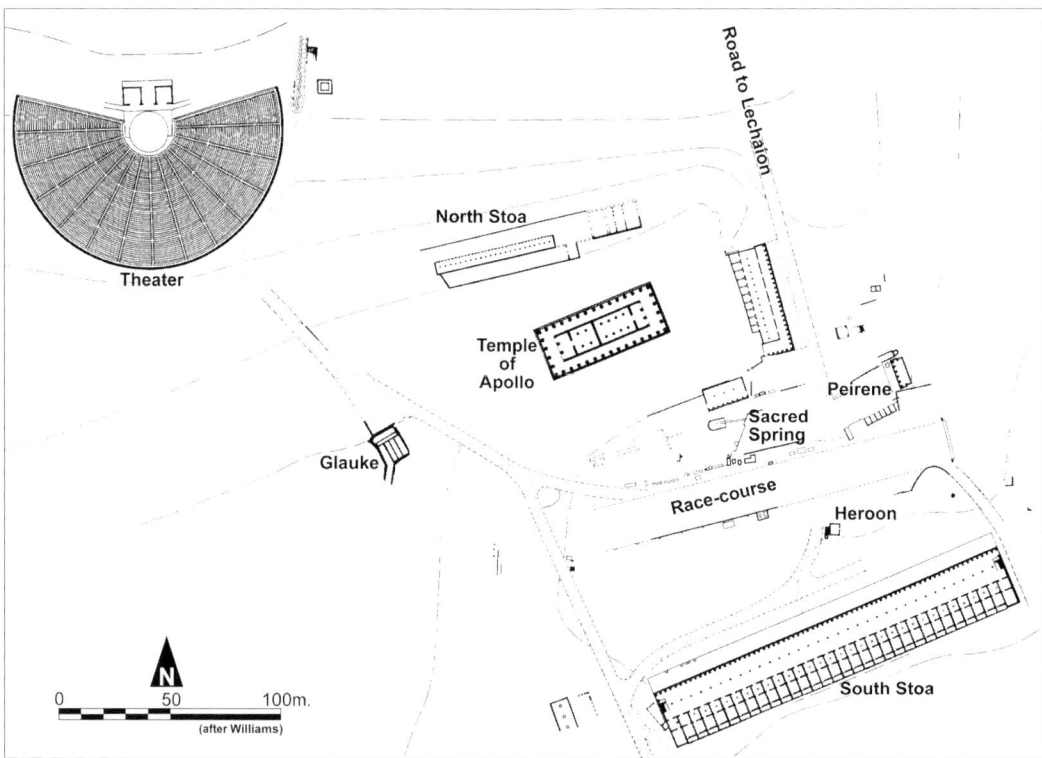

Figure 3
Greek site of Corinth, circa 400 B.C.E.

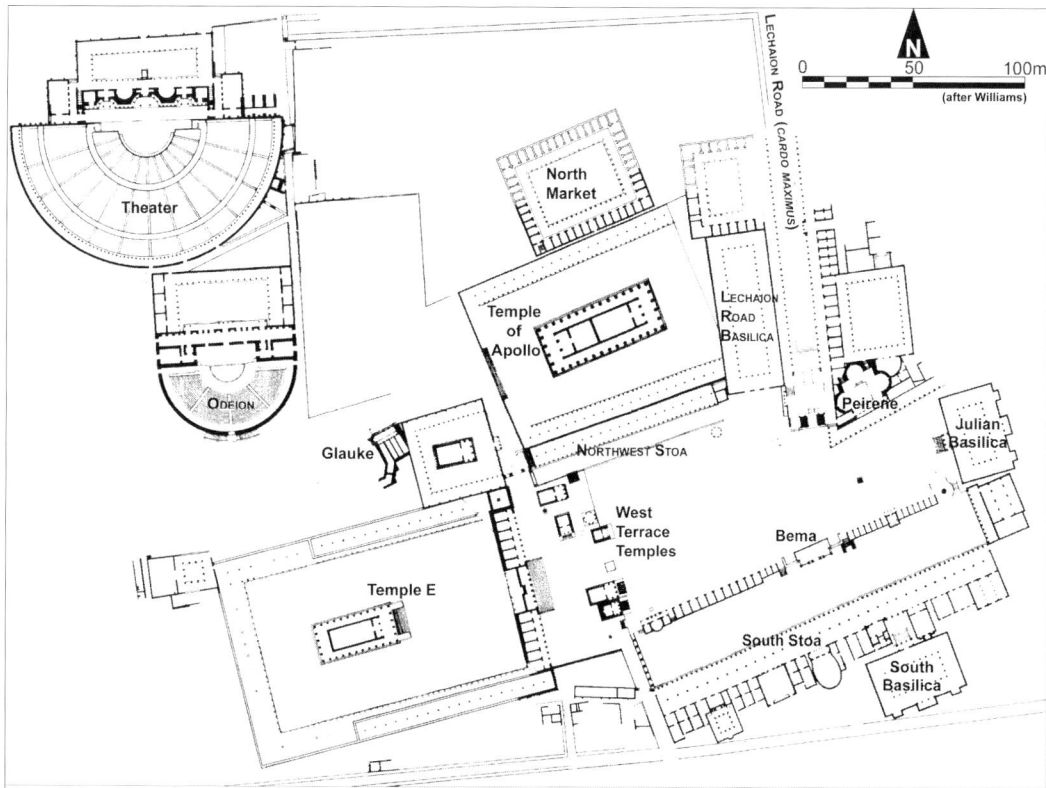

Figure 4
Roman site on Lechaion Road, circa 150 C.E.

laid out from scratch on an orthogonal plan. In the main site the *cardo maximus*, a broad marble-paved street, ascends to the paved Roman forum (Fig. 4). The forum is surrounded by *stoas* with shops, basilicas, and, at the west end, Roman podium temples. The Temple of Apollo (Fig. 5) and the South Stoa were both retained and modified for new uses (see Figs. 3, 4). Of the public monuments, the Peirene fountain is the best preserved and most impressive structure (Fig. 6). Nearly all traces of the medieval city have been removed with the exception of a recently excavated complex that may have once been a hospital or hospice (Fig. 7). To the north of the main site is the Asklepieion, which was excavated in the 1930s. The Asklepieion consists of the foundations of the temple and *stoas*, and the Lerna fountain court below. On one side of the complex are the remains of a gymnasium. On the slopes of Acrocorinth are the excavated remains of the Demeter Sanctuary, while further afield are portions of the Roman

Figure 5 (left)
Temple of Apollo at Corinth.
Figure 6 (right)
The Peirene fountain at Corinth.

Figure 7
Medieval site of Corinth, circa 1300 C.E.

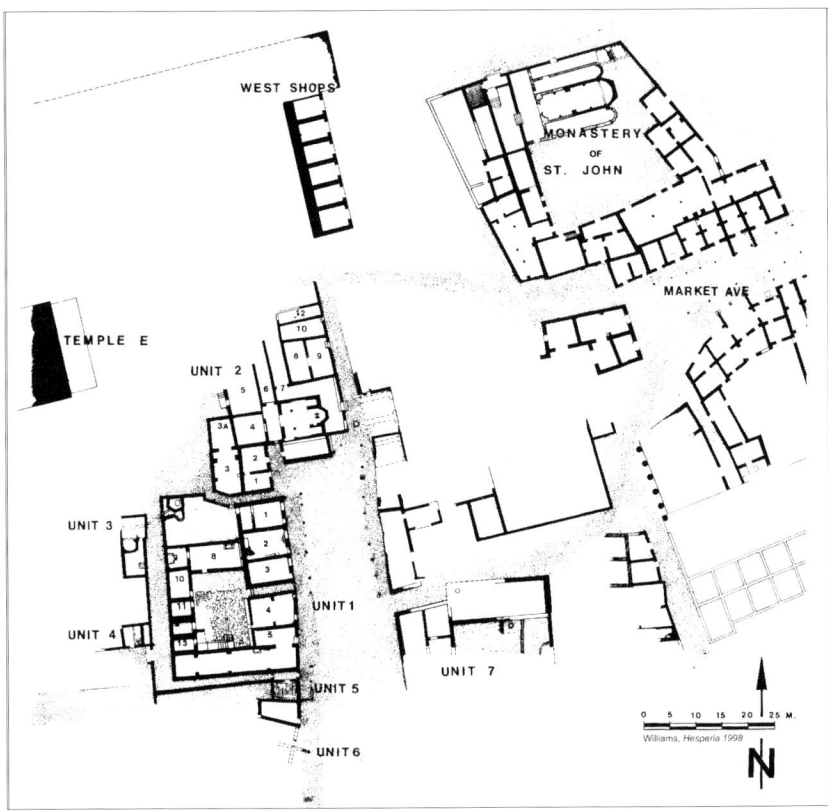

city wall and the amphitheater, both unexcavated, cemeteries, and three excavated early Christian basilicas.

A number of important sites within the territory of Ancient Corinth have been excavated. These include the following:

- **Acrocorinth.** Excavations on the summit of the acropolis, at the site of the Temple of Aphrodite, took place in 1920. The fortifications were planned and are fully published. Parts of the walls, especially the gates, are undergoing consolidation, but most of the enclosed area is a wasteland of undocumented postmedieval structures. The site is a romantic ruin that is found quite appealing by visitors.
- **Lechaion.** The western harbor of Corinth lies within the long walls, which are part of the ancient fortifications (Fig. 8). It consists of several excavated harbor basins, which it is believed were dug in the Classical period. Harbor moles extending out into the gulf are of early Roman date. A huge sixth-century Christian basilica, the second largest in Greece, was excavated by the Archaeological Society in the early 1960s. The basins are now seasonal lagoons that support a large variety of rare resident and migratory birds. It also has a variety of common and not so common plant species.
- **Korakou.** American excavations at Korakou on the bluffs east of the ancient harbor revealed parts of an important Bronze Age settlement. The ceramic finds were important in developing Mycenaean chronology, and the site is generally considered to be a vital archaeological resource for future excavations. The site has been encroached on by new housing developments.

Figure 8
Lechaion Road looking toward the Acrocorinth.

- **Isthmia.** Corinth's pan-Hellenic sanctuary dedicated to Poseidon at Isthmia is located on the Saronic Gulf at the south end of the Isthmus. It consists of a temple, a stadium, and a theater. When the Isthmus was fortified by a wall in the Late Roman period, Isthmia was the site of a major fortress guarding the road to Athens. The site has been extensively published, and its museum is one of the richest, most interesting, and best presented in the Peloponnese.
- **Diolkos.** This roadbed was supposedly built by Greek tyrant Periander (d. 586 B.C.E.) to facilitate portage of merchant and war ships across the Isthmus until the ninth century C.E. Several plans were made from circa 300 B.C.E. to replace the roadbed with canals, most notably by the emperor Nero. Large sections of the road on the Corinthian Gulf side of the Isthmus were excavated by the Greek Archaeological society and can still be seen beside the road to Loutraki.
- **Kenchreai.** The eastern harbor of Corinth is located at Kenchreai on the south coast of the Saronic Gulf. Underwater excavations produced data on the buildings located on the harbor moles and the important glass opus sectile panels displayed in the Isthmia Museum.
- **Perachora.** The Corinthian Sanctuary of Hera is located on a promontory, on the north coast of the Corinthian Gulf opposite the ancient city of Corinth. Excavations by the British School in the 1930s revealed a temple with a unique triglyph and metope altar, dining rooms, and quantities of Geometric and Archaic votives. The site is one of outstanding natural beauty.

In an educational sense, the site offers the opportunity to learn about multiple phases of Greek art and architecture. For instance, Corinth boasts the earliest Archaic stone-built temple and a diversity of Archaic architecture. In the Roman period, Corinth's status as a Roman colony as opposed to a Greek city under Roman rule affords a unique contrast in ancient planning and administration (Fig. 9). A quarter of the visitors to Corinth, some forty thousand people each year, obtain entry gratis or at

Figure 9
Topographical plan of village with Roman site superimposed.

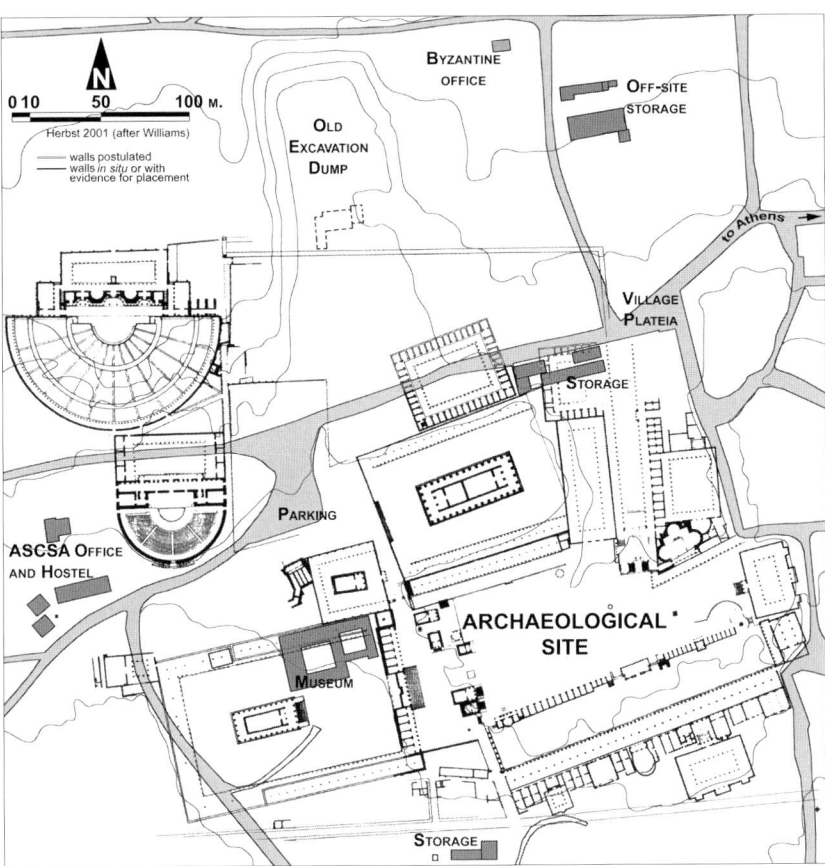

reduced rates, as students or members of school groups, and so on, to encourage appreciation of antiquity.

Officers of the American School conduct frequent tours of the site for groups of university students from various countries. These generally last several hours in duration and occasionally amount to full day seminars. Altogether, thirty-seven full volumes and several hundred articles on primary material, and many more on secondary material, have been published on the archaeology and history of Corinth. A volume that summarizes the present state of scholarship and the literature is due to be published in 2002.

Collections

The museum boasts a collection of over ninety thousand coins. In addition, about ninety thousand other inventoried objects form the basis of a comparative collection for visiting scholars to consult. About 40 tons of excavation finds, all univentoried and mainly ceramics from saved contexts, are stored for reference and study. On a research level Corinth continues to embrace archaeological science; in 2001 a facility to house Corinth's human bone collection was opened. This building now houses several hundred skeletons representing an almost unparalleled array of human pathologies. Corinth is also actively seeking to create a relational database to integrate and manage all phases of recording and collections management from excavation to publication. The archives of the excavation include an almost complete record of the excavations, including hundreds of fully catalogued plans and thousands of photographs.

The museum display consists of a static collection, which by modern standards is unappealingly presented in cramped quarters in old cabinets. There is little latitude for expanding or changing the display given the constraints of space and existing rules governing museum collections. There is nothing to link the objects on display with the site(s) that produced them, with the history of the region, or with their function. Certain periods are not well represented or are completely omitted. There is also nothing that informs the public how archaeologists treat the material during the excavation and postexcavation process. There is no attempt to cater to the religious pilgrims who make up a significant minority of the tourist numbers.

The museum itself is dated; old-fashioned, its storage areas are completely full. The workrooms are cold and damp in winter and hot in summer, and objects are kept in conditions that are detrimental to the collection. No bespoke office space exists for the local archaeological authority, which presently shares the small prehistoric gallery with the museum guards and the prehistoric display. No space exists for a proper conservation laboratory. Storage for context material is restricted to one wing of the museum and several buildings scattered around the village. These buildings are dilapidated, vermin-ridden, and filled to capacity.

The monuments on the site require extensive consolidation; they are in places falling into ruin, and many buildings are hazardous to the public. Every summer the vegetation on most of the excavated area is sprayed with herbicide, but the dead stalks are often not removed until the autumn. There are no pathways laid out, and visitors are permitted to wander as they please. There is no modern guidebook nor is there any on-site explanation of the architectural spaces. Wheelchair facilities are nonexistent, and toilet facilities are limited to two stalls, not adapted for wheelchair access, which are completely insufficient for the requirements of the staff and the general public.

Tourism and Transport

Ancient Corinth is currently about the tenth-ranked tourist site in Greece, drawing some 160,000 visitors a year (Figs. 10, 11), although this number has dropped appreciably over the past decade (which is obviously of concern to the community). In the village of 2,000 people, the revenues generated by the site support thirty-five full-time state employees in the museum and archaeological authority offices, yet there are insufficient funds for many essential administrative materials. The American School employs thirteen full-time and twenty seasonal employees. Archaeology, centered in Ancient Corinth, is thus one of the largest employers in the region.

The direct benefits of tourism to the community are limited and could be developed further. A majority of tourists arrive at Corinth via a bus tour of Corinth, Mycenae, and Epidaurus. Generally, the tour schedule rarely affords tourists the opportunity to shop or eat. Many tourists who arrive at Corinth independently of a tour are en route to other destinations. Saint Paul spent eighteen months at Corinth, and his letters to the Corinthians form a significant part of Christian doctrine. The bema, where Paul was brought before the Roman governor, is the focus of a small but

Figure 10
Income from ticket sales.

1999				
	106,600	full price at 1,200 ($4.00) = 127,920,000 drs		$426,400
	15,742	half price at 600 ($2.00) = 9,445,200 drs		$ 31,484
	39,090	free tickets		
TOTAL	161,432			$457,884

1998				
	129,050	full price at 1,200 ($4.00) = 154,860,000 drs		$516,200
	7,930	half price at 600 ($2.00) = 4,758,000 drs		$ 15,860
	17,778	free tickets		
TOTAL	154,758			$532,060

Half-price entry is given to European Union (EU) pensioners and non-EU students. Free entry is given to educational groups, museum personnel, children, and visitors on Sundays from November to March.

	Full	Half	Free	Total
1. Acropolis	1,165,742	82,727		1,248,469
2. Knossos	655,845	35,210	119,370	810,425
3. Lindos	504,440	21,534	67,658	593,632
4. Delphi	364,000	14,800	166,200	545,000
5. Epidaurus	361,845	24,871	58,540	445,256
6. Olympia	314,645	16,918	99,962	431,525
7. Mycenae	268,258	16,145	15,671	300,074
8. Sounion	170,060	8,689	47,350	226,099
9. Palamidi	95,600	14,700	55,600	165,900
10. Corinth	129,050	9,930	17,778	154,758
11. Aphaia	85,351	2,487	31,743	119,581
12. Ath. Agora	74,100	11,800	32,800	118,700
13. Ialisos	88,500	3,400	7,150	99,050
14. Olympion	40,649	3,467	19,584	63,700

Source: Kathimerini (English Edition), Thursday, April 22, 1999, showing receipts for 1998 and Corinth gate receipts for the year 1998.

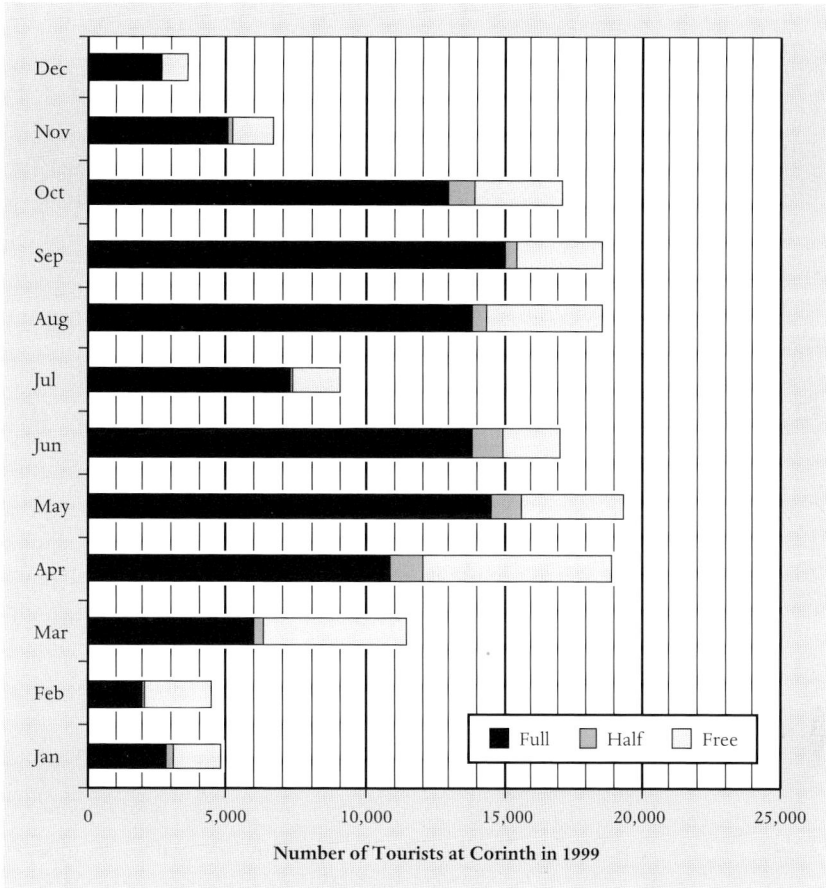

Figure 11
Monthly distribution of tourists at Corinth in 1999.

significant pilgrimage. Several thousand visitors a year, mainly Baptist Americans and Catholic Asians, take group tours that follow the footsteps of Saint Paul, and assemble to sing hymns in front of the bema. The Orthodox clergy of Corinthia (the county of Corinth) assemble to celebrate holy liturgy on the bema each year on June 29. A pavement next to the theater dedicated by Cornelius the Aedile, a friend of Saint Paul, preserves part of the dedication and is of interest to the better informed religious tourists.

Access to the site by road from Athens is a six-lane highway as far as the Tripolis and Patras interchange three kilometers east of Ancient Corinth and then a two-lane highway to the turnoff. The trip from central Athens takes about one hour and fifteen minutes if traffic is light between the center of Athens and Elevsina. Usually the trip takes two hours, sometimes longer. From Patras the trip is two hours on a one-lane highway that is soon to be upgraded to a three-lane highway. Travel by car is the most convenient mode of getting to the site. Ancient Corinth is not sign-posted from the Athens approach, which results in many drivers mistakenly taking the Tripolis Road at the interchange, which causes them to take a long drive before they can turn around. By train, the journey from Athens and Patras takes about one hour and thirty minutes to reach Corinth. The Athens station is linked to the newly opened underground system, which is undergoing expansion. Links at the Corinth end are improving—the local bus station has moved to an office opposite the railway station where there is a taxi stand but rarely any taxis. A new high-speed rail link is being built to link Athens, Corinth, and Patras. In future the journey will take less than one hour to a location about 6.5 kilometers east of Ancient Corinth where there will be taxi and bus services to the village and to New Corinth. The new link will make rail travel to Corinth very convenient for commuters and tourists alike, and increased tourist traffic and more Athenian commuters settling in the area must be expected. Depending on traffic in Athens, the local direct bus takes about one hour and thirty minutes from the suburban bus station to New Corinth; this bus runs hourly from New Corinth to Ancient Corinth, where there are bus stops by both site entrances.

There is an extensive network of roads in the village that reflects the Roman to early modern requirements of the settlement before the development of the archaeological site and its attraction for mass tourism. Nearly all outside visitors converge on the small village *plateia* (central plaza) along narrow two-lane village streets before taking the road to the site entrance. With rising rural incomes, the number of locally owned cars has increased dramatically, and locals using the village retail and recreation facilities park close to the village's center, restricting roads to one single lane for two-way travel. At the height of tourist season from late March to the end of September, with an average of 650 tourists a day, there is a serious problem with traffic congestion in the village.

The parking lot is a widening in the road from the village's center at a point where it forks to one of its suburbs and to Acrocorinth; it has a capacity of about ten coaches. At peak hours during the tourist season many coaches are forced to park alongside the road, which reduces it to a single lane and causes traffic jams.

Current Management Structure for the Site

The site and museum at Ancient Corinth are open from 8:00 A.M. to 5:00 P.M. in the winter and from 8:00 A.M. to 7.30 P.M. in the summer. The guards work independently of the Greek Archaeological Service. There are a total of about eighteen guards working two rotating shifts and taking turns on evening and night duties. Numbers only allow one guard on site at a time, and guards also staff the entrance and exit gates (selling tickets, cards, and guides); the remainder guard the museum.

The head office of the authority for Prehistoric and Classical Antiquities is in Nauplia, a 45-minute drive to the south. This office covers a large territory spanning the Argolid and the Corinthia; in addition, it embraces many major tourist sites including Tiryns, Mycenae, Argos, Epidaurus, Isthmia, Perachora, Nemea Valley, and Corinth. It also embraces a large number of ongoing excavations and surveys (the Swedish School in Berbati Valley and at Asine; Germans at Tiryns; French at Argos; Americans at Isthmia, Nemea Valley, Lerna, and Corinth; the Greek Archaeological Society at Mycenae, and so forth). A branch office operates out of Corinth and is in charge of the northern part of the region. The Corinth office has a limited budget, and the staff includes two senior archaeologists and one junior archaeologist, a draftsperson, and three laborers. Their office consists of the small prehistoric gallery in the museum. There is also a rudimentarily equipped conservation laboratory in one of their storerooms. Their brief is to examine building permits and to undertake rescue excavations.

The head office of the authority for Byzantine Antiquities is in Patras, located two hours to the west. This office oversees the provinces of Corinth, Achaia, and Elis. The local branch of the authority employs two full-time archaeologists, and a laborer, a cleaner, and a guard.

Postscript

Following the Loutraki conference, excavations at Corinth and the IV Ephoreia of Prehistoric and Classical Antiquities cooperated in drafting a proposal for the enhancement of the site for visitors in anticipation of designing a management plan for the site. This proposal was submitted to the Greek Ministry of Culture in July 2001 and embraced immediate problems of access, off-road parking, wheelchair access, hygienic facilities, marked paths, fire hydrants, and educational materials on site. The plan was accepted by the Greek Ministry in February 2002. The program is, however, no more a solution to the problems facing the site than a tourniquet is sufficient treatment for a serious wound. It was designed to reduce drastically the gradual but chronic damage done by unrestricted access to monuments that can no longer sustain larger numbers of visitors and to close off areas that are dangerous to the public. Instead, visitors will be channeled along temporary marked routes to *topoi* where viewing areas and information is provided. At the same time, the program intends to improve the grossly insufficient existing amenities offered. The process of planning an interim solution has, however, served the positive purpose of gaining the attention of both the cultural and political authorities at regional and state level. It has helped to build the mutual trust and respect of the various responsible bodies and there is now general agreement that the site be managed in a coordinated fashion.

The next steps are to establish policies, set objectives, develop strategies, and prepare plans with a view to implementing a heritage management plan for Corinth. This process must be achieved by consulting all those with a stake in the site, including local residents and visitors, in addition to those with more scholarly, economic, and political interests in the site such as archaeologists, employees, tourist companies, and local authorities. The process of site documentation is an ongoing one and old records are currently being upgraded and integrated. Beyond, but synchronous with this phase, we must assess and analyze the condition, significance, and values of the various monuments and examine the actual management structure.

Summary of Discussions

Jeanne Marie Teutonico and Gaetano Palumbo

THE DEVELOPMENT OF SITE MANAGEMENT plans based on a clear understanding of a site's values and broad participation is increasingly seen as an effective way to ensure the sustainable conservation and management of archaeological sites. Building on previous experience in this field, the Corinth Workshop was designed to discuss the most current management planning concepts, to explore their applicability in countries of the eastern Mediterranean, and, ultimately, to develop approaches useful to the future stewardship of archaeological sites in the region.

The workshop was structured to include a series of presentations on values and the theoretical principles of site management planning, followed by a number of case studies in which the theoretical model could be critically analyzed in the context of practical realities. Participants were also divided into smaller working groups for three collective exercises centered around specific issues emerging from the presentations. The first examined the issue of values—what they are and how they are, or should be, articulated in the context of a management plan. The second utilized the case of Corinth as an opportunity to discuss the development of a management planning process with specific policies in mind, and the third looked at the issue of barriers to the implementation of a values-based planning approach and how to overcome such barriers.

Many ideas and recommendations emerged from the discussions held throughout the event, both those associated with the presentations and case studies and those developed by the working groups. The main points are summarized below.

Values

- Values are often considered self-evident and thus taken for granted. As a result, they are not articulated at the beginning of a planning process but rather emerge at the end when policies and approach have already been decided.
- Local stakeholders must have a clear voice in articulating the values of a site; this cannot be accomplished by outsiders working in isolation.

- Economic values often predominate over all others, especially where tourism is seen as a potential source of income. Education is necessary to raise awareness of the many other values (historical and artistic, social, symbolic, natural, and so on), which should be considered alongside economic values if a site is to be conserved in its complexity.
- Values may be in conflict, requiring negotiation among stakeholders and balancing of interests. It is recognized, however, that reconciliation of conflicting values is not always possible and compromise or prioritization of values may be necessary.
- Heritage sites often contribute to enhancing cultural identity. The assessment of values related to cultural identity must be undertaken with due regard to moral and ethical implications.
- Lack of administrative infrastructure and education in conservation and management planning hinders the acceptance of values and their use.
- Values are dynamic and may change over time; the planning process must take account of this.

The Management Planning Process: Overcoming Obstacles to Integrated Planning

- The management planning process is often perceived as overly complex or as an end in itself. It is important to educate decision makers, professionals, and other stakeholders regarding the real benefits of the process and to show examples where the process has been successfully implemented in practice.
- The management planning process must have a clearly identified leader with well-defined responsibilities. Local professionals must have a strong role in the process.
- The management planning process must be coherent in methodology but also flexible and adapted to local conditions. The process should be perceived as iterative rather than linear.
- Not enough attention is paid to the identification of stakeholders. All groups with an interest in a particular site must be included in the planning process. Effective communication tools must be explored and adopted in order to build trust and promote real dialogue.
- Public awareness regarding cultural heritage should be promoted through effective use of mass media and through educational initiatives at all levels, from primary school through university.
- Management planning must be truly interdisciplinary and participatory; only then is it possible to understand the motivations and values of each of the stakeholders and to reach a consensus on priorities and policies.
- Decision makers must be convinced that an integrated planning approach is critical to the effective conservation and management of archaeological sites. This requires dialogue and an understanding of sometimes divergent priorities.

- National legal and administrative systems may not be suited to the adoption of an integrated planning process, and this needs to be addressed; however, a values-based process may also be used as a tool to build collaboration between different ministries and government departments.
- Archaeological sites should be considered within larger initiatives of urban and regional planning.
- It is often difficult to acquire funding for planning; many funders are only interested in implementation. This stance is slowly changing, but a concerted effort should be made to rectify this situation on both the national and international levels. The involvement of donors in the planning process may be one way to promote better understanding of the importance and efficacy of planning.
- A management plan will be most effective if it is recognized as an official, and if possible, legal document.
- To ensure the effective implementation and review of management plans, the role, qualifications, and responsibilities of the site manager must be clarified. It is important to establish how decisions are made and by whom.
- Education and training in conservation and site management planning are crucial at all levels, from decision makers to specialists, craftsmen, and local stakeholder groups. National and international agencies should cooperate to develop appropriate training opportunities for all those involved in the conservation and management of archaeological sites.
- There is often a perception that conservation is antithetical to development and improvement in the quality of life. It is the responsibility of the profession to show that good conservation can still promote economic development in a way that respects multiple values and is sustainable in the long term.

The Corinth workshop created an opportunity for professionals representing many different countries, disciplines, and cultural environments to discuss issues of common concern. The fact that there was general agreement on the basic principles of values and significance, and on the importance of planning for the long-term management of cultural heritage, indicated the relevance of the proposed approach. It is hoped that the event has helped to strengthen a network of institutions and professionals committed to advancing the practice of archaeological site management in the Eastern Mediterranean region, and that there will be future opportunities to share ideas and experiences.

Annotated Bibliography on Management of Archaeological Sites

Martha Demas

THE PURPOSE OF this annotated bibliography is to provide practitioners with an overview of the published literature related to the management of archaeological sites. The bibliography is divided into three subject areas; the focus and rationale of each is explained below. These are to some degree artificial divisions, and there is considerable overlap and relationship among the areas. Nevertheless, both the issues themselves and the literature that gives expression to them argue for splitting rather than lumping. While all of the citations in the bibliographies are annotated, most of them are simply indicative of the contents; some are more analytical; and a few contain editorial remarks.

The published literature on the management of cultural resources, and archaeological sites in particular, has grown substantially in the last two decades. Each of the bibliographies is selective and current only through 2000; citations from 2001 are opportunistic rather than the result of a literature search. While the scope of the bibliography is intended to be global, the literature on these subjects is overwhelmingly from English-speaking countries (Australia, the United States, and Britain). This is a reflection, on the one hand, of the origins of heritage management theory in these countries, and on the other hand, the fact that most of the international conference proceedings are in English.

Archaeological Heritage Management (Bibliography 1)

Archaeological heritage management is a subset of what is widely known as cultural resource management, which encompasses a broad range of issues related to the protection, preservation, and use of archaeological resources. Its origins relate to the many threats against archaeological resources and the means and methods of mitigating their impact, by, for instance, the development and implementation of policy and legislation (both nationally and internationally); the survey, collection, and management of data; the protection and/or salvage of resources in the face of modern development and illicit trafficking; the education and training of professionals and the public; and the integration with the allied disciplines of nature conservation and environmental protection.

Increasingly, however, the rights of indigenous peoples and their varied responses to their past, theoretical developments in archaeology, issues of development in the Third World, and the marketing and exploitation of heritage for tourism have given rise to new approaches and perspectives and have brought archaeological heritage management into greater discourse with academic archaeology, as well as with government agencies and nongovernmental organizations. That these issues are of global concern is well illustrated in the many publications of collected papers from international congresses.

Individual bibliographies could be generated for most of the themes that constitute archaeological heritage management; this is particularly true of legislation, policy matters, and issues and approaches to rescue or salvage archaeology, which has been a major focus of professionals since the 1960s. The literature on this subject is extensive, however, and these issues are not the focus of this publication (which is the individual, not the cumulative, resource). It is intended that this bibliography be inclusive with regard to issues but selective in citations.

Site Management (Bibliography 2)

Whereas archaeological heritage management is aimed principally at the cumulative resource, the focus of the site management bibliography is the individual site, or classes or spatial groupings of sites, which come under a single management scheme. Although all the issues that constitute archaeological heritage management are also part of managing the individual site, the literature emphasizes the impact of these issues on a specific site or group of sites and how they have been addressed in the development of management plans; many issues become more prominent when they are addressed at the site level (for example, presentation and interpretation) or when they are focused in their solutions (for example, visitor management).

Both the process of site management and the final product (the management plan) are included in the bibliography, but the emphasis is on process. Site management plans are numerous, but they are as difficult to obtain as they are to implement. A few examples are cited in order to call attention to these very important but largely ignored documents and to illustrate some of the approaches to site management. The individual elements of a management plan and the strategies for their implementation (for example, condition recording, interpretive programs, and visitor management) could each be a separate bibliography; only assessment of significance has been singled out for such treatment in Bibliography 3, since significance assessment is central to the values-based approach to planning advocated in this publication.

Assessment of Significance (Bibliography 3)

The literature in this bibliography covers the process of evaluation and the selection of sites for preservation and protection, generally within the context of legal protection, and the role of values in decision making and management planning for the individual site. Many of the assessment models and criteria have been devised as a tool of cultural resource management, where the focus has been on criteria for determining scientific significance in order to establish priorities for research (especially as a part of rescue or contract archaeology), or for protection and preservation. Nevertheless, the approaches and criteria are potentially applicable to decision making for the individual site.

Formulated as a statement of significance, the assessment of values becomes a critical component of the site management plan. The importance of assessment in the selection and management of individual resources and the difficulty of achieving a consensus on how this should be achieved account for the extensive literature on this topic, of which this bibliography provides only an overview.

Acknowledgments

The author acknowledges the assistance of Anne Oliver in the compilation and annotation of this bibliography. Authors of annotations are indicated as follows: Martha Demas (md) and Anne Oliver (ao).

Annotated Bibliography 1 — Archaeological Heritage Management

Antiquity 67, no. 255 (1993): 400–45.

In this issue, a special section is devoted to "Heritage and the ICAHM Charter." The charter was developed by the ICOMOS International Committee on Archaeological Heritage Management. Following an introduction by Henry Cleere, the text of the charter is presented, followed by two commentaries on the charter, its creation, and its legal implications. Several articles on the state of archaeological heritage management in Great Britain and the United States are also included. See also Elia 1993. (ao)

Ashworth, Gregory, and Peter Howard, eds. *European Heritage: Planning and Management.* Exeter, England: Intellect Books, 1999.

This textbook is the result of cooperation among seven European Union universities and was developed for use in postgraduate courses offered at the institutions involved. The geographical scope of the book is Europe, with topics ranging from an historical overview of policy on and interest in the preservation of the past to identity issues and uses of heritage, with case studies on eco-museums, "heritage gem cities," gardens, theme parks, and heritage centers. Throughout the text are exercises and discussion questions for students. An appendix offers a review of the historical development of national policies in selected European countries. This is heritage management for the heritage industry. (md)

Barnes, Mark R. "Preservation of Archaeological Sites through Acquisition." *American Antiquity* 46, no. 3 (1994): 610–18.

While the focus of this article is the history and role of the various governmental agencies in the United States engaged in the acquisition of archaeological sites for long-term preservation, the author also includes a section on private sector acquisition of sites—an important tool for the preservation of sites that is rarely discussed. The Nature Conservancy, established in 1951, is dedicated to the preservation through acquisition of natural areas, but takes into consideration the cultural resources that exist within these areas. The Archaeological Conservancy, modeled on the Nature Conservancy but dedicated to preserving archaeological sites through acquisition, was newly established when this article was written. Other private foundations and initiatives, such as agreements with landowners, are also briefly mentioned. (md)

Bourke, Max, Miles Lewis, and Bal Saini, eds. *Protecting the Past for the Future: Proceedings of the UNESCO Regional Conference on Historic Places* (Sydney, Australia, 22–28 May 1983). Canberra: Australian Government Publishing Service, 1983.

This collection of articles from a UNESCO conference provides an overview of the state of cultural heritage preservation in the Asia-Pacific region in the early 1980s. The papers included in the sections *Regional Overview* and *Protection* discuss the legislation and management policies of many of the nations of this region (for example, Australia, China, India, Japan, Korea, Malaysia, New Zealand, and Thailand). (md)

Castillo Ruiz, José. *El Entorno de los Bienes Inmuebles de Interés Cultural: Concepto, Legislación y Metodologías para su Delimitación: Evolución Histórica y Situación Actual.* Granada: Universidad de Granada, 1997. (In Spanish.)

A comprehensive examination of the issues that relate to the surroundings or physical contexts of cultural properties, with a full account of the development of legislation to define and protect them in Spain, France, and Italy. Case studies of existing cultural properties and their surroundings are given, and a new methodology is proposed for the definition, delimitation, and regulation of surroundings in the future. (ao)

Chapelot, Jean, and Alain Schnapp. *La Politique de l'Archéologie en Europe.* Paris: Centre National de la Recherche Scientifique, 1984. (In English, French, and Italian.)

> The results of a roundtable held in Paris in 1978, these collected papers explore the status and health of archaeology in Europe in the 1970s by investigating national institutions and governmental organizations responsible for guiding policy. (md)

Cleere, Henry, ed. *Approaches to the Archaeological Heritage: A Comparative Study of World Cultural Resource Management Systems.* Cambridge: Cambridge University Press, 1984.

> A collection of essays on the national cultural resource management policies of twelve countries, mostly in Europe but also including Mexico, Peru, Japan, India, and the United States. Individual essays describe the legislative framework and organizational structure for protecting archaeological resources and explore such issues as public attitudes and archaeological training and education. (md)

Cleere, Henry, ed. *Archaeological Heritage Management in the Modern World.* London: Unwin Hyman, 1989.

> This volume constitutes the published results of one of the sessions of the first World Archaeological Congress (WAC) held in Southampton, England, in 1986. It also includes a few commissioned papers. The book is international in scope (with contributions from eighteen countries) and covers a broad range of issues relating to cultural resource management such as its history and legislation, training, and data management. It also provides a series of case studies. For the proceedings from the Third WAC, see McManamon and Hatton 2000 (those from the Second Congress have not been published). (md)

Cooper, Malcolm A. et al., eds. *Managing Archaeology.* London: Routledge, 1995.

> This publication brings together papers from the Theoretical Archaeology Group (TAG) conference held in Southampton, England, in 1992. The editors convened the conference with the intention of exploring divergent ideas and perspectives on management and archaeology. While the emphasis of the essays is on the United Kingdom, their ideas have international relevance. Of particular interest are the discussions of the philosophy and nature of management and its relationship to the theory and practice of archaeology. The sequence of papers attempts to bridge the gap between "management theory and practical management," with topics ranging from ways of valuing archaeological resources through marketing strategies for archaeology. (md)

Council of Europe. "Archaeology and Planning" (An international colloquy organized jointly by the Council of Europe and the Region of Tuscany, Florence, Italy, 22–25 October 1984). *Architectural Heritage Reports and Studies*, no. 5. Strasbourg: Council of Europe, 1987.

> This wide-ranging series of articles comprises the published results of a colloquy held in Florence, Italy, on the theme of archaeology and planning in Europe. A major emphasis is on strategies for conserving archaeological resources in the face of rural and urban development. Planning techniques, developing cooperative relationships between archaeologists and planners, the integration of archaeological resources into the urban fabric, and computerized documentation and cartography are highlighted. (md)

Cultural Resource Management. Australian Heritage Commission Bibliographic Series, no. 3. Canberra: Australian Government Publishing Service, 1990.

> This annotated bibliography on cultural resource management was produced from the Australian bibliographic database HERA. It covers all aspects of cultural resource management, focusing on Australian literature in particular, and including some United States literature. (md)

Darvill, Timothy. "Ancient Monuments in the Countryside: An Archaeological Management Review." *English Heritage Archaeological Report*, no. 5 (1987): 25–31.

> The theme in this article is management of archaeological resources in the larger context of their related countryside and landscape. The three main aspects of management are curatorial management (conservation and protection); exploitation (use of sites by the public and researchers); and rescue excavation. Integration with other land use demands, especially in the realm of private ownership, and drawing up a management plan and communicating it to those who may be impacted are emphasized; a schematic is provided outlining the stages of management planning. (md)

Darvill, Timothy, and Geoffrey Wainwright. "The Monuments at Risk Survey: An Introduction." *Conservation and Management of Archaeological Sites* 1, no. 1 (1995): 59–62.

> This brief article summarizes the aims, methodology, and management of the MARS (Monuments at Risk Survey) Project, an initiative designed to provide a systematic quantification of the current state of England's archaeological resource. The MARS project will examine levels of documentation for single monuments, landscapes, and districts; the scale and rate of physical impact on the sites over time; the present condition of the sites; the effectiveness of different management techniques; and the relation between the state of preservation of a monument and the information it preserves. (ao)

Davis, Hester A. "Public Archaeology Forum." *Journal of Field Archaeology* 16 (1989): 233–36.

> The full text of the British Code of Practice for developers and archaeologists is presented with background information and commentary. The code attempts to foster mutual understanding and cooperation between developers and archaeologists, and to reduce the conflicts that arise between these two groups. Publication and review of the code can also be found in *British Archaeological News* 1, no. 1 (June 1986) and *British Archaeological News* 1, no. 6 (August 1986). (md)

Economic Development and Archaeology in the Middle East. Amman: Department of Antiquities of the Hashemite Kingdom of Jordan and the American Schools of Oriental Research, 1982.

> This booklet, published by the American School of Oriental Research in Jordan in conjunction with the Jordanian Department of Antiquities, addresses cultural resource issues in the country and represents an unusual and welcome departure from the standard activities and concerns of foreign archaeological schools. A further development in this direction is the Cultural Resource Management Project begun in 1987 by the Antiquities Department of Jordan and the American Center of Oriental Research, described in *ACOR Newsletter* no. 3 (November 1990). (md)

Elia, Ricardo J. "United States Cultural Resource Management and the ICAHM Charter." *Antiquity* 67, no. 255 (1993): 426–38.

> In a critical comparison of the practice of archaeological heritage management in the United States with the principles and standards expressed in the ICAHM Charter, the author concludes that philosophy and legislation are in accord with the Charter but that the United States falls short in practice. This is ascribed to the nature and predominance of contract archaeology, the lack of consistent enforcement of standards, and a shortage of professional training programs. (ao)

Frankel, David. "The Excavator: Creator or Destroyer?" *Antiquity* 67 (1993): 875–77.

> While acknowledging the destruction inherent in excavation, the author argues that archaeologists also create sites by establishing a context for what they unearth and constructing a history through comparative analysis. The trend of cultural resource managers to equate archaeology only with destruction, and thus to limit or forbid excavation, also limits the discovery and interpretation of our history. (ao)

Gay, Honor. "Integrated Conservation of Natural and Historical Aspects of the Countryside." *Journal of Architectural Conservation* 1, no. 3 (1995): 70–88.

> Historically, the conservation of historic (including archaeological) and natural environments have developed independently, resulting in an artificial division between two allied fields of endeavor. The author explores this division in Britain and argues for the necessity of integrating these two strands of conservation. The first part of the article analyzes whether the separation of these fields is justified. Of particular interest for archaeological sites is the discussion on the impacts and potential benefits of colonization of ruined structures by plants. The second part of the article examines the development of legislation on the historic and natural environment in Britain. The case for better communication and a much stronger link between conservation of nature and culture is well made. (md)

Greenberg, Ronald M., ed. "Archaeology and the Federal Government. *Cultural Resource Management* 17, no. 6 (1994): 36.

> This thematic issue defines the roles of the numerous federal agencies and private organizations involved in archaeology in the United States, outlines the legislation that guides them, and contains descriptions and commentary on archaeological activities occurring under Federal jurisdiction. These include excavation, database management, site stabilization, site protection, public outreach, and education. While the articles are brief and expository, they present a good cross-section of federal activities and the organizations and people involved. (ao)

———. "Parks Canada: Archaeology and Aboriginal Partners." *Cultural Resource Management* 20, no. 4 (1997): 64.

> This thematic issue presents the experiences of Parks Canada (the federal agency equivalent to the National Park Service in the United States) in managing its archaeological resources. The relevant agencies and legislation are described, followed by articles on ecosystem management, cultural landscape studies, monitoring, inventory and database management, rescue archaeology, cooperative management strategies (particularly with aboriginal partners), and site-specific studies. (ao)

Greene, Joseph A. "Preserving Which Past for Whose Future? The Dilemma of Cultural Resource Management in Case Studies from Tunisia, Cyprus, and Jordan." *Conservation and Management of Archaeological Sites* 3, nos. 1–2 (1999): 43–60.

> The author examines how three countries in the Mediterranean region—Tunisia, Cyprus, and Jordan—have approached the demands of preserving sites in the face of major development pressures. The responses include a UNESCO campaign involving multiple funding sources and allocation of concessions to international teams (Tunisia); a reliance on foreign expeditions and the national antiquities service to respond to rescue excavations (Cyprus); and the establishment of a cooperative program among government and private organizations and universities to address preservation of antiquities in the face of economic development (the Jordan Cultural Resource Management Project). (md)

Greeves, Tom. "Archaeology and the Green Movement: A Case for *Perestroika*." *Antiquity* 63, no. 241 (1989): 59–66.

> The relationships between archaeological sites or features and their landscape, and archaeological and nature conservation are explored. The author argues that archaeologists must share the blame for the destruction of resources through the practice of excavation. Neither archaeologists nor society understand the role of conservation, which is associated exclusively with nature conservation. Archaeological conservation can make a significant cultural contribution to the conservation or green movement and would also benefit from such an association. (md)

Healy, Paul F. "Archaeology Abroad: Ethical Considerations of Fieldwork in Foreign Countries." In Ernestene L. Green, ed., *Ethics and Values in Archaeology*. New York: The Free Press, 1984.

> The author explores the ethics and etiquette of excavating in foreign countries. In a section entitled "Cultural Resource Management and the Foreign Archaeologist," the very important question of the responsibility of foreign archaeologists for the protection, restoration, and preservation of sites is raised. The critical role of funding agencies, the need for clarification of responsibilities by the host government, and the moral and professional obligation of developed nations to assist in protecting and preserving resources of less developed nations are discussed. (md)

King, Thomas F. "Prehistory and Beyond: The Place of Archaeology." In Robert E. Stipe and Antoinette J. Lee, eds., *The American Mosaic: Preserving a Nation's Heritage*, 236–64. Washington, D.C.: US/ICOMOS, 1987.

> This article is a historical overview of archaeology's role in the United States National Historic Preservation program, especially since the passage of the National Historic Preservation Act of 1966 and the growth of the historic preservation movement. Such issues as academic vs. public archaeology, the emergence of a conservation ethic, and the interchange of ideas and methods between archaeology and historic preservation are discussed. (md)

Lambrick, George, ed. *Archaeology and Nature Conservation*. Oxford: Oxford University Department for External Studies, 1985.

> These conference papers explore the "mutual interests, problems and experiences of nature conservationists and archaeologists in protecting Britain's countryside heritage." The management of natural and archaeologically important areas for their mutual benefit is emphasized. Papers are grouped under the following categories: the relationship between archaeology and ecology; statutory provisions and the role of government agencies, the role of nonstatutory organizations; conservation management policies; and case studies. (md)

Lipe, William D. "A Conservation Model for American Archaeology." *The Kiva* 39, nos. 3–4 (1974): 213–45.

> The author of this seminal article proposes a conservation model to replace the current exploitative model of archaeology, which emphasizes excavation rather than conservation of resources. Conservation strategies, including education, integration of archaeology and planning, and the establishment of archaeological preserves, are discussed. In the latter context, the author deals with the question of significance and the need for representative sampling. (md)

McIntosh, Susan Keech. "Archaeological Heritage Management and Site Inventory Systems in Africa: The Role of Development." In Ismail Serageldin and June Taboroff, eds., *Culture and Development in Africa* (Proceedings of an International Conference held at the World Bank, Washington, D.C., April 2–3, 1992), 387–409. Washington, D.C.: The International Bank for Reconstruction and Development/The World Bank, 1994.

> Based on her experiences in West Africa, the author argues that in order to promote effective archaeological heritage management in the region, basic site inventory methods must be restructured and African archaeologists must be trained in the use of computerized information systems, air photo interpretation, management theory, and conservation practice and methods. Policy recommendations to international development agencies are to fund long-term national site inventory work and database management, and to fund an intensive training program in archaeological heritage management for Africans (a sample course outline is provided). (ao)

McManamon, Francis P., and Alf Hatton, eds. *Cultural Resource Management in Contemporary Society: Perspectives on Managing and Presenting the Past*. London: Routledge, 2000.

> This collection of papers derives from the sessions of the Third World Archaeological Congress, held in New Delhi in 1994. The papers were updated through 1999 and new contributions were commissioned. The scope is interna-

tional, with contributions from Africa, the Americas, Asia, and Europe. The issues covered are equally broad, representing a spectrum of concerns in archaeological heritage management, including impact from modern development, policy and legislative issues, education and interpretation, rescue archaeology, and illegal trafficking. For the proceedings from the First World Archaeological Congress, see Cleere 1989 (those of the Second Congress have not been published). (md)

Morales Juarez, Roberto. "In Central America: Archaeological Heritage and Sustainable Development Planning." In *Vestiges Archéologiques, la Conservation In Situ* (Actes du deuxième colloque international de l'ICAHM, Montréal, Québec, Canada, 11–15 October 1994), 235–41. Ottawa: Publications de l'ICAHM, 1996.

The author discusses the relationship between cultural heritage conservation in Central America and issues of sustainable development and cultural identities. Heritage conservation has received little attention and is not highly valued in Central America, except where tourism can be exploited. In the context of a United Nations Development Program project to support sustainable development, a land-use planning model is proposed to integrate heritage conservation with economic development and public participation. The planning model is briefly described. (md)

O'Keefe, P. J., and L. V. Prott. *Law and the Cultural Heritage*. Abingdon, Oxon: Professional Books Ltd., 1984.

Five volumes are envisioned for this series entitled *Law and the Cultural Heritage*; two of which (vols. 1 and 3) have been published to date. The series is comprehensive and comparative in scope, covering legislation from all parts of the world. *Discovery and Excavation* (vol. 1) focuses on moveable archaeological heritage and discusses the need to protect antiquities and the historical development of legislation. *Creation and Preservation* (vol. 2) deals with the creation of cultural objects and the legal rights associated with them. *Movement* (vol. 3) deals with the legal control of trade in cultural objects. *Monuments and Sites* (vol. 4) is a survey of the law on immoveable cultural heritage. *Principles* (vol. 5) will assess the changes in the law brought on by development of special regulations to protect the cultural heritage. (md)

Prinke, Andrzej. "Landscape Parks in Poland: A Multidisciplinary Approach to Natural and Cultural Resources." In *Vestiges Archéologiques, la Conservation In Situ* (Actes du deuxième colloque international de l'ICAHM, Montreal, Quebec, Canada, 11–15 October 1994), 369–74. Ottawa: Publications de l'ICAHM, 1996.

The author describes an initiative in Poland to create a series of landscape parks with natural and cultural values in an attempt to break down the barriers between the disciplines. The parks selected are located near urban areas so they are easily accessible to the public and are included in the Regional Development Plan for the area. The cultural resources in the parks are historical and archaeological sites and are interpreted in conjunction with the natural values in an integrated way to the public. (md)

Rotroff, Susan I. "Archaeologists on Conservation: How Codes of Archaeological Ethics and Professional Standards Treat Conservation." *Journal of the American Institute for Conservation* 40 (2001): 137–46.

This article provides an historical overview and current status of codes of practice and professional standards developed by archaeological societies in the United States as they relate to conservation. While the emphasis is on the conservation of objects, the various codes and the author's discussion of them elucidate the evolution of issues and concerns of archaeologists. Although there has been progress in making a conservation ethic more central to the archaeological community, the author argues that a holistic approach (on the model of an ecosystem) has yet to be achieved. (md)

Schiffer, Michael B., and George J. Gumerman, eds. *Conservation Archaeology: A Guide for Cultural Resource Management Studies*. New York: Academic Press, 1977.

This is an early and very influential collection of articles on cultural resource management in the United States. Individual papers are grouped into nine topics: cultural resource management, conservation archaeology and research orientations, research designs, acquisition of survey data, estimating the nature and extent of the resource base, assessing significance, forecasting impacts, mitigation, and research contributions. (md)

Schmidt, Peter R., and Roderick J. McIntosh, eds. *Plundering Africa's Past*. Bloomington: Indiana University Press, 1996.

While this publication emphasizes the problem of the looting of cultural heritage sites (particularly archaeological sites), the wide range of articles provides a good overview of important issues in cultural resource management in Africa, including interpretation of cultural heritage and conflict of values. (md)

Serageldin, Ismail, and June Taboroff, eds. *Culture and Development in Africa* (Proceedings of an International Conference held at the World Bank, Washington, D.C., April 2–3, 1992). Washington, D.C.: The International Bank for Reconstruction and Development/The World Bank, 1994.

This compilation of papers from "Culture and Development in Sub-Saharan Africa," an international conference of 1992, explores many issues directly relevant to archaeological resource management in Africa. The papers provide an overview of the role and relationship of culture to economic development within the social and political context of sub-Saharan Africa. Of particular interest are the themes on cultural institutions, conservation of the built historic environment, and development, archaeology, and the environment. (md)

Silva, Roland. "The Cultural Triangle: International Safeguarding Campaign." In *The Cultural Triangle of Sri Lanka*. Paris: UNESCO, 1993.

The author narrates the efforts to have the "Cultural Triangle," which encompasses seven major sites across Sri Lanka, adopted by UNESCO as the focus of an international campaign for funding and technical support. Once this was achieved, an autonomous management structure was created from within the existing government to oversee the work, and a cultural resource management plan was developed. This includes guidelines that govern excavation and conservation at the sites. (ao)

Smith, Laurajane. "Heritage Management as Postprocessual Archaeology?" *Antiquity* 68, no. 259 (1994): 300–309.

Postmodern, or "postprocessual," archaeology is a theoretical movement that recognizes the place and seeks the integration of archaeology in a social, cultural, and political context. The author articulates the divide between theory, which is espoused by academics but not practiced, and practice, which is employed by heritage managers without benefit of a coherent theory. Heritage management is often discounted as the commercial bastardization of academic archaeology, and the field has been hindered by this approach. As the author concludes, however, "unlike postprocessual archaeology . . . it is heritage management and its position within the state that is actively impacting upon and defining the political uses of archaeology." (ao)

Society for American Archaeology, *Save the Past for the Future II: Report of the Working Conference, Breckenridge, Colorado, September 9–22, 1994*. Washington, D.C.: Society for American Archaeology, 1995.

The goals of the conference were to assess the state of archaeological site protection and the prevention of archaeological looting on public lands in the United States and to develop strategies to improve and implement protection. In this special report, the conference proceedings are presented and include general papers summarizing the history of resource protection in the United States, legislation and recent legal actions in support of protection, the need to integrate agencies and efforts, and the need to educate both professionals and the public. Of greater importance are the workshop proceedings, which discuss the issues of education, integrated resource management, and law enforcement and present recommendations for future actions. (ao)

Tilley, Christopher. "Excavation as Theatre." *Antiquity* 63, no. 239 (1989): 275–80.

> This is a revision of a paper originally delivered at an ICAHM conference in 1988. The author questions and challenges the notion that rescue excavation is a means of preservation in the face of development, arguing that archaeologists have emphasized excavation and the concomitant compilation of data to the detriment of developing conceptual structures and actively engaging in the interpretation of the past. The solution proposed is large-scale excavation conceived as an experiment in interpretive activity involving the public. It is a provocative challenge to what the author sees as a trend among cultural resource management professionals and the heritage industry to move archaeology toward a "form of production and marketing of the past." (md)

Wainwright, G. J. "The Management of the Archaeological Resource in England." In *Archaeology and Society: Large Scale Rescue Operations—Their Possibilities and Problems* (Papers presented at the symposium in Stockholm, Sweden, 12–16 September 1988). ICAHM Report No. 1, 321–30. Stockholm: ICAHM, 1989.

> The author presents management of archaeological resources as generally practiced by English Heritage. The management cycle is defined in the following three stages, which are fully discussed: identification and recording, deciding on the management option (curatorial or exploitative management), and excavation and recording, where preservation is not possible. Criteria for allocation of limited funds for rescue operations are defined; these are the same criteria used for scheduling sites. (md)

Wildesen, Leslie E. "The Study of Impacts on Archaeological Sites." *Advances in Archaeological Method and Theory* 5 (1982): 51–96.

> This study of impacts—defined as measurable change in the characteristic or property of an archaeological site—looks at types of impacts, how they are measured, and how a better understanding of their cumulative effects can be used to manage archaeological resources. The author puts forth a "value conservation" approach, which represents a middle course between site exploitation (removal of the resource) and site conservation (removal of the impact). A review of the studies undertaken to date and an extensive bibliography make this article particularly valuable. (md)

Wilson, Rex L., ed. *Rescue Archeology* (Proceedings of the Second New World Conference on Rescue Archeology, Dallas, Texas, 1984). Dallas: Southern Methodist University, 1987.

> Published under the same title are the papers from the First New World Conference (1982); those of the Third New World Conference, held in Venezuela in 1987, are in Spanish (*Arqueología de Rescate*). The focus of the proceedings is the Western Hemisphere. All the important issues associated with rescue archaeology are covered and include perspectives from both developed and developing countries. The papers cover the philosophy and principles of rescue archaeology; legislative, economic, social, and political issues; the interface between archaeology and engineering; current practice and strategies; and professional standards; the recommendations and resolutions of the conference are also published. (md)

Annotated Bibliography 2 — Site Management

Addyman, Peter V. "The Stonehenge We Deserve." In H. F. Cleere, ed., *Archaeological Heritage Management in the Modern World*, 265–74. London: Unwin Hyman, 1989.

> Perhaps Britain's most famous archaeological monument, Stonehenge has long been in need of a management policy; however, it has been difficult to reach a consensus on how the site should be presented to the public. The author discusses two conflicting presentation philosophies for the site. The Historic Buildings

and Monuments Commission is attempting to attract the serious visitor by requiring a real investment of time and intellectual commitment. The philosophy of Heritage Projects Ltd., a private company, assumes a degree of self-selection among visitors and believes that visitation should be encouraged by making the experience physically and intellectually appealing. (md)

Aguilar Piedra, Carlos. "Archaeological Parks: Guayabo de Turrialba and El Caño." In *Rescue Archaeology* (Papers from the First New World Conference on Rescue Archaeology), 163–71. Washington, D.C.: The Preservation Press, 1982.

The author discusses the challenges and problems involved in the establishment of archaeological parks based on his experience with parks in Costa Rica and Panama. The lack of financial support and the absence of a national park service tradition hamper the establishment of archaeological parks in Central America. Emphasized are the importance of establishing the boundaries of the park for its legal protection, integration with the community, and the role of research. (md)

Australian National Parks and Wildlife Service. *Australian Ranger Bulletin* 4, no. 1 (1986).

This issue of the bulletin is devoted to cultural resource management in Australia. Many of the articles are case studies of rock art sites. A broad range of issues is addressed—education, tourism, vandalism, erosion, and more. The management principles and many of the specific strategies developed to deal with these problems are generally applicable to archaeological sites. (md)

Bahçeci, Müge. "The Pamukkale's Preservation and Development Plan." In *Vestiges Archéologiques, la Conservation In Situ* (Actes du deuxième colloque international de l'ICAHM, Montréal, Québec, Canada, 11–15 October 1994), 45–53. Ottawa: Publications de l'ICAHM, 1996.

Pamukkale, Hierapolis, a site on the World Heritage List, combines white travertine formations produced by thermal springs with archaeological deposits from different historical periods. In 1990 a preservation and development plan was created in order to define and address the problems confronting the site, particularly in relation to regulating and accommodating tourism. The author outlines the plan, which is in the implementation stage. (ao)

Clark, Kate, ed. *Conservation Plans in Action: Proceedings of the Oxford Conference*. London: English Heritage, 1999.

This publication includes the papers, with selected discussion, of a major conference on conservation planning in Britain, entitled "Conservation Plans for Historic Places" and held in March 1998. Papers include an overview of the conservation plan and planning process by the editor of the volume, examples of conservation planning by various practitioners, the role of conservation planning in the Heritage Lottery Fund, and sage advice from such long-time practitioners as James Semple Kerr. The planning process advocated is essentially that of the Australian Burra Charter, adapted to the experience and needs in England. The epilogue, written one year later, is an interesting assessment of problems encountered in the development of conservation plans. (md)

Feilden, Bernard, and Jukka Jokilehto. *Management Guidelines for World Cultural Heritage Sites*. Rome: ICCROM, 1993.

These guidelines for the management of World Heritage sites originated in a meeting of ICCROM and ICOMOS in 1983 under the auspices of the cultural heritage division of UNESCO. The aim of the guidelines is to "provide advice and suggestions for implementing the intentions of the World Heritage Conventions." Beginning with a review of the policies of the Convention, *Management Guidelines* includes chapters on assessment of values, management planning, staffing and personnel considerations, physical interventions and the concept of authenticity, planning for historic towns, and visitor management and interpretation. A summary article of the main issues can be found in Jukka Jokilehto, "Conservation Management of World Heritage Sites." In *The Safeguard of the Rock-Hewn Churches of the Göreme Valley* (Proceedings of an International Seminar, Ürgüp, Cappadocia, Turkey, 5–10 September 1993), 49–56. Rome: ICCROM, 1995. (md)

Gutiérrez, María de la Luz et al. "The Management of World Heritage Sites in Remote Areas: The Sierra de San Francisco, Baja California, Mexico." *Conservation and Management of Archaeological Sites* 1, no. 4 (1996): 209–25.

The creation of a management plan for a remote area presents special problems and demands thoughtful solutions. In this article, the authors describe the development and implementation of a management plan for a group of World Heritage rock art sites in Baja California, Mexico, using a participatory and collaborative approach; their experiences and conclusions will be valuable to those seeking to create effective plans for similar sites. (ao)

Hawass, Zahi. "Site Management at Giza Plateau: Master Plan for the Conservation of the Site." *International Journal of Cultural Property* 9, no. 1 (2000): 1–22.

The development of a Master Plan for the Giza pyramids is the focus of this article. The author, with long experience of the Giza plateau, describes in some detail the threats to the site (including development pressures, rise of the water table, tourism, pollution, and inappropriate past interventions), then outlines the implementation of the plan for management. Phase four of this plan—the development of a Master Plan—concludes the article. (md)

Hughes, Mike, and Linda Rowley, eds. *The Management and Presentation of Field Monuments*. Oxford: Oxford University Department of External Studies, 1986.

These published proceedings of a conference held in Oxford in 1985 are concerned with the management and presentation of field monuments in England. The papers are grouped under the following headings: "The Role of Historic Buildings and Monuments Commission," "Ancient Monuments and the Landowner," "The Preservation and Integration of Monuments," "The Management of Monuments," "The Regional Approach," and "Case Studies." (md)

Johnson, Stephen, and Christopher Young. "A Management Plan for the Hadrian's Wall World Heritage Site" (1994); "Managing Hadrian's Wall" (1995); and "Hadrian's Wall Management Plan" (1996). *Conservation Bulletin (English Heritage)* (March 1994): 4–5; (July 1995): 5–8; and (July 1996): 1–3.

This series of three articles provides a continuous overview of the process of creating a comprehensive management plan for Hadrian's Wall. The plan is based on a clear articulation of the values of the resource and extensive consultation with the multiple private and public bodies that own, manage, or have an interest in parts of the wall. The first article of 1994 reviews the challenges and the need for a comprehensive plan, and the general approach to be taken in developing a plan. Short-term (five year) and long-term (thirty year) objectives are set forth in the articles of 1995 and 1996, with a review of the consultation process in 1996. The process is intended to be a model for management of World Heritage sites in Britain. (md)

Jones, Rhys. "Recommendations for Archaeological Site Management in Kakadu National Park." In idem, ed., *Archaeological Research in Kakadu National Park*. Canberra: Australian National Parks and Wildlife Service, 1985.

These recommendations for the management of archaeological sites in Kakadu evolved from three major considerations: the attitude of the Aboriginal owners toward the park; the impact of visitors on the physical fabric of the rock shelters; and the immense scale of the archaeological resource, especially with respect to research potential. Specific recommendations for the management of the sites are set forth following a brief statement of strategy that emphasizes the need to restrict access to sites. (md)

Kerr, James Semple. *The Conservation Plan: A Guide to the Preparation of Conservation Plans for Places of European Cultural Significance*. Sydney: National Trust of Australia (NSW), 1996.

> This is the fourth revised edition (the first was published in 1982) of a manual describing the process of preparing a conservation (management) plan for cultural sites. This process, involving assessment of significance and development of policies and strategies, reflects Australian practice, based on the Australian Burra Charter for the conservation of places of cultural significance. The emphasis in this manual is on historic sites, but the principles are applicable to all types of cultural sites, including archaeological sites. (md)

Kimball Brown, Margaret. "Mothballing Albany Mounds." *American Archaeology* 3, no. 3 (1983): 214–16.

> The author outlines a management plan for this North American Indian village and mound site that will be appropriate to the existing constraints (no personnel, budget, or facilities available). Given these constraints, it was decided to "mothball" the site in order to preserve it in a stable condition for the future. Mothballing consisted primarily of returning the site to a prairie ground cover, using a herbicide to destroy the existing hay crop. (md)

Klok, R. H. J. "Managing Megalithic Tombs as a National Resource in the Netherlands." In *ICOMOS Eighth General Assembly and International Symposium*, vol. 2, "Old Cultures in New Worlds," 938–44. Washington, D.C.: US/ICOMOS, 1987.

> The author describes the management scheme for a class of monuments—the fifty-four surviving megalithic tombs of the Netherlands, which are of exceptional scientific and public value and were being threatened by natural erosion, vegetation, development, and vandalism. The management process consisted of establishing a central documentation system; safeguarding the tombs from vandalism by installing glass tiles to seal the chamber floor; establishing a protected archaeological zone around each monument, either by land acquisition or land management contracts with owners; and the designation of eighteen representative tombs that would be open to the public and interpreted. (md)

Kwas, Mary L., ed. *Archaeological Parks: Integrating Preservation, Interpretation, and Recreation*. Nashville: Department of Conservation, Division of Parks and Recreation, 1986.

> This series of papers, the result of a symposium on archaeological parks in the United States, describes the experience of park managers in dealing with problems of education, interpretation, resource protection, land management, and facility development. There are seven case studies of specific sites, focusing on a wide range of issues, and five more general contributions. A preeminent concern in all the papers is the public use aspect of cultural parks and the development of education and interpretive programs. (md)

Lambert, Dave. *Conserving Australian Rock Art: A Manual for Site Managers*. Canberra: Australian Institute of Aboriginal Studies, 1989.

> This manual is designed for rock art sites in Australia, but the approach and many of the specific recommendations are applicable to archaeological sites in general. The first half deals with deterioration of the resource (from water, salts, vegetation, microflora, and animals), and the second half includes chapters on managing sites to reduce adverse impacts from visitors and site vandalism. (md)

Leay, Martin J., Janet Rowe, and John D. Young. *Management Plans: A Guide to Their Preparation and Use (Prepared for the Countryside Commission)*. Cheltenham: Countryside Commission, 1986.

> This manual outlines the principles and practice of preparing management plans for natural and cultural heritage sites. The stages of the process are as follows: aims, survey, analysis, objectives, prescription, implementation, and monitor and review. The process is clarified in examples of management plans for

the following categories: whole-farm, woodland, estate (a cultural site managed by the National Trust), and recreation. (md)

Lertrit, Sawang. "Who Owns the Past? A Perspective from Chiang Saen, Thailand." *Conservation and Management of Archaeological Sites* 2, no. 2 (1997): 81–92.

A preservation plan for the fourteenth-century Buddhist community of Chiang Saen has been administered by the Thai government since 1957; however, problems of site looting, damage, deterioration, and encroachment persist. Research was conducted to determine local attitudes toward the site; the results indicate that these problems stem from the disassociation of the local population from the process of preservation and management. The author describes the methodology and results of the research project and suggests ways to gain the concern and cooperation of the local population. (ao)

Marquis-Kyle, Peter, and Meredith Walker. *The Illustrated Burra Charter: Making Good Decisions about the Care of Important Places*. Sydney: Australia ICOMOS, 1992.

A step-by-step explication of the Burra Charter, the Australia ICOMOS charter on conservation and management of heritage sites. Commentary on each article is provided, and concepts are clearly explained with the aid of photographs and informative captions. The full text of the charter, as well as guidelines for establishing cultural significance, developing conservation policy, and undertaking studies and reports, are appended. The utility of this publication has not been diminished by the revisions to the Burra Charter in November 1999, for which, see Marilyn Truscott and David Young, "Revising the Burra Charter: Australia ICOMOS Updates Its Guidelines for Conservation Practice," *Conservation and Management of Archaeological Sites* (2000), 4, 101–16. (ao/md)

Miller, Hugh. "International Technical Assistance: Park Planning in Jordan." *Cultural Resource Management Bulletin* 10 (1987): 7–9.

The author reviews the history and accomplishments of the international park-planning project in Jordan. The project began in 1965 as part of a USAID economic development program, with the intention of developing and enhancing the tourism industry as a foreign currency earner for Jordan. Master plans were prepared for three antiquity sites (including Jerash and Petra). The sites were to be developed as parks, administered by a newly established National Park Service of Jordan, and managed according to the park master planning process developed over many years by the United States National Park Service for their parks. (md)

National Park Service. *Director's Order #28: Cultural Resource Management*. United States Department of the Interior (*http://www.nps.gov/refdesk*).

This is the manual used by managers of National Park Service (NPS) cultural properties. In addition to establishing NPS policy with respect to the management of cultural resources, it outlines the planning process, including documentation of the resource, and sets forth the standards for the management of historic and prehistoric structures, with specific chapters on management of archaeological resources, cultural landscapes, historic and prehistoric structures, and museum and ethnographic resources. Appendices include a glossary, bibliographies, and relevant laws, guidelines, and standards. (md)

Ndoro, Webber. "The Preservation and Presentation of Great Zimbabwe." *Antiquity* 68, no. 260 (1994): 616–23.

The author presents the history of preservation at the site, including the most recent strategies and interventions. Of greater importance are the discussions on site presentation (reconciling the needs of the site, the indigenous population, and the foreign tourist) and on the justification of conservation in a developing country. See also Pwiti 1996. (ao)

Park Planning Team. *Troy Historical National Park, Master Plan for Protection and Use.* 1971.

> This master plan is one of fourteen plans developed by the United States National Park Service (NPS) in cooperation with local planning teams; eleven of the plans were developed for sites in Turkey (1969–71) and three for those in Jordan. The guiding themes of all NPS plans are protection, development, and interpretation of the resource. The plans usually contain the following sections: an historical review of the resource; background information (for example, geology, climate, and existing facilities); development and management proposals (visitor use, infrastructure development of facilities and utilities, and administration and staff); interpretive program; and conservation. See also Miller 1987 for a contextual review of NPS planning in Jordan. (md)

Pearson, Michael, and Sharon Sullivan. *Looking after Heritage Places: The Basics of Heritage Planning for Managers, Landowners and Administrators.* Carlton, Victoria: Melbourne University Press, 1995.

> A detailed explication of site management planning as practiced in Australia according to the process in the Burra Charter, the Australia ICOMOS charter on conservation and management of heritage places. Each step delineated in the Burra Charter is explained, with numerous examples from real-life practice in Australia by professionals with extensive experience. (md)

Pessis, Anne-Marie. "Parque Nacional Sierra de Capivara (Brasil): Políticas y acciones de preservación." In Matthias Strecker and Freddy Taboada Tellez, eds., *Administración y Conservación de Sitios de Arte Rupestre* (Contribuciones al Estudio del Arte Rupestre Sudamericano, no. 4), 82–91. La Paz: Sociedad de Investigación del Arte Rupestre de Bolivia, 1995. (In Spanish.)

> The author describes the process of creating and managing a large cultural and natural park containing numerous rock art sites in northeast Brazil. Topics include the recruitment of appropriate personnel and organizations to protect, preserve, and manage the cultural and natural resources; the development of visitor infrastructure appropriate to each site within the park; and scientific investigations into the deterioration and conservation of the pictographs and petroglyphs. (ao)

Pitts, Michael. "What Future for Avebury?" *Antiquity* 64, no. 243 (1990): 259–74.

> Avebury is a World Heritage Site incorporating a unique complex of prehistoric features, which include megaliths, settlement, and barrows. The site's protection, preservation, and presentation are complicated by the presence of a village situated in the midst of these features and plans for the development of the site for tourism. The author reviews efforts to document, excavate, protect, preserve, and develop the Avebury monuments—both historic and prehistoric—during the last four centuries. This review highlights changing philosophies for preserving the site from complete removal of the village in favor of the prehistoric monuments to an equal appreciation of the historic values of the village. In the context of the most recent development pressures on Avebury, the author urges archaeologists to become more actively involved in the long-term planning and development of the site. (md)

Pwiti, Gilbert. "Let the Ancestors Rest in Peace? New Challenges for Cultural Heritage Management in Zimbabwe." *Conservation and Management of Archaeological Sites* 1, no. 3 (1996): 151–60.

> The current management of Great Zimbabwe is explored through the lens of the history and politics of Zimbabwe. The central theme is the evolving role of the local community in the postcolonial management of the site. The community continues to relate to the site as a religious center, resulting in conflicts with intervention needs. The challenges presented by growing tourism to the site are also explored. The author discusses how the current management is attempting to reconcile these conflicts (developing a "corporate strategy" for conservation, which links cultural heritage and economic benefits; and "adopt a site" approach to directly involve the local community as custodians). See also Ndoro 1994. (md)

Rauch, M., and C. Weber. "The Rapa Nui National Park: Management and Maintenance of the Archaeological Heritage of Easter Island." In A. Elena Charola, Robert J. Koestler, and Gianni Lombardi, eds., *Lavas and Volcanic Tuffs* (Proceedings of the International Meeting, Easter Island, Chile, 25–31 October 1990), 259–67. Rome: ICCROM, 1994.

The authors review the history of Rapa Nui National Park and its management since its creation in 1935. The changing issues and problems confronting management and the current aims and objectives of the park and its management plan are described. Some of the problems that management is addressing are the need for long-term maintenance of the site, lack of understanding and awareness by researchers of postexcavation/investigation needs, and the impact of increasing visitation to the island. The importance of planning and coordination among government agencies, research institutions, the local population, and the tourist industry is emphasized. (md)

Sullivan, Sharon. "Aboriginal Site Interpretation: Some Considerations." *ACT Heritage Seminars* 3 (1985): 11–22.

This author's considerable experience with site management enables her to discuss the issues involved in interpreting Aboriginal sites for the general public. The process of establishing the site's significance—the cornerstone of management—is outlined. The importance of understanding the values of Aboriginal sites to the Aboriginal community is underscored and must form the basis of an interpretive plan. Interpretive themes and strategies for implementing them are discussed. (md)

Sullivan, Sharon. "A Planning Model for the Management of Archaeological Sites." In Marta de la Torre, ed., *The Conservation of Archaeological Sites in the Mediterranean Region* (Proceedings of an International Conference organized by the Getty Conservation Institute and the J. Paul Getty Museum, May 1995), 15–26. Los Angeles: The Getty Conservation Institute, 1997.

In Australia, the principles of the Burra Charter have been used to create a simple and logical planning model for the management of archaeological sites. The model is presented and discussed in detail, and with appropriate adaptations, it can be implemented at sites worldwide. (ao)

Thorn, Andrew, and Andrew Piper. "The Isle of the Dead: An Integrated Approach to the Management and Natural Protection of an Archaeological Site." In Ashok Roy and Perry Smith, eds., *Archaeological Conservation and Its Consequences* (Preprints of the Contributions to the Copenhagen Congress, 26–30 August 1996), 149–52. London: International Institute for Conservation of Historic and Artistic Works, 1996.

The Isle of the Dead retains an historic cemetery, an aboriginal shell midden, and an internationally significant high-water mark. With careful management and accurate environmental impact assessment, the site has been protected through natural means requiring minimal intervention. The natural isolation of the island has been used to control visitor access, and tree plantings have been used to stabilize the environment around the headstones. (ao)

de la Torre, Marta, ed. *The Conservation of Archaeological Sites in the Mediterranean Region* (Proceedings of an International Conference organized by the Getty Conservation Institute and the J. Paul Getty Museum, May 1995). Los Angeles: The Getty Conservation Institute, 1997.

This publication of a conference is focused on conservation and management of archaeological sites in the Mediterranean, with papers on the planning process (see Sullivan 1997), issues of reconstruction, and presentation of archaeological sites and management considerations at the site of Akrotiri, Thera. In a series of case studies, the history of excavation, conservation, and management at three major Mediterranean sites is thoroughly considered: the late Roman villa of Piazza Armerina, Italy; the Minoan palace at Knossos, Crete; and the Hellenistic-Roman city of Ephesus, Turkey. (ao/md)

Valiente Cánovas, Santiago. "Parques y excavaciones arqueológicas: experiencias en el Yucatán, México." In *Cuadernos 3 Conservación Arqueológica: Reflexión y debate sobre teoría y práctica* (Contenido del Curso-Debate realizado en Sevilla del 30 de noviembre al 4 de diciembre de 1992), 50–57. Sevilla: Consejería de cultura y medio ambiente, 1994. (In Spanish.)

The author presents a very general survey of the current state of Maya sites in the Puuc area, Mexico, and makes broad suggestions for the creation of archaeological parks to attract visitors and make the sites economically viable. (ao)

Veliz, Vito, John W. Bright, and James R. Barborak. "Planning and Managing Honduras's Copán Ruins World Heritage Site: The Role of Cultural Parks in Contributing to Education and Economic Development." In *International Perspectives on Cultural Parks* (Proceedings of the First World Conference, Mesa Verde National Park, Colorado, 1984). Denver: United States National Park Service in association with the Colorado Historical Society, 1989.

This paper affords an unusual look at the international, national, and regional institutions and agencies that provided material, financial, and training support for the development and management of Copán. Also discussed are the lessons learned from the development and implementation of a master plan: the need for high-level government commitment and quality planning documents; the inclusion of rural development of adjacent areas; the suitability of labor-intensive development rather than high-tech solutions for developing countries; the upgrading of existing infrastructure over new development; and the regional exchanges of personnel and cooperative training programs. (md)

Wager, Jonathan. "Zoning and Environmental Management Plan (ZEMP) for the Angkor World Cultural Heritage Site, Cambodia—A Case Study." In *The Safeguard of the Rock-Hewn Churches of the Göreme Valley* (Proceedings of an International Seminar, Ürgüp, Cappadocia, Turkey, 5–10 September 1993), 57–75. Rome: ICCROM, 1995.

This paper describes the work of the Zoning and Environmental Management Plan for Angkor (ZEMP), undertaken by UNESCO from 1992 to 1994. The author reviews the history of Angkor, UNESCO's involvement at the site, and the ZEMP process. The objective of the process was to produce a comprehensive zoning plan for Angkor to address and reconcile the main planning issues at the site—cultural conservation, tourism, and rural development. Guiding principles for sustainable development are outlined. The article ends with a useful summary of the main lessons learned from carrying out the process. (md)

Wood, J. B., and A. Warren. *A Handbook for the Preparation of Management Plans* (Discussion Papers in Conservation 18). London: University College London, 1978.

This handbook, commissioned by the Nature Conservancy Council to the Conservation Course at University College London, describes the process of preparing a management plan for natural reserves. Although the focus of this manual is natural reserves, the process is equally applicable to the management of cultural resources. The three main stages of the process are defined as the collation of descriptive information, a description of policies, and a prescription for action. (md)

Zilhão, João. "The Rock Art of the Côa Valley, Portugal." *Conservation and Management of Archaeological Sites* 2, no. 4 (1998): 193–206.

The author provides a full description of the efforts to create and manage the Côa Valley Archaeological Park (inaugurated in 1996), which contains numerous rock art sites dating from paleolithic to historic times. In many ways, these efforts represent the state of the art in conservation and management of a heritage site, including research and scientific dating to determine the significance of the site; documentation and information management; legal protection of both the cultural heritage and its natural context; involvement of local, national, and international groups in all aspects of the process; interpretation; and development of a well-considered visitor and site management plan. (ao)

Annotated Bibliography 3   Assessment of Significance

Attenbrow, Val, and Tia Negerevich. "The Assessment of Sites: Lucas Heights Waste Disposal Depot: A Case Study." In S. Sullivan and S. Bowdler, eds. *Site Surveys and Significance Assessment in Australian Archaeology* (Proceedings of the 1981 Springwood Conference on Australian Prehistory, Department of Prehistory, Research School of Pacific Studies, Australian National University, Canberra), 1984, 136–37.

Described in this case study is an assessment of the scientific significance of a group of prehistoric sites in Australia. Assessment was undertaken within a regional context and in terms of criteria such as size, contents, preservation, representativeness, as well as the site's potential contribution to research questions. (md)

Australian Heritage Commission. *What Do We Want to Pass On to Future Generations? An Overview of Criteria and Assessment Procedures for the Register of the National Estate.* Australian Heritage Commission, 1990.

This study constitutes a full review of the process and criteria for assessing the significance of Australia's natural and cultural heritage. (md)

Avrami, Erica, Randall Mason, and Marta de la Torre, eds. *Values and Heritage Conservation* (Research Report, The Getty Conservation Institute). Los Angeles: The J. Paul Getty Trust, 2000.

This is a report on the results of a research initiative undertaken by the Getty Conservation Institute to explore the role of values in the conservation of cultural heritage. The aims and initial results and an overview of the meaning and practice of conservation, values and valorization, and the need for a conceptual framework constitute the first part of the report. A series of commissioned essays in the second part explore these issues from diverse perspectives. An extensive annotated bibliography related to values completes the report. Economic values in the context of cultural heritage are the focus of another report emerging from this research initiative (Randall Mason, ed. *Economics and Heritage Conservation* [a meeting organized by the Getty Conservation Institute, December 1998]). Los Angeles: The J. Paul Getty Trust, 1998). (md)

Bickford, Anne, and Sharon Sullivan. "Assessing the Research Significance of Historic Sites." In S. Sullivan and S. Bowdler, eds. *Site Surveys and Significance Assessment in Australian Archaeology* (Proceedings of the 1981 Springwood Conference on Australian Prehistory, Department of Prehistory, Research School of Pacific Studies, Australian National University, Canberra), 1984, 19–33.

The criteria of the Australian Heritage Commission regarding historic sites stress historic and public values and do not take into account scientific and research values. The authors devised three general questions to guide the assessment of the scientific significance of historic sites: Can the site contribute knowledge that no other resource or no other site can? Is this knowledge relevant to general questions about human history or other substantive problems? Does this knowledge contribute to other major research questions? (md)

Bowdler, Sandra. "Unconsidered Trifles? Cultural Resource Management, Environmental Impact Statements, and Archaeological Research in New South Wales." *Australian Archaeology* 12 (1981): 123–33.

In the context of Australian legislation to protect archaeological resources, the author discusses the question of significance as the justification for deciding which resources should be preserved. The American experience with defining scientific significance is reviewed. Assessment based on both research questions and representativeness is recommended, but the issue of who should undertake research and assessment needs to be addressed. Research consultants may provide the answer. (md)

————. "Archaeological Significance as a Mutable Quality." In S. Sullivan and S. Bowdler, eds. *Site Surveys and Significance Assessment in Australian Archaeology* (Proceedings of the 1981 Springwood Conference on Australian Prehistory, Department of Prehistory, Research School of Pacific Studies, Australian National University, Canberra), 1984, 1–9.

The author illustrates with case studies the changeability and relativity of significance as it applies to archaeological sites. As the level of research and the nature of research questions change, so will an assessment of a site's scientific significance. The important point is made that is only implicit in most discussions of scientific significance as research potential; namely, once a site is excavated, the "focus of [its] significance has moved elsewhere." (md)

Cleere, Henry. "Cultural Landscapes as World Heritage." *Conservation and Management of Archaeological Sites* 1, no. 1 (1995): 63–68.

In the context of the UNESCO World Heritage Convention of 1972, the author explores the concept of cultural landscapes as a distinct category of heritage and traces the attempts to establish criteria to assess these landscapes. The discussion is useful in thinking through the values attributed to cultural landscapes. (md)

Clegg, John. "The Evaluation of Archaeological Significance: Prehistoric Pictures and/or Rock Art." In S. Sullivan and S. Bowdler, eds. *Site Surveys and Significance Assessment in Australian Archaeology* (Proceedings of the 1981 Springwood Conference on Australian Prehistory, Department of Prehistory, Research School of Pacific Studies, Australian National University, Canberra), 1984, 10–18.

Groube's model (see Groube 1978) for significance assessment utilizing three levels of research design—initial, integrative, and theoretical—is adapted to the assessment of Australian rock art. (md)

Coster, John. "Exotic Forestry and Site Management in the Auckland Region." In J. R. McKinlay and K. L. Jones, eds., *Archaeological Resource Management in Australia and Oceania*, 89–94. Wellington: New Zealand Historic Places Trust, 1979.

The author critically examines two systems that have been used in the forestry service for selecting sites for protection and preservation. One of the systems comprises three sets of guidelines: scientific criteria (with emphasis on a representative sample, intact sites, and unique sites); management criteria (in this case, the forestry service requirements and needs); and secular criteria (for example, aesthetics, educational value, and traditional importance). A second, more utilitarian system is based on management criteria: sites to be permanently preserved (in practice, this refers to sites that are intact and whose preservation is viable); sites that require further investigation; and sites that require no further management. (md)

Crosby, Anthony. "Ruins Stabilization—the Value Implied." In *International Perspectives on Cultural Parks* (Proceedings of the First World Conference, Mesa Verde National Park, Colorado, 1984), 101–6. Denver: United States National Park Service in association with the Colorado Historical Society, 1989.

Explored in this text are the values of archaeological resources and how they are affected by preservation actions. Values can be broadly classified as symbolic or religious, economic or functional, educational or informational, and aesthetic, but they are inevitably relative, dependent on time, place, and culture. Physical interventions undertaken to preserve a site will respond to different values and may well result in a conflict of values. Compromise is inevitable, but one must always ask whether a preservation action will complement or detract from the important values of a site. (md)

Darvill, Timothy. "Value Systems in Archaeology." In Malcolm A. Cooper et al., eds., *Managing Archaeology*, 41–50. London: Routledge, 1995.

The author looks at the origins, formation, and evolving nature of value systems, and relates this to the ways in which society values archaeological resources. Three categories, or gradients, of values are defined and explored: use value (the exploitation of the resource for some kind of tangible return in the present, such as archaeological research, education, recreation, social solidarity, and economic gain); option value (the potential of the resource for use in the future); and existence value (the feeling of well-being that comes from knowing the resource exists). This value system is also discussed by the author in "Value Systems and the Archaeological Resource." *International Journal of Heritage Studies* 1, no. 1 (1994): 52–64. (md)

Darvill, Timothy, Andrew Saunders, and Bill Startin. "A Question of National Importance: Approaches to the Evaluation of Ancient Monuments for the Monuments Protection Programme in England." *Antiquity* 61, no. 233 (1987): 393–408.

The evaluation system for archaeological sites and monuments established as part of English Heritage's Monuments Protection Programme is set forth in some detail. The aim of the program, begun in 1986, was to identify sites of national importance for statutory protection. Procedures to evaluate monuments on a systematic and nationwide basis were developed. Selection criteria, based on earlier nonstatutory criteria (see Saunders 1984), are applied at three levels of evaluation: characterization, discrimination, and assessment of resources. (md)

Davis, Hester. "Is an Archaeological Site Important to Science or to the Public, and Is There a Difference?" In Davis L. Uzzell, ed., *Heritage Interpretation*. Volume 1, *The Natural and Built Environment*, 96–99. London: Belhaven Press, 1989.

In North America, the significance debate has arisen largely in the context of expenditures of public money and the federal mandates to assess significance. The use of public money has implications for how we assess whether sites are important. The author explores the importance of sites from the perspective of the general public, and the conflict among the public, archaeologists, and Native American interests in archaeological resources. (md)

Dunnell, Robert C. "The Ethics of Archaeological Significance Decisions." In Ernestene L. Green, ed., *Ethics and Values in Archaeology*, 62–74. New York: The Free Press, 1984.

Significance assessment is a moral and ethical issue due to the non-renewable nature of archaeological resources. The author argues against problem-oriented assessments since they restrict the value of the archaeological record to contemporary problems. A representative sample is the only way to ensure future research needs. (md)

Flood, Josephine. "More or Less Significant." In S. Sullivan and S. Bowdler, eds., *Site Surveys and Significance Assessment in Australian Archaeology* (Proceedings of the 1981 Springwood Conference on Australian Prehistory, Department of Prehistory, Research School of Pacific Studies, Australian National University, Canberra), 1984, 55–60.

The criteria used by the Australian Heritage Commission for listing Aboriginal sites include "outstanding quality" and "representativeness." The emphasis in assessment has now shifted to "representativeness," as the most outstanding sites have already been listed. Representativeness is defined as characteristic examples of each type of site by biophysical region. (md)

Fowler, Peter J. "Archaeology, the Public, and the Sense of the Past." In David Lowenthal and Marcus Binney, eds., *Our Past Before Us: Why Do We Save It?*, 56–69. London: Temple Smith, 1981.

The author explores the meanings of a "sense of the past" for educators, academics, and the public, particularly as they relate to the conflict between preserving the past for archaeological/academic purposes and for public consumption. The criteria for preservation will differ: archaeology requires preservation of its resources for its own survival but the public's expectations will not always correspond with this scholarly need. (md)

Francis, Peter D., and Eric C. Poplin, eds. *Directions in Archaeology: A Question of Goals* (Proceedings of the Fourteenth Annual Conference, The Archaeological Association of the University of Calgary, November 12–14, 1981). Calgary: The University of Calgary, 1982.

Part six of these conference proceedings, *Approaches to the Evaluation of Cultural Resources: Canadian Perspectives,* includes seven papers and a final review paper on evaluation and significance assessment in the context of cultural resource management issues. The major arguments are similar to those in the literature of the United States: problem-oriented research vs. representative sampling and the use of humanistic vs. scientific criteria as the means of assessment. Both historic and prehistoric resources are considered. (md)

Glassow, M. "Issues in Evaluating the Significance of Archaeological Resources." *American Antiquity* 42, no.3 (1977): 413–20.

The author argues for assessment based on categories of significance that will reflect a quantitative analysis of site attributes or properties: variety, quantity, clarity, integrity, and environmental context. (md)

Groube, L. M. "Priorities and Problems in Dorset Archaeology." In *New Approaches to Our Past* (Proceedings of the Southampton University Archaeological Society, 1978). Monograph Series, University of Southampton, no. 2, 29–52.

This is an earlier version of what was more fully set forth in Groube and Bowden 1982, in which the author develops the method of ranking archaeological problems in order to establish priorities for protection and excavation. Delivered at a conference, the author notes in a postscript the hostile reaction of some in the audience, which he attributes in part to "square-root phobia." This remark refers to the rather complex mathematics that informs this particular approach to site ranking. (md)

Groube, L. M., and M. C. B. Bowden. *The Archaeology of Rural Dorset: Past, Present and Future* (Dorset Natural History and Archaeological Society, Monograph 4). 1982.

This report on Dorset archaeology investigates the causes of destruction to resources and the role of legislation and other measures to protect them. It also focuses on establishing priorities for future archaeological work and protection of resources in the region. A cumbersome ranking of archaeological problems as initial, integrative, and theoretical is proposed as the basis for assessing priorities. Initial archaeological problems are of the lowest level, requiring basic data gathering; integrative problems involve correlations, relationships, and patterns among sites and artifacts; theoretical problems encompass the broad issues of cultural change, social and economic structures, relationships among man, culture, the environment, and so on. These three levels of problems are applied to the main archaeological periods. In addition to the ranking of problems, a flow and feedback score is applied, which attempts to compensate for the inevitable feedback between the problem levels. A third scale of assessment is based on the importance of the problem to local Dorset archaeology. (md)

Johnston, Chris. *What Is Social Value? A Discussion Paper* (Technical Publication Series, Number 3. Australian Heritage Commission). Canberra: Australian Government Publishing Service, 1994.

> This brief publication explores social value—the meanings attached to heritage places by groups of people—through a thoughtful analysis of its many facets and manifestations, its connections and differences with other values, and its transitory nature. Approaches to assessing social value are discussed, and issues such as whether social value needs to be protected, the conflicts between protecting fabric and function of a place as expressed in social values, and the tensions between economic growth and community identity are raised. (md)

Kalman, Harold. "An Evaluation System for Architectural Surveys?" *Association for Preservation Technology Bulletin* 8, no. 3 (1976): 3–23.

> The use of evaluation systems, selection criteria, and scoring systems utilized for evaluating historic resources in the United States is explored as background to the presentation of the author's evaluation of historic buildings in Vancouver, Canada, undertaken in the early 1970s. Appendices include criteria established for the United States National Register and National Trust and the Historic Sites and Monuments Board of Canada. (md)

Lancaster, Osbert. "What Should We Preserve?" In Jane Fawcett, ed., *The Future of the Past*, 65–74. London: Thames & Hudson, 1976.

> In the context of historic preservation, the author allows for only three grounds for preserving a building: intrinsic aesthetic merit, *pietas*, and scenic usefulness. While this narrow approach does not reflect current trends, it is typical of the visual and symbolic approach to cultural heritage. (md)

Lipe, William. "Value and Meaning in Cultural Resources." In Henry Cleere, ed., *Approaches to the Archaeological Heritage*, 1–11. Cambridge: Cambridge University Press, 1984.

> This article defines four types of values that may be assigned to cultural resources: economic, informational, associative, and aesthetic. These values are fully explored as a means of understanding how cultural resources can be of use and benefit to society. The author does not formulate a system whereby these values can be assessed but recognizes that they can be used for selecting which resources should be preserved. (md)

Moratto, M. J., and R. E. Kelly. "Significance in Archaeology." *The Kiva* 42, no. 2 (1976): 193–202.

> Traditionally, significance has been measured in terms of size, condition, depth, richness, age, uniqueness, or presumed scientific value. A broadly based system that will address all the relevant issues (governmental and archaeological) is needed. The authors propose an interrelated set of criteria: historical, scientific, geographic, ethnic, public, monetary, legal, and managerial. These criteria are each briefly explored in the context of assessing significance. (md)

———. "Optimizing Strategies for Evaluation of Archaeological Significance." In *Advances in Archaeological Method and Theory*, vol. 1, 1–30. New York: Academic Press, 1978.

> In an amplification of Moratto and Kelly 1976, the problems and concepts associated with resource assessments are clearly reviewed, and criteria for evaluating cultural resources are set forth in some detail. These criteria are historic, scientific, ethnic, public, legal, and monetary. "Specious" criteria, such as egocentrism and sensationalism, are usefully explored. The extensive bibliography includes additional sources not cited herein. (md)

O'Keefe, P. J., and L. V. Prott. *Law and the Cultural Heritage,* vol. 1. Abingdon, Oxon: Professional Books Ltd., 1984.

The question of significance is discussed within the legal framework of site protection. The authors point out the ambiguity surrounding the use of such terms as *significance, interest,* and *value* in legislation designed to protect cultural resources. (md)

Plog, Fred. "The Ethics of Excavation: Site Selection." In E. L. Green, ed., *Ethics and Values in Archaeology,* 89–96. New York: The Free Press, 1984.

This article addresses the specific question of how to select sites for excavation. The author singles out the following seven questions that must be addressed to justify excavation: Has a research question been identified to which the site is pertinent? Does the research design specify the minimal amount of work necessary? Are the archaeological techniques available adequate to address the problem? Can the problem be addressed using existing data? Can a less well-protected site be used? Can a partially disturbed site be used? Can a site with greater interpretive potential be used? The author also sets forth standards for the evaluation process. (md)

Raab, L. Mark, and Timothy C. Klinger. "A Critical Appraisal of 'Significance' in Contract Archaeology." *American Antiquity* 42, no. 4 (1977): 629–34.

The authors critically evaluate four current strategies for assessing significance, as measured by the National Register criteria, a consideration of monetary values, unique characteristics, and problem-oriented research. This type of research is judged to be the best approach. (md)

Saunders, Andrew. "Integrated Conservation." In *Interchange of Experience Concerning the Care of Archaeological Remains* (Seminar in Stockholm, Sweden, 7–9 November 1983), 15–18. Stockholm: Central Board of National Antiquities, 1984.

The inventory and legal protective systems in Britain are reviewed. The proposed criteria for selection of scheduled monuments are set forth and briefly defined: survival and condition, period, rarity, fragility and vulnerability, diversity, documentation, group value, and potential. (md)

Schiffer, Michael B., and George J. Gumerman. *Conservation Archaeology.* New York: Academic Press, 1977.

Part IV, "Assessing Significance," includes an introductory statement and four papers devoted to the problems of significance assessment from the American perspective of cultural resources management. This volume, one of the most frequently cited in cultural resource management literature, is a good starting point for exploring these issues. (md)

Sharrock, Floyd W., and Donald K. Grayson. "'Significance' in Contract Archaeology." *American Antiquity* 44, no. 2 (1979): 327–28.

The limitation of problem-oriented strategies for assessing archaeological resources must be recognized. They are inevitably biased toward current research problems; sites that may be important for future research will not be properly represented. The author points out that the National Register criteria at least have the virtue of being broad and recognizing potential values. (md)

Stanley Price, Nicholas. "Conservation and Information in the Display of Prehistoric Sites." In Peter Gathercole and David Lowenthal, eds., *The Politics of the Past,* 284–90. London: Unwin Hyman, 1990.

The decision to conserve an archaeological site for public presentation raises questions of interpretation and legibility. The three well-accepted conservation principles of reversibility, minimum intervention, and compatibility of materials should guide every intervention, but the type of intervention will depend on the values ascribed to a site: aesthetic and artistic, economic and utilitarian, associative and symbolic, and historic and informational. The author discusses the conflict of values in the light of conservation theory, public vs. professional interests, and types of interventions. (md)

Stehberg, Rubén. "In Chile the National Museum of Natural History Develops Archaeological Sites." *Museum* 34, no. 2 (1982): 114–16.

Criteria were developed specifically for selecting prehistoric archaeological sites for excavation and public presentation around Santiago, Chile. The criteria chosen were representativeness, significance, variety, geographical situation, ease of access, preservation, monumentality, and location on state property. (md)

Sullivan, Hilary. "Mornington Peninsula Archaeological Survey: Assessing Significance in a Local Context." In S. Sullivan and S. Bowdler, *Site Surveys and Significance Assessment in Australian Archaeology* (Proceedings of the 1981 Springwood Conference on Australian Prehistory, Department of Prehistory, Research School of Pacific Studies, Australian National University, Canberra), 1984, 119–26.

In this case study, scientific significance of prehistoric sites was evaluated within a survey area for the management and protection of sites. Criteria were designed to determine research potential and provide a representative sample of sites; these included preservation, structure, and contents of sites. (md)

Sullivan, S., and S. Bowdler, eds. *Site Surveys and Significance Assessment in Australian Archaeology* (Proceedings of the 1981 Springwood Conference on Australian Prehistory, Department of Prehistory, Research School of Pacific Studies, Australian National University, Canberra), 1984.

This series of conference papers focuses on defining the scientific significance of sites. The adaptation of the concept of scientific significance as research potential was the main theme of the conference. The papers deal with both historic and prehistoric sites and are equally divided between general discussions and case studies. Selected papers are annotated herein. (md)

Tainter, Joseph A., and G. John Lucas. "Epistemology of the Significance Concept." *Antiquity* 48, no. 4 (1983): 707–19.

The concept of significance as articulated in United States legislation and regulations is explored from an historical and philosophical perspective. This concept is traced to the Western tradition of empiricism or positivism, in which the meaning perceived in phenomena does not vary or change. The authors argue that this is epistemologically unsound; significance is not a quality inherent in cultural resources but is assigned to them and will change. (md)

Thompson, Raymond H. "Archaeological Triage: Determining the Significance of Cultural Properties." In Rex L. Wilson and Gloria Loyola, eds., *Rescue Archaeology* (Papers from the First New World Conference on Rescue Archaeology), 40–46. Washington, D.C.: The Preservation Press, 1982.

The United States needs a national system of archaeological "triage" to save its resources. The author suggests a regional evaluation system and the use of commonly recognized categories of archaeological information. The categories can be used as the basis for a statement of significance, for comparison, and as a justification for decisions. Categories include chronology, ethnic identity, rich assemblage, degree of disturbance, uniqueness of cultural expression, and more. (md)

Titchen, Sarah M. "On the Construction of 'Outstanding Universal Value.'" Some Comments on the Implementation of the 1972 UNESCO World Heritage Convention." *Conservation and Management of Archaeological Sites* 1, no. 4 (1996): 235–42.

The criteria for nominating a World Heritage site center on the concept of "outstanding universal value." This article traces the changing perceptions of the meaning of that phrase, and the subsequent modification of the criteria as embodied in the Operational Guidelines for the Implementation of the World Heritage Convention. The ambiguity of the phrase, while presenting some difficulties, also accommodates changing attitudes toward the cultural and natural heritage. The author argues that as the criteria continue to be modified, they will allow for the inscription of a continuum of sites from cultural to natural and thus help to balance the World Heritage List. In the same volume, see also Henry Cleere, "The Concept of 'Outstanding Universal Value' in the World Heritage Convention," 227–33. (ao)

Weinland, Marcia. "Archaeological Significance: A Ten-Year Review of Nominations from Kentucky." *American Society for Conservation Archaeology Newsletter* 7, no. 1 (1980): 12–19.

A brief review of the earlier literature on significance assessment precedes this overview of the specific criteria that were actually used for justifying National Register listings in Kentucky. Of the thirty-seven criteria identified, those most frequently cited as justifications were impact and integrity, but this must be seen in the context of contract projects and damaged sites. Other criteria were rarity of culture or site type, subsistence pattern, stratified deposits, local chronology, intensity of occupation, and visual impression. (md)

List of Participants
Corinth, Greece

19–22 May 2000

First Name	Last Name	Title*	Affiliation*	Country
Fouad	Aghabi	Assistant to Secretary General for Technical Affairs	Ministry of Tourism and Antiquities	Hashimite Kingdom of Jordan
Aysar	Akrawi	Executive Director	Petra National Trust	Hashimite Kingdom of Jordan
Ihab	Amarin	Architect, Second Tourism Project	Ministry of Tourism and Antiquities	Hashimite Kingdom of Jordan
John	Ashurst	Director	Ingram Consultancy Limited	United Kingdom
Zoe	Aslamatzidou	Archaeologist	IV Ephoreia of Prehistoric and Classical Antiquities	Greece
Zaki	Aslan	Coordinator of SITES Near East Programme	ICCROM	Italy
Gideon	Avni	Director of Excavations and Surveys	Israel Antiquities Authority	Israel
Issam	Awad	Chief Architect	Al-Aqsa Mosque, Dome of the Rock Restoration Committee	Palestinian National Authority
Nissim	Bados	Manager of Beit Shean National Parks	Israel Nature and National Parks Protection Authority	Israel
Leila	Badre	Director	The Museum of the American University of Beirut	Lebanon
Esti	Ben Haim	Masada Mountaintop Project Coordinator	Israel Nature and National Parks Protection Authority	Israel
Carolina	Castellanos	Conservator	Private Consultant	Mexico
Uzi	Dahari	Deputy Director, Head of Archaeology Administration	Israel Antiquities Authority	Israel
Martha	Demas	Senior Project Specialist, Field Projects	The Getty Conservation Institute	USA
Françoise	Descamps	Senior Project Specialist, Field Projects	The Getty Conservation Institute	USA
Hani	Falahat	Assistant Inspector of Antiquities/Petra	Department of Antiquities	Hashimite Kingdom of Jordan
Suleiman	Farajat	Assistant Director General, Inspector of Antiquities	Petra Regional Planning Council	Hashimite Kingdom of Jordan
William	Fulco	NEH Chair in Ancient Mediterranean Studies	Loyola Marymount University	USA
Osama	Hamdan	Architect	Al Fonoon Engineering Office	Palestinian National Authority
Mahmoud	Hawari	Coordinator, Palestinian Scientific Committee	Museums With No Frontiers	Denmark
Joseph	Jabbra	Academic Vice President	Loyola Marymount University	USA

*Titles and affiliations are current at the time of publication and do not necessarily reflect those held at the time of the workshop.

First Name	Last Name	Title	Affiliation	Country
Maria Teresa	Jaquinta	Project Manager, Architecture and Archaeological Sites Program	ICCROM	Italy
Zaidan	Kafafi	Dean of Research and Graduate Studies	Yarmouk University	Hashimite Kingdom of Jordan
Gjerak	Karaiskaj	Chief, Ancient and Medieval Monuments Department	Istituti i Monumenteve te Kultures	Albania
Effie	Karpodini-Dimitriadi	Director	Euroskills S.A. Educational Services	Greece
Saleh	Lamei	Director General	Center for Conservation and Preservation of Islamic Cultural Heritage	Egypt
Angelos	Manolakis	Prefect	Prefecture of Corinth	Greece
Ze'ev	Margalit	Manager of the Development Division	Israel Nature and National Parks Protection Authority	Israel
Yoel	Marinov	Director General	East Jerusalem Development Company	Israel
Sally	Martin	Project Manager	Butrint Foundation	United Kingdom
Randall	Mason	Assistant Professor and Director of Historic Preservation, School of Architecture	University of Maryland	USA
Lida	Miraj	Master Researcher	Institute of Archaeology, Tirana, and Archaeological Museum of Durres	Albania
Mohammad	Najjar	Director of Excavations and Surveys	Department of Antiquities	Hashimite Kingdom of Jordan
Yusuf	Natsheh	Director, Department of Islamic Archaeology	Awqof Administration	Palestinian National Authority
Gaetano	Palumbo	Director of Archaeological Conservation	World Monuments Fund France	France
Iris	Pojani	Director	International Center for Albanian Archaeology	Albania
Hamed	Salem	Lecturer	Institute of Palestinian Archaeology	Palestinian National Authority
Guy	Sanders	Director, Corinth Excavation	American School of Classical Studies at Athens	Greece
Sandra	Scham	Associate Curator	Pontifical Biblical Institute	Israel
Walid	Sharif	Acting Director General	Ministry of Culture, Directorate of Cultural Heritage	Palestinian National Authority
Ali	Shuaibi	President	ICOMOS Saudi Arabia	Saudi Arabia
Giora	Solar	Architect	Private Consultant	Israel
Elisabeth	Spathari	Ephor of Antiquities	IV Ephoreia of Prehistoric and Classical Antiquities	Greece
Lazar	Sumanov	Advisor Coordinator	Republic Institute for the Protection of Cultural Monuments (RZZSK)	Former Yugoslav Republic of Macedonia
Hamdan	Taha	Director	Palestinian Department of Antiquities	Palestinian National Authority
Jeanne Marie	Teutonico	Associate Director	The Getty Conservation Institute	USA
Tsvika	Tsuk	Director, Department of Archaeology and Heritage	Israel Nature and National Parks Protection Authority	Israel
Ariel	Weiss	Director	Yad Hanadiv Foundation	Israel
Adel	Yahya	Chief Archaeologist	Palestinian Association for Cultural Exchange	Palestinian National Authority
Christopher	Young	Head of World Heritage and International Policy	English Heritage	United Kingdom

Author Biographies

Aysar Akrawi is the executive director of the Petra National Trust (PNT) in Amman, Jordan. Responsible for the preparation and execution of the organization's many projects and publications, she coordinates with the Jordanian government, nongovernmental organizations, and international donor agencies. She studied at the Lebanese American University in Beirut and serves on the boards of the Petra Regional Planning Council (PRPC) and the National Committee of the International Union for the Conservation of Nature (IUCN).

Erica Avrami was a project specialist at the Getty Conservation Institute from 1994 to 2001, where she was involved in education initiatives, field projects, and research related to the values and economics of heritage conservation. She received her undergraduate and graduate degrees from Columbia University, where she studied architecture and historic preservation. She is currently a private conservation consultant.

Esti Ben Haim is coordinator of the Israel Nature and National Parks Protection Authority's mountaintop project at Masada. Before joining the authority's project, she was a researcher and lieutenant colonel in the Israeli army. Prior to that, she worked as an archaeologist in the field for the Israel Antiquities Authority. She studied archaeology and geography at the Hebrew University in Jerusalem.

Carolina Castellanos is an independent conservator who specializes in conservation and management of archaeological sites. She works as a consultant to institutions such as the Getty Conservation Institute and ICCROM developing management plans for sites such as Chan Chan, Peru; Joya de Ceren, El Salvador; and the Mimbres-Paquime Connection Project in Mexico and the United States. Having studied conservation, archaeology, and anthropology, she has taught site management and conservation planning at a variety of regional courses.

Martha Demas joined the Getty Conservation Institute in 1990 and is now a senior project specialist in Field Projects. She is currently managing the Mosaics Project, which addresses issues of in situ conservation of mosaics, and the China Principles project, which is aimed at developing and applying national guidelines for conservation and management of cultural heritage sites in China. She studied Aegean archaeology at the University of Cincinnati and historic preservation at Cornell University, specializing in conservation of the archaeological heritage.

William J. Fulco, S. J., has been the National Endowment for the Humanities professor of Ancient Mediterranean Studies at Loyola Marymount University in Los Angeles, California, since 1997. Prior to that position, he was adjunct professor of archaeology at the University of Southern California. He has published numerous articles and books on Near Eastern archaeology and classical numismatics. His areas of interest include comparative Afroasiatic linguistics, Canaanite epigraphy, archaeological ceramics, and numismatics.

Randall Mason is assistant professor and director of historic preservation at the University of Maryland's school of architecture. He is also a partner in the nonprofit conservation firm Minerva Partners, which develops projects and research to strengthen the connections between heritage conservation and social development. From 1998 to 2000 he was senior project specialist at the Getty Conservation Institute, researching economic and social issues relating to the conservation of cultural heritage. He studied geography, urban planning, and history, and holds a doctorate from Columbia University.

Gaetano Palumbo is director of archaeological conservation at the World Monuments Fund in Paris. Previously, he coordinated the master's program in managing archaeological sites at University College London's Institute of Archaeology and was a project specialist at the Getty Conservation Institute at the time of the Corinth workshop. He holds a doctorate in archaeology from the University of Rome and has served as a consultant for international organizations on issues related to site inventories, cultural resources management, and site management planning.

Guy Sanders has held the titles of associate director and now director of the American School of Classical Studies Excavations at Corinth since 1996. Before that, he was assistant director of the British School in Athens. He studied archaeology, geography, art history, and ancient history at the Universities of Southampton, Missouri, and Birmingham.

Jeanne Marie Teutonico is associate director of the Getty Conservation Institute. An architectural conservator with over twenty years of experience in the conservation of buildings and sites, she was previously on the staff of the International Centre for the Study of the Preservation and Restoration of Cultural Property (ICCROM) in Rome and then of English Heritage in London. She studied art history at Princeton University and holds a master's degree in historic preservation from Columbia University.

Christopher Young has been head of World Heritage and International Policy for English Heritage since 1999. Prior to that, he was director for the Hadrian's Wall World Heritage Site, working on the completion and implementation of its management plan. He has assisted the development of management plans for World Heritage Sites, potential and actual, and has contributed to the revision of the World Heritage Committee's Operational Guidelines. He studied history and archaeology at the University of Oxford.